NEVER
QUESTION
THE
MIRACLE

NEVER QUESTION THE MIRACLE

A Surgeon's Story

Rose-Marie Toussaint, M.D.

with Anthony E. Santaniello

One World
The Ballantine Publishing Group • New York

I would like to dedicate this book
to the Conscious Inner Self of all

A One World Book
Published by The Ballantine Publishing Group

http://www.randomhouse.com

LIBRARY OF CONGRESS CATALOGING-IN-PUBLICATION DATA
Toussaint, Rose-Marie.
    Never question the miracle : a surgeon's story / Rose-Marie Toussaint, with
Anthony E. Santaniello.
        p.   cm.
    ISBN 0-345-40723-7 (alk. paper)
    1. Toussaint, Rose-Marie.   2. Women surgeons—United States—
Biography.   3. Women surgeons—Haiti—Biography.   4. Afro-American
surgeons—Biography.   I. Santaniello, Anthony E.   II. Title.
RD27.35.T68A3   1998
617'.092—dc21   97-37566
[B]

Text design by Mary A. Wirth

Manufactured in the United States of America

First Edition: March 1998

10 9 8 7 6 5 4 3 2 1

NEVER QUESTION THE MIRACLE

CHAPTER 1

When people ask me, "How did you get here?" I know they are asking many questions at once. They're asking how I got to be a surgeon, but not just a surgeon, because I am a surgeon specializing in liver and kidney transplantation. They want to know how I came to be in charge of a transplantation service with a large city-based operation, a doctor on a round-the-clock watch, waiting for the always scarce organ to become available, waiting for the chance to perform the surgery that will remove one more patient from the "desperately waiting" list, a list from which names are removed more often by death than by surgical intervention.

But when people ask, "How did you get here?" I know they are really asking, "How did *you*, a woman, a black woman from

Haiti, the poorest country in the Western Hemisphere, get here?"

An unlikely series of events brought me here, a series of events of the most ordinary, nose-to-the-grindstone variety. No one has to be told that becoming a surgeon is an arduous task under any circumstances. My circumstances made it harder, of course. But I had the most extraordinary help along the way, always when my need was greatest, help that came like a miracle out of the blue, turning the ordinary into, well, the miraculous.

I think the best way for me to tell how I got here is to take it a step at a time, perhaps from the beginning when I, grand-daughter of Haitian farmers, was told that one day I would become a healer, a physician ministering to my fellow human beings.

I'll do that, but first there is the present moment, typical of all my moments, today's work of seeing and treating the desperate individuals who seek me out, knowing that transplantation is their only chance, the last chance. My patients are of all types, a cross section of humanity, man, woman, and child, but they are all facing death because few come to me except as the last resort. And yet, in spite of the similarity that this death sentence gives all of them, each patient retains his or her own individuality, each remains unique, one of a kind. That is one reason why the effort to give each a chance for renewed life is so important—and so rewarding. Another is that nine out of ten patients with terminal liver disease who receive transplants when they are in good physical condition are alive one year after surgery. But when transplantation is a last resort, only five of ten patients are alive a year after the surgery. We have a saying in the transplant community: If you can walk to the hospital for your liver transplant, it is likely that you will walk out in two weeks. If you are wheeled in comatose, you are more likely to be wheeled to the rehabilitation center in three to six months. Worse yet, you might be wheeled to the morgue.

I would like you to know some of my patients in all their uniqueness. They are the reasons why I, a black woman, an outsider, opened myself to the many miracles that have made my life's work possible. For one, each encounter with a patient is a different challenge and the chance for a different kind of miracle. Stan, the patient who burst into my life unexpectedly one morning, more than proved the point.

I looked across my cluttered desktop and thought: At least you have to give this guy credit. Instead of a proper medical file with his case records, he's showing me a fistful of old newspaper clippings.

"I don't see patients unless they are referred by their primary physicians," I said, about to add, "not just off the street," but he cut me short.

"You see, Doc, my cousin works here in your hospital, and she sent me these."

He leaned closer and I saw his eyes, not only the ominous yellow tint to the whites but the intensity with which they fixed on me.

"She says you do livers. Like in the newspaper story. See, that's you, ain't it?"

It was the story: YOUNG TRANSPLANT SURGEON GIVES NEW LIVER, NEW LIFE TO BOY, 13. Same ghastly photograph. Not one of my better days. Or was it because I had been up all the night before, chasing after another liver, getting ready for another operation. I'll never forget about leaving on the glasses again.

No glasses, no matter what, not with photographers.

"You did that," he said, as if I needed reminding. It was Mitchell's operation, and it was a success. The new liver kicked in almost at once. He's home now, ready to celebrate his fourteenth birthday. Probably the first birthday party he's ever enjoyed. Here's to you, Mitch! Many more.

"So I need a liver, too, and this is the place."

His self-assured tone went with the rest of him, jolting me out of my pleasant reminiscences. My patients usually plead for, not demand, my intervention.

I couldn't stop saying them, but as soon as the words were out I regretted them. I heard myself say, "Well, just tell me what size you are."

He sat back, looking puzzled. Only for a second, though; then his big handsome face broke open in a wide grin, his teeth flashing in his broad black face, laughing at himself, at the world, probably.

"That's good, Doc! That's good. Like I'm coming in here asking for a liver like livers come in boxes and sizes like shoes."

"They don't," I said.

The nonsense was over. He took a breath and fixed me with the first direct look of the interview.

"I appreciate that. I do. I read all what that kid had to go through. It was moving. And what you did saved his whole life—and no question about that."

He was quiet, looking away from me. Then the tremor came into his voice, one that I had not yet, maybe never will, get used to: the sound of someone asking for a miracle.

"I need that liver, Dr. Toussaint. I'm going to die."

I shuffled some papers, some other potential transplant patient's file—official, neat, and organized, ready to be considered officially. But he hadn't offered me any file, nothing but a newspaper story about one of my better days.

"Your regular physician, the doctor who has been seeing you. I need a referral, something telling me what he thinks."

I don't think he was listening because he just repeated, "I'm going to die."

"Is that what your doctor told you?"

Every muscle in his face—his whole torso—seemed to tighten in anger as if even the memory of whatever confrontation he had had with his physician still aroused his every instinct for survival.

"Told me there wasn't anyplace going to give *me* a liver. No place he was going to send me to, anyways. Told me to go home and wait. He meant, wait to die."

"He didn't . . . no one would say that," I heard myself muttering without conviction.

He leaned back, looking at me with a critical, almost pitying gaze. "What do you think he meant?"

"I really don't know anything about your case," I said, at once ashamed of the lie. I knew all about cases like his.

"I'm end-stage liver failure. My liver's shot. Yeah. Cirrhosis. I blew it. You know my case now? Know the end of the story?"

He was posing it as a question, but he and I both knew the answer.

If he waited, he would die. If he waited much longer, he would certainly die. Within months, within the year. At least this guy recognized what his doctor wouldn't—waiting often equals death. The sooner the job is done, the better chance of survival. That's the simplest part about organ transplantation. The part most people still haven't learned.

"You going to decide if you can take me as a patient?" he asked with patience. "How much time do you need to make up your mind whether I live or die?" was what he was asking.

"You mean, can I list you?"

"That how you say it, 'list me'?"

"Organs, especially livers, are in short supply. There's always a waiting list."

"What more do you need to know than that I need it?"

He was right. It was the only question worth asking. But it never had a simple answer. So I just repeated the obvious: "The supply is limited, the need isn't."

We both fell silent for a moment. I almost felt as if he were deliberately giving me time to think, to work my way through all the negatives he had already heard. He held my eyes with his for a moment, and I think he just shrugged his shoulders. *We're both in this together. It's not a perfect system, but you can make it work. You're going to make it work for me.* I was reading his mind, but I was probably right.

"I read about that. I'll donate mine when the times comes if it would help," he said abruptly, startling me out of my trance.

"It won't, not after all it has been through."

"I mean the new one. When I'm through with it."

He had gotten up while I was trying to get the point of this last remark and was offering me his large, work-worn hand across the desk. A deal completed.

"I need a referral from your physician before I can consider your case. Then there's the question of insurance, payment . . ."

Again he cut me short, still holding my hand, lost in his, holding too tight for comfort.

"I sometimes need that hand . . . you know . . . to operate with," I said.

He dropped the precious object, and I got it out of sight, away from the apologetic administerings I feared he was about to offer.

"You have to make an appointment at the desk. You have to be examined. We need your records."

"How soon do I go on the list?"

"I really don't even know enough yet to make any evaluation, let alone a final decision. It can take months. I can't promise anything," I replied, reasonably enough.

"Come on, Doc!" he boomed, looking for a moment as if he were going to reach over the desk and jolt me into getting the point with a swift one to the jaw. "You ain't gonna let me die right after gettin' to know me so well."

And he was out the door, all jaunty steps and arms swinging, mission accomplished. Yes, in Stan's opinion his life-and-death mission had been accomplished.

"Was that typical male assurance?" I asked myself, or just plain ignorance of what this business—the art and craft of organ transplantation—was all about? Or was that the kind of absolute confidence some patients insist on placing in us surgeons, who are the last chance before the inevitable, the predictable, the unacceptable?

From the first meeting with Stan, I got to know the essential thing about him. Stan wasn't going to go without a fight. That made him a good transplant candidate. He'd be part of the team. He still had the spark in him. If he had come to me sooner, with more of his body intact . . . Unfortunately, even without knowing his case in any detail I knew that official medical opinion at this late stage in his deterioration was against him. He was too far gone to be a good transplant candidate. Why he wasn't sent to me sooner, why so many other patients weren't, was a question that continually plagued me. It was against official medical opinion, that's all. Official opinion would probably also be against me if I decided that Stan, in spite of his present condition and past life, was worth the risk.

It was quiet in Mr. Grand's room. Too quiet and too dark, no TV, no music, no light sufficient to read by. But to read, Mr. Grand would have to be sitting up in a chair, or at least in his hospital bed. But he wasn't and probably had not been all day. Probably had not sat up or moved, certainly had not gotten out of his bed, no matter how much he was coaxed.

It took a lot of coaxing to get Mr. Grand to move, but you couldn't do it without his cooperation. Even as sick as he was, Mr. Grand continued to live up to his name. "On the grand scale," as his daughter described him, with great affection. Something about his size and his sheer bulk had the power to draw amazed looks from other patients. On the rare occasions when he felt up to a walk around the nurses' station, the image of his six-foot-six frame moving slowly, like some slow-motion natural force, brought a hush that lasted till he passed. People then looked at one another, almost in embarrassment, thinking they had given in to some kind of superstition and had been caught worshiping a graven image, a cultured icon.

I didn't have to check the chart to remind myself of the orders: Mr. Grand had to sit up, get up from the bed, and be encouraged to walk each day, several times a day.

"It usually takes at least three of us, and even then most of the time he just goes dead in our arms," I heard the small voice behind me say, but I didn't turn around. I wasn't pleased.

"I don't want him dead. I want him alive and moving. Let's try it now." I know I wasn't being polite, but orders were orders, and I had written them.

Giving a politely suppressed but still audible sigh, tiny Janet, Mr. Grand's usual nurse, got around the other side of the bed and bent over his impressive bulk, whispering gently, as if to let him know that she was calling him back with as much reluctance as he had to be called back.

With Mr. Grand, that was not how my orders were going to be carried out. "Get someone to help. Someone big." Again, I was not being polite. Pulling rank, for the moment at least. "Make up for it later," I promised myself.

"There isn't anyone as big as Mr. Grand."

I just motioned to her to get behind the man's shoulder and heave. I called out to him in a louder than normal voice, "Mr. Grand! Mr. Grand! Have to sit up now. Sit up. Up. Have to get your feet over the side of the bed. Now, Mr. Grand. Up, now!"

We had already, over the last months, twice drained fluid from Mr. Grand's grotesquely swollen abdomen and then sent him home to wait for the liver that could, possibly, save his life. And each time he had returned to us as swollen, as reluctant to move as before. But only by some physical activity, even a slow—monumentally slow—walk around the corridor, could we give his body a chance to cooperate with us, use whatever resources were left to keep himself going until the operation when someone else's liver would take over for his.

We had even inserted a line to feed him when he began to refuse food and had sent him home with that, making sure a nurse came regularly to watch the line for infection, which of course happened, meaning another admission and another week in the hospital. How Mr. Grand retained his monumental size on that liquid feeding was part of the mystery of Mr. Grand.

I spoke louder, determined to get his eyes open. I was determined to settle for that outward sign, even though I couldn't be sure I had actually caught his attention or interest.

"Mr. Grand! When the nurse, when Janet, asks you to do something, I want you to know that is something I have asked—something I have ordered. It's on your chart because I ordered it."

Something in the tone of my voice, or perhaps in the words I had used, finally connected. Mr. Grand stopped letting us do the work and was actually helping Janet and me raise him to a sitting position in the bed. I let go, moving back, then motioned to Janet to do the same. Mr. Grand made the last few inches on his own, sitting upright now, his hands reaching for the covers and pulling them up slightly. He opened his eyes and looked directly into mine.

I assumed he was asking me to clarify my last statement, so I repeated with some slight emphasis: "I ordered it."

Let him figure that one out on his own, I thought, as I took the chart and repeated the orders. I have more important things to deal with than wondering if this large, dying man is comfortable knowing that I, a small female, am giving the orders. I don't even have time to wonder if he, a large black male, is comfortable knowing that he is in the care of a woman of color who is much younger. What really troubles me is that he is my patient, but he doesn't seem to be interested in the only thing I can do for him at this stage—save his life, if that's at all possible—with all the effort and expertise and experience I can bring to it—me and the others on the transplant team.

Mr. Grand just didn't seem to care. I had gotten the impression that the whole thing wasn't Mr. Grand's idea at all. It was true and a truth I had often tried to avoid. There are patients like Mr. Grand, patients who are no longer willing to participate in their own recovery. Where there's a will there's a way, and where there isn't . . .

Still, I had to care, and I had to get him to care. But how could I do that when he seemed unwilling to meet me even halfway? Whether I could get him to care or not would make a difference, because transplantation surgery is possibly the most cooperative kind of endeavor in all of surgery. It depends not just on my skill but on the patient's spirit. How to evaluate that spirit is always a problem, one that medical science alone cannot answer. Science can determine whether the patient is physically able to withstand the ordeal of surgery and the long follow-up. But how can a doctor know if the patient has the strength of character, the will to become a critical part of the process of recovery? Of course I listen, and I watch how each patient responds. I read and interpret subtle signs that always do manage to come across—the sudden downcast eyes, the tightening of a muscle in the face, signs of weariness and uncertainty. The signs of determination and strength as well are there to be read and evaluated. Perhaps I have learned to make these judgments from patients whose transplants succeeded or failed. But now I trust my instinctive evaluation of the patient before embarking on an operation. In my field—surgery— where it is almost always a matter of life or death, there is little room or time for pretense. So what I intuitively sense about a patient is true because the patient and I have arrived at the trite phrase: the moment of truth.

And this was why I wondered about Mr. Grand and his chances.

* * *

The next week Stan came back. He called, several times, and I said I would consider his case. This time he had his file, but no referral. There wasn't any real mystery about that. He had end-stage liver disease, end-stage kidney disease.

What's more, his only contact with a physician was through his HMO, which was unlikely to be interested in footing the bill for Stan's liver transplant. And there was another critical factor: The physician who would make the decision also happened to be sitting on the HMO board that would make the medical-financial decisions that would decide Stan's future. One of those unlucky coincidences for Stan. Unlucky, in this case even possibly deadly.

You get to realize that medical decisions are never purely medical. Someone is always deciding if someone else's life is worth it, worth the dollars and cents, the time and effort it will cost to save it. It's the kind of lesson you don't start getting until long after you leave medical school.

I didn't want to bring the matter up with Stan, not then, with him stripped in front of me and my wondering if we should admit him then and there and get some of that fluid drained from his swollen abdomen. Give him that much relief at least. He had lost a bit of his swagger as he took off his clothes, I figure probably he was embarrassed at having to let me peer and poke at what he had made, what time and circumstances and just plain bad luck had made of what must have been a shape he was proud of, glad to work to keep in shape . . . no gain without pain and all the other locker-room slogans. For the moment, as I explained to him what I had in store for him, I felt like cheering him up with a good "no gain without pain."

But he might have thought I was mocking him. He was probably still enough of a jock to think that if it came from someone like me. In any case, I could reassure him that the CT scan showed no cancer in his liver. And he wasn't suffering from malnutrition, at which news he laughed outright, grab-bing a handful of his distended abdomen as evidence of the truth of that statement. I couldn't correct him and say that it wasn't because he was overeating that he had that belly on him now, at his still-young forty-eight years.

Most of my patients can't bear the thought of food and weaken themselves through malnutrition. Let Stan eat as long as he could and wanted to. The desire to eat would disappear along with everything else enjoyable in his life if he didn't get transplanted soon.

From a strictly rational point of view, Stan could be consid-ered typical, the end-stage patient in a more or less general state of denial, so focused on the possibility of a cure that he didn't have the time or perhaps didn't want to waste the psy-chic energy thinking about all the things that stood in his and, of course, my way to that cure.

The first hurdle was the thing itself, the liver that would have to be found for him, assuming that his depleted body would hold out that long. The scarcity of organs is something we have had to live with for decades (okay, that's a contradic-tion in terms, saying *live with* when what actually happens is that patients who need transplants *die from* the scarcity).

The second hurdle, something Stan seemed willing to let me bring up on my own, was money. His insurance was not go-ing to cover the operation, nor would his physician recommend that his HMO foot the bill. After all, the rational argument goes, in times of diminishing resources, such expensive proce-dures as organ transplantation must be rationed. But in times of rationing, guess whose belt gets tightened another notch?

I kept him in for a few days of tests and let him know he would be listed. I told him he could start really worrying now, and he said, "Don't worry, Doc. You can trust me."

"You're supposed to trust *me*," I replied in my starchiest pro-fessional manner, which I knew he wasn't buying.

"Maybe it works both ways," he answered quietly, and I had to agree with him.

The questions remained about Mr. Grand. Was he ready, was he ever going to be ready or, instead of worrying about that, why not just decide to do him the second a liver is available? Just assume he would be ready by the time we were.

Again I spoke with him about what the operation would demand of him and asked if he felt up to it. Because if he couldn't muster the strength, we couldn't, in conscience, subject him to all those hours of surgery, the risk of rejection, infection, or death. I don't know if he grasped what I was saying, although he listened and nodded and said yes to everything.

What I really wanted to tell him was that he, too, had to participate. He had to want the procedure, the organ itself, even come to think of it as a kind of harmonizing union.

His wife and daughter were anxiously waiting, knowing the time was getting close as he inched his way to the top of the list. That's when I noticed what I had probably been avoiding for weeks. It was in their eyes and anguished looks. They simply could not imagine life without him. The possibility, the very real, almost immediate possibility of his death, had terrorized them. I couldn't grasp the concept they had of their lives together, but I knew they wanted his life more than he did.

Suddenly, the waiting was over. A call from a nearby hospital informed us that a suitable organ was available. Things would move now, at a pace that would not even give us time to consider how fast and frantic it was. Events would whirl past us, but we would have to be calm, cool, collected, plying our trade, our skills, in the eye of the storm. That was a way of looking at it, but most of the time I felt as if my head were in the calm eye while the rest of my body was being buffeted by mighty-high winds and I had to struggle to keep my balance.

The donor was a twenty-seven-year-old motor accident victim, brain-dead but with intact and excellent liver and kidneys. Ideal. Tragic, yet ideal for my patient. I could not even begin to question the mystery of the gift.

I would be doing the donor hepatectomy, the one-and-a-half-hour-to-two-hour procedure to recover the still living organ from the brain-dead accident victim. I would also be doing the recipient operation, a long day and night overall.

But first the patients, Mr. Grand and Stan. I had to make sure Stan was at the hospital and completely prepared. He was not going to have first shot at the liver, Mr. Grand was one step above him. Stan was just a standby. I would also, in the few minutes I would have with him, have to help him deal with both the excitement of maybe getting a life-extending liver and the possibility that he would remain just a standby.

As usual with everything connected with organ transplantation, there's more to it than these emotions. Stan would also have to deal with the natural anxiety about the operation itself, about the risk of his body rejecting the organ in the days and weeks after the operation. And if he actually got to the operating table, he would also have to know that he was there only because someone else wasn't. Stan knew enough to understand that someone, the unknown someone who was giving him a chance at a new life by not being strong enough to take the chance himself, may have just received a death sentence.

They were doing the preoperative—preop—prep on Stan when I got to his room on the regular floor, not in the ICU—the intensive care unit—where Mr. Grand was being worked up. As I expected, Stan was ready with a joke when I arrived.

"Always a bridesmaid, never a bride. Ain't that it, Doc?"

"I think it's always an understudy, never a star," I said, trying to be professional and poking about his only slightly swollen abdomen. He had been following orders. He was in good shape, considering he was end-stage, not for one vital organ but for two, liver and kidney.

"You great surgeons are all show-biz!" he retorted. And he knew I suspected he was right.

I had to get down to business, so I motioned for him to sit on the bed and pulled my chair up close. Then, surprisingly, I couldn't find a way to begin.

Seconds, precious seconds, ticked by, and then, as if aware of the clock, we began speaking together, Stan saying, "The organ, it's someplace close?" I responding, "At least the organ is close."

We were both silent until he said quietly, "If you see any of the family . . ." But he didn't go on.

"I mean," I picked up when we had both faltered again, "I used to have to fly all over the place, wherever an organ was available. Accidents happen all over the place, like sudden death. . . . Got to see a lot of America in the dark. Anyway, this one is a taxi ride away."

"You're taking a taxi?" he asked with surprise.

"Sometimes I do. Or a limo. I'd take a dogcart if necessary."

"Give you more time to do a leisurely job . . . on the other guy . . . if not me."

"You'll be next, if not this time."

"Thank them for me if you have time. Tell 'em I appreciate the gift—not just the organ, if things work out I get it, but what they are giving. Someday I hope I can find them and thank them for having enough love to think of someone else. Doc, they think just like you. Don't matter I'm not deserving. I'm just alive and suffering."

Stan, my deserving patient, had gotten it right again.

The donor procedure was routine, if you could ever get used to opening up a strong young body and seeing the still living organs, the liver still smooth and pink, remarkably, beautifully smooth, soft, and pink, yes, like a baby's bottom, and still performing its miraculous functions of purification. But not for this poor soul. The organs perform just as long as the machinery can hum quietly along, keep them going, keep the heart and the blood pressure normal—until we take what is needed and let them turn off the respirator, shut it all down, for good this time. You have to keep reminding yourself that turning off the machine is not really a second death, just the culmination of a death begun.

Whatever of this person is eternal had gone before us, whatever is still living and mortal we are taking with us. It helps, it always has helped, to remember that this person's last act, even though involuntary, was an act of love. There is always an aura of reverence in the place where we perform this first act in the drama of organ transplantation.

The removal of the liver, technically speaking the hepatectomy, was going beautifully, on schedule, every second saved here giving us more time later in the evening when the grueling, hours-long transplantation itself would be done. With the help of two assistants I had entered the abdominal cavity via a long midline incision, then saw at once that the liver was in excellent shape. Every other step followed almost automatically, by the book, with great attention.

We have the liver but won't wait to get the kidneys, although we want to lay claim to them now. I tell the organ-procurement coordinator that we will call as soon as possible when we know which of our patient's medical statuses warrants immediate transplantation. I'm thinking of Stan and the chance that he will graduate from standby to star tonight. We could do his kidney right after the liver transplant if necessary. I feel confident he's up to the eighteen or so hours the kidney-liver transplant operation will need. I don't want to think that I have already, in my mind at least, given him the liver destined for Mr. Grand.

I know I will have about two hours between securing the organ and the transplant procedure. I'll need the break. I'm looking forward to at least twenty more hours of work, if not more, and even though I have a team that has learned to work together superbly, instinctively, I'm still in charge. I will have a bonus for this procedure, I remember. David, Dr. Dave, my mentor from my fellowship days at what we all called Mecca, the great Mecca of transplantation where I studied for three grueling years. Dave has promised to assist me during the operation. With Dr. Dave assisting you get that special feeling that your own guardian angel has suddenly appeared in the flesh. It gives you a kind of slightly ambivalent feeling. You love having someone you can lean on, but you also get the feeling you don't dare risk making a mistake. Guardian angels notice everything. But tonight Dr. Dave would be my assisting surgeon. I would be in charge, I again reminded myself. In charge, responsible for the outcome.

I rested for a few minutes, then went to see Stan, who was sitting quietly in his room, alone. He had already been prepped and had the procedure described to him again, just to get his official and legal consent, although we knew we had that from the first day he arrived in my office. There wasn't much we had to say now, but I asked him anyway if he had any questions.

"Just one, Doc. You didn't forget about the kidney, did you?"

"Best I could do was put a reserve on it."

"Reserve? How long that last?"

"Kidney or reserve?"

"Okay," he conceded. "Either one."

"Don't worry," I answered, holding out my hand, wanting instead to give him a big hug just to tell him I cared, was worried, couldn't do any more than that at the moment.

Then he did it, reached out and took my hand, gently this time, in both of his, shaking his head. "Doc," he said, "I'm not worried. I'm impatient, that's all. You know me well enough now to know that I'm impatient. And all this has been taking time."

He didn't have to add "time I don't have to spare."

What he said was "Doc, be with me. Help me find the way."

Every minute counted now, but I had by this time learned how to tune out time, sidestep the minutes shouting for me to get moving. I would stay until I knew that Stan had begun to move, away from his anxiety and fear, into the kind of necessary calm that would do as much for him now as anything I could prescribe. I said, "You're there."

His answer seemed to me tinged with sadness, almost shame. He said quietly, "No."

I knew when not to argue with Stan, so I just said, "Close."

He hesitated a split second, then agreed. "Okay."

His hands still held mine, but now so gently I could not tell. We were together, listening to what might have been time itself passing quietly, not hurrying, giving us space. I did not have to nod in agreement or coax him. He was listening, as I was, to his breathing, each breath yielding completely to the next and the next, without a seam, life itself.

I left him embraced by the calm that would protect him as he yielded his hurt body for us to administer to.

Outside his room, hurrying now that I knew the minutes had started to tick past and fast again, I had my mind fixed again on the coming hours.

The kidney, if we were going to have a chance to use it, should be used within forty-eight hours. It would last that long, even slightly longer, on the perfusion machine. But if the chance came to do a liver transplant on Stan and we had a good kidney on reserve, waiting, it was going to be something of a race with time, or, more likely, a race against time, to transplant both.

Doing both a liver and a kidney transplant back to back, as it were, makes doing the kidney risky. If the new liver doesn't work well, uncontrollable bleeding will ensue and the new kidney will have to be given to the next medically stable candidate. The kidney transplant itself becomes more risky because of increased chance of bleeding even if the liver works immediately. If things work out so that we actually do Stan's liver and then begin the kidney procedure, he will have been on the operating table for at least twelve hours. If there are any problems with the liver procedure, we may need up to twenty-four hours for that procedure alone. If all these ifs become real, he would be lying there, unconscious, wide open, all that time. It gets real cold when the body is wide open—worse than standing in a blizzard with your mouth wide open. Stan's heart will not like it one bit.

After the hushed quiet of the operating room where I had removed the donor liver, my own operating room seemed irreverently casual, with enough just plain chatter and gossip interspersed with the reassuring technical jargon to put one at ease. But by now we were a team, had trained mostly together, respected one another's expertise. No one on the team was especially uptight about this procedure, no more than usual, that is. My second assistant had also trained under Dave, so that made it cozier, or perhaps added just the right amount of apprehension to keep us all on our toes.

Mr. Grand looked monumental under the surgical cap, but he did not look good. Again I could feel my instincts calling out that this was not going to go, this was not going to work. I wasn't alone in this, apparently, because I caught the questioning glances going from one to another of our anesthesiology team. (The anesthesiologists are truly essential members of the liver transplant team, responsible for putting the patient into deep sleep, monitoring and medically treating him, basically ensuring that he is alive during the entire transplant operation.)

They were taking Mr. Grand's blood pressure and temperature. Neither was encouraging; both were worse than they had been just a short time ago, before the lines were inserted. We can tolerate a certain bit of elevated temperature in some pre-transplant patients, but not this sudden rise. The pressure was dropping by the second. We couldn't tolerate that, either. If one or the other of these warnings had flashed before, hours certainly but even moments before, we would have known what to do. It was quiet in the room now. The only activity was in the next room at the back table, where two surgeons were preparing the organ. The liver transplant could not be delayed indefinitely, for it has its own timetable independent of ours.

Then Dave motioned for me to follow him outside. "He doesn't look good. Low pressures, high pulses and temperature . . . And still you brought him in here?"

"He didn't have them before he was brought in here," I answered, not even bothering to hide the defensiveness in my voice. Dave had been part of my training, he should have known better than to accuse me of making such elementary mistakes.

"You want my opinion?"

"Why did I ask you to be here?"

"This one will wind up on your record as a surgical death," he said simply, firmly, unequivocally.

"I'm not interested in my record!" I almost snarled at him.

"Okay, look at it another way. This one will wind up dead. And on your record anyway. If you don't make up your mind soon, this liver will have to be trashed, wasted, even though there are many candidates out there waiting for it."

What else but impeccable, irrefutable, infallible argument from a guardian angel?

I tried to turn away, but he would not let me. We were face-to-face, and he was talking quietly, only to me, quietly even though I was the only one there. He said, "You get attached to your patients. It happens with every surgeon, especially transplant surgeons. We want to do everything to keep them alive. Without the liver they will die. They'll be miserably sick and then die. You want to prevent that, do your duty to the patient and the family. But you have to learn when it isn't possible anymore. Sometimes there comes a time when you can't do any more, and it is no reflection on you that you can't. No one likes to make such a life-and-death decision. But we all have to face the decision at some time, sooner or later. Remember the three years we worked together? You saw me facing decisions like this. The most difficult ones. Learning how to make them was part of your training, too."

I did lean on him then, felt his reassuring bulk and strength. That is sometimes the best (or maybe the most comforting?) part of men—their reassuring bulk and presence when you need something to lean on, against, one place to give you a few seconds of security.

We went back in and faced the others, now watching us without a sound or movement. Lucky for me a gesture was enough, a shrug and some small turning up of my hands. Good team players that they were, they seemed to mirror my feeble gestures, a nice way to let me know they agreed, would have advised the same, done the same.

And then they began to move as only a surgical team under pressure can move, as only a transplant team with the clock ticking away the life of a precious organ can move. We all knew we were going to use that organ, and the kidney I had on reserve was only a phone call away.

We knew we had a patient who was ready, body, mind, and soul.

*   *   *

It was Stan's turn now, his turn because we had both the organs he needed on ice, waiting, in a kind of suspended animation. And as I tried to relax, maybe even drop off for a few minutes while waiting out the two hours it would take to prep Stan, the three hours to get the OR ready for this second operation, I kept thinking of those organs.

The liver was already four hours old, still in its ice cooler.

I hoped it was still as soft and rosy as a baby's bottom. I guess I have grown particularly attached to this image because I hadn't yet had my own baby, close, at home, reassuring to touch, bottom and all. Maybe I'll give up transplantation and do pediatrics, or perhaps there's a better way to get close to a baby. My own biological clock is ticking away, time is running out, I better meet Mr. Right fast, get married, and have my own babies soon, before it is too late.

The kidney would fare a bit better, I kept reassuring myself.

It was hooked up to the perfusion apparatus, artificially maintained, being flushed continually. Nevertheless, it, too, was aging. I checked my watch: It had been six hours since it was removed. Not too much in itself to worry about, but the kidney had a long way to go before Stan would be prepared to accept it.

I found myself going through the grade school arithmetic of the thing: five hours in all preop; more or less ten hours for the old liver out, new liver in procedure; with any luck and no complications (if we had difficulty establishing hemostasis, bleeding would delay us until we could slow it down), then the kidney implant would take about three hours. Did I need toes as well as fingers to figure out the hard numbers here?

Did I lose the exact count at this point? Or maybe I did not want to recognize that my patient, Stan, would be on that table for seventeen hours—a day in Stan's life. Let it be the first day in Stan's new life.

The beeper demanded my attention. But before I could handle whatever was important enough to intrude on my time before going off to surgery (not exactly like being buried alive, but close), I had to think about Mr. Grand—no, not about him but his wife and daughter. They would, of course, have been there to receive him when he was taken back to the intensive care unit after the aborted attempt at transplantation. The surgical resident would have explained. I hope, yes, I knew, he would have found some way around the obvious, some way to turn "hopeless" into something more tolerable. I would have to go and meet them soon, within the hour. It was cowardly of me to hope that the beeper was announcing some emergency that would occupy every available second before Stan's operation.

The call was from a hospital only a few miles away—being more than a bit travel-shy, I heaved a little sigh of relief at that. The emergency you can drive to is always preferable to the emergency you have to fly to. This is going to be one of the first maxims in "Advice to the Young, Overworked Transplant Surgeon," my best-selling exposé of life in and around the OR. But the emergency was real enough, for all its accessibility.

The patient was a twenty-seven-year-old black female diagnosed with end-stage liver failure, acute fulminant type of unknown etiology. Pick the phrase that disturbed you the most: twenty-seven-year-old, female, black, end-stage, acute fulminant liver failure, unknown etiology.

I listened to a quick run-through of the slow agony this woman, her husband, her family had been going through for the past few weeks, made even worse by the brutal abruptness with which it had fallen on them, like being taken in ambush by unknown assailants, like being robbed at gunpoint, like waking up suddenly paralyzed, speechless, blind.

She went home from work at her steady, stable government job with what everyone said was a bad case of flu. And she went to bed. And stayed there. For days, sleeping hour after hour after hour until day or night came to mean nothing to her. When she woke she was confused, irritable, irascible, argumentative. Her husband gave her the benefit of the doubt: She's sick and out of sorts, so maybe her mother should deal with her.

It's still really strange to me that people don't automatically think the worst. Why didn't they think something was terribly wrong instead of just a routine case of the flu when she slept endlessly, waking up only to wander in a kind of stupor around the house. The medical people she had first seen had done their work dutifully. The lab test documented high liver function tests one day after she managed to get to the health department at her job.

If I had seen her sooner I would not have worried about the "etiology unknown," not worried about finding a cause. Patients with fulminant liver failure don't usually survive in spite of all the intensive care they are given. Brenda had received some of this care. They had placed a nasogastric tube in her in an effort to reduce her ammonia level and treated the swelling of her brain with diuretics and steroids. Because she was half comatose they had to watch so that she would not regurgitate into her lung and either choke to death or develop pneumonia. Strenuous measures, and all of them temporary, marking time. Patients such as Brenda don't survive without the ultimate heroic measure, the one I could perform.

Yes, I heard myself assent, I would come over and examine the patient, talk to the family, see what I could—what could be done. I hung up the phone and then realized I had not asked one critical question: What had already been done? Not what efforts had been and were being made to stabilize her, but what, if any, effort had been made to save her. There was a difference. I still had to learn that the efforts I had by now taken for granted, assumed had to be done, would not necessarily be done by other physicians and wouldn't be seen as automatic for a patient like Brenda. What I had come to know and believe in as salvation, and thus necessary, obligatory, was also being seen as too costly, experimental, untested, untried, unnecessary. For myself, I did not have to meet Brenda and her family before I made up my mind that nothing about them was unnecessary.

I went into the OR for Stan's liver and kidney transplant knowing I would not be free for at least a day, a day and some more hours tacked on. And I knew I would have the next day and night and most likely more already spoken for. The next challenge—no, that wasn't right, I knew at once—the next chance for life was called Brenda.

CHAPTER 2

Yes, it's an indulgence, but I never apologize. In any case, people expect doctors to ride around in expensive cars and I don't
have it in my heart to disappoint the public. Now, it's entirely
likely that the "public," on seeing me behind the wheel, assume
some really eccentric M.D. has gone and hired himself a lady
chauffeur. How else to reconcile those intimidating letters before
the numbers on the license plate with my presence up front
in this most luxurious, polished-to-perfection, gently humming
along vehicle?

But as I say, I never apologize. I have even learned to
smother any possible sprouts of guilt by putting my time behind the wheel to good use. As I am doing now, dictating the
operative report covering my share of the work just done
on Stan as I coast along through one of the nicer sections of

Washington, D.C. (how my vehicle, if not its driver, must feel
at home!), heading for my first encounter with Brenda and her
desperately anxious family. The thought of them, the remembered tremor in the mother's voice as she tried to describe the
young woman's sudden, violent collapse, energizes me and I
want to speed up my dictation, it being now impossible, in the
late afternoon near rush hour, to increase the speed at which
I am traveling. As the traffic snags at a packed intersection I
note with a certain satisfaction that even the most affluent sections of the city bear burdens similar to those carried by the
less fortunate among us. Nevertheless, these tree-lined streets,
set-back houses—sorry, residences—surrounded by dollops of
well-trimmed shrubs like sober green statues in attendance,
clean windows, clean gutters, all this was in stark contrast to
the tired, workaday neighborhoods that circled my own hospital for miles. I heard my involuntary thought as if I had asked
the question out loud: "How much is a stay out this way—to
say nothing of treatment—costing Brenda and her family?"

I play back what I had dictated, seeing in my mind's eye the
body that had lain on the table under my scalpel for so many
hours and was probably only just now being closed and made
of one piece again. I had wisely turned over Stan's kidney transplant to Dr. Jones, one of my favorite teachers and mentors
during my general surgery residency. This would be the first of
many such combined liver and kidney procedures we would
do, building in the process a complete transplant team.

Liver is my specialty, and I rejoiced in being able to say at
the end, "The patient tolerated the procedure well, in a critical
but stable condition." I guess if you had to write the opposite,
as I have had to do, you could forgive the emotion the words
call up in a transplant surgeon. So by now Stan's new kidney
had probably settled in along with his new liver, and the kidney team's report would, with continuing good luck, strike the

same satisfied note as mine: The patient's responses demon-
strated good function of the graft.

I hadn't, of course, turned Stan over to the kidney transplant team led by Dr. Jones with a casual "He's all yours, Doc."
Months before the operation I had alerted our nephrology
team (rather kidney dialysis service) that Stan would require
continuous blood filtration during the operation. The filtration process, called continuous veno-venous hemofiltration,
was essential in first ridding Stan of excess fluid and second in
removing excess potassium, which could compromise his heart
function. To be on the safe side, two nurses alternated being
on beepers around the clock for months while waiting for the
moment when we had secured the organs for the operation.

Stan had been on dialysis for his failed kidney, and this
meant that he had required dialysis throughout the liver transplant, especially prior to unclamping the vessels when blood
flow starts through the new liver. That was the most dangerous
moment, the seconds you have nightmares about. For immediately after unclamping, the transplant patient is in the greatest
danger of hyperkalemia—the sudden upsurge in potassium
that can bring the heart to a standstill, all your work coming
undone and the patient slipping away from you.

I played it extra-safe with Stan, making sure the continuous
hemofiltration was actually started as soon as he went to sleep,
hours before I estimated we would be ready to unclamp and
enter the ultimate danger zone. As usual, experience gave us
the edge and the hemofiltration carried out during the operation safeguarded Stan until he was out of the OR and in the
intensive care unit. That year, this successfully performed combined liver and kidney transplant was only one of forty-nine
such procedures performed in the United States. We made history that day for our hospital. It was a national and worldwide
first for our African-American Dialysis and Transplant Center.

*   *   *

I fiddle with the tape recorder and hear myself saying, "The hepatectomy was continued and terminated without much difficulty. The native liver was removed from the operative field. It was very small." A shorthand way of summing up hours of meticulous cutting away of surrounding tissues until the vessels were identified and isolated, dissected, and ligated: hepatic artery, common bile duct, portal vein, and its venous tributaries.

Naturally, Stan's liver was very small. As he was the first to admit, he had blown it with his long history of end-stage alcoholic cirrhosis. Long meant long—at least twenty years, although he had sworn off drinking a good seven years before appearing at my door, finally driven there by the recurring episodes of confusion, easy fatigability, and, most ominous, encephalopathy. Simply put, Stan had been hard at work poisoning himself, letting spill into his brain the toxins his liver could no longer filter, putting himself at the increased risk of confusion, stupor, and ultimately coma. He knew it was happening to him; he had understood it without benefit of the medical terminology he had recently learned. His mother and two brothers were all dead of complications of alcoholic cirrhosis. By some free gift of grace he had come to his senses before they were taken from him.

And now, still eyeing the vehicles on either side of me as they eyed mine, I began again to describe for the record the most taxing hours of the operation, placing the donor liver into the space I had created for it, uniting it with the waiting vessels we had clamped shut: suprahepatic vena cava, infrahepatic vena cava, portal vein, joining Stan's own vessels to these foreign conduits with sutures that must not be too tight, not too loose, only just right. Meticulous work of stitching that makes me think, How nice my hands are so small that I can do this "woman's work" without getting in my own way. There have been some advantages to being a woman that I should remember to be more appreciative of in the future.

Technically, this stitching is called anastomosis, and it can make or break you as a transplant surgeon, an attempt at a seamless joining of vessel to vessel, so delicately done that the body never realizes that one is its own, the other a gift.

Most of all I relive the critical moment of unclamping, the final test of all the previous work. I indulge myself with a bit of theatrics here, knowing that the tape will be erased, my voice with it, as my secretary types the final report. I say, rather grandly, "The patient tolerated the reperfusion well without hypotension." And then, even more grandly, "Minutes post reperfusion, profuse production of bile was evident." It came, the golden flow, as we call it, the flow of bile that was final evidence of the immediate functioning of the transplanted liver.

We still had to work on Stan for several hours after this, doing the arterial anastomosis, stopping bleeding, removing bypass tubes that were no longer necessary, washing the abdominal cavity with antibiotic and antifungal warm fluids, suctioning and mopping the fluid and blood, inserting the three drains that would remain in place for the next several days, beginning to close the peritoneal cavity, reuniting the three flaps into which we had divided the abdominal wall. We first had to join the underlying fascia in two layers and then stapled the skin in a great inverted Y pattern, not unlike the metallic Mercedes-Benz insignia.

And then I play back that amen for which I am always so grateful, "The patient tolerated the procedure well, in a critical but stable condition."

Traffic, even in the better neighborhoods, eventually eases up and lets you through, and I was at long last entering the parking lot of the hospital where Brenda and her family awaited me. The sense of urgency I had kept under control so far was now too strong to give me the luxury of time to search out a legitimate parking place in the lot. I sailed into an empty space clearly marked Staff Only and put on my Sue Me face. In any event, I knew the chief of gastroenterology, and he would be in charge of this case. We had served on some of the same review boards, and he had offered encouragement at first when I was struggling to get the liver transplantation unit on its feet. He had even promised me referrals, although I had learned, in the last year, not to take this promise too literally. But he probably owed me a favor or else I would have to owe him one. We'd even up later. I had scribbled down the building and floor in my book and double-checked them as I thrust myself between the closing doors of what I hoped was the right elevator.

I didn't have to worry that I wouldn't find my way because she was there, in the hallway, outside the closed door to the room where her daughter was fighting for life—or perhaps losing it. No mistaking the anguish on her face, but no mistaking either the determination to fight this inexplicable menace that threatened all she loved. She was wife, mother, grandmother, ageless, our classic woman, recognizable as a rock, the mainstay, where we look instinctively for help and hope. She looked nothing like my own mother, except that they were indistinguishable, identical in the strength they projected. She was indomitable, not to be cowered by anything, not the presence of death itself. And the minute I came into sight she fixed me with a look that said, "No! I won't let her die, nor will you."

Two nurses, stiff, tight-lipped, and disapproving, materialized on either side of Brenda's mother, not as if to offer support but rather to bar entry to the room. One, the stiffer, addressed her, not me, saying, "Any disturbance, visitors, is likely to set her off again. We are doing our best to keep her calm. You must cooperate." They were clearly out of patience and did not hesitate to show it. And because I still had my coat buttoned up against the cold, they could not read my hospital ID card, so they could be excused for not showing the proper deference due a doctor.

The woman ignored them, taking me by the arm and with her free hand pushing open the door, a gesture so quick and forceful it resulted in a mild collision, me with one of the two nurses, that my weak smile of apology did little to atone for. Drawing back out of any further contact, the nurse measured me for a split second, found something or perhaps everything apparently lacking, and announced in two sentences, "Family. Only." I saw I had missed my chance to identify myself. But Brenda's mother fixed her for a moment with a stare that had nothing of contempt in it, only a kind of resigned hopelessness, perhaps doubting if the message would ever penetrate. She said, "It's Dr. Toussaint. You don't recognize her from the newspapers and TV? She's family."

As she pulled me into the room, the door almost closing on me as I wiggled through the space she gave, I saw that the two starched professionals had been joined by several other people, patients perhaps, or visitors, all well dressed with none of the usual hospital slouch about them. The group looked at the two of us with some bewilderment, not unkindly, just puzzled by whatever fuss we had been bringing into their world. Nobody said it, not a shoulder shrugged, but you could hear the words: "What can you expect?" Later I would learn the cause of these looks of apprehension and distress: Brenda had been going in and out of a wild delirium. She could be heard all up and down the corridors, and she had been making the residents' and nurses' lives miserable by tearing out the nasogastric line they had inserted to administer medication to cool her off and ward off coma and death. As usual, nobody was being intentionally unkind, they were just eager to have the source of the disturbance, these alien people, removed.

The room was dark, but I could make out two shapes huddled close; the young man, sitting on the edge of the bed, had his arms around the woman and her head was buried against his chest, hidden by the bedcovers he had wrapped protectively around her, although the room was not cold, only dark and filled with tension and rank fear. Before I could come any closer the older woman again took my arm and pulled me gently toward her, whispering in the quiet, "My name is Bernice. We are not going to let her die."

At first I thought the words ended in a kind of question mark, but when she repeated them, with increased pressure from her hand on my arm, I knew there was no question about it. "We are not going to let Brenda die," she said, and then released me, standing aside, consigning Brenda to me with a kind of blind faith I had experienced before but at which I still trembled.

Perhaps the whispered words or the awareness of me, a stranger, another presence in the room, stirred the silent figure—whatever it was, its effect on Brenda was instant, explosive. She shot up, pushing the man, her husband, away so unexpectedly he slid from the bed and had to steady himself momentarily by grabbing for the bedside chair. The covers fell in a tangle about her bare feet so that she stumbled as she tried to move. She looked down, her face contorted, her eyes blazing, and then she swooped up all the covers and flung them away, the source of all her anguish.

"It's all this!" she screamed in a voice full of fury. "I don't need all this! I'm tired of all of you! Get out! Get the hell out of my life!"

Unsteady on her feet, the hospital gown falling from her shoulders, her braided hair wild, flying about her drawn and twisted face, she looked like some centuries-old picture of a patient in an insane asylum, except that we do not have such institutions any longer, we have drugs to sedate the mentally disturbed before they reach such a state of incoherence, before they come to look like ancient images of madness and say things they never even thought before.

I didn't need a CT scan to tell me what was happening to Brenda, although the scan would later confirm what I immediately suspected. The brief description of her condition

I had already been given—easy fatigability, then round-the-clock sleep, personality changes, irritability, abusiveness, incoherence—all of it prepared me for this late stage, where the poisonous ammonia level was so high that it now interfered with normal brain functions. Brenda was going "mad," but she was being driven there by the failure of her liver, the sudden buildup of ammonia that was, in a sense, drowning her brain and with that the person her family knew as Brenda.

I was jolted from almost automatic and logical assessment of the case before me into the present reality by another outburst from the distraught woman, who had turned to face her husband. For the first time I saw his young strong face and the terror aroused by this unknown person confronting him. He seemed at once to be both shrinking back from this madness and trying to reach out to catch her, to stop her from tumbling down into further madness.

She did fall on him, against him, with tight fists hitting rapidly on his solid shoulders, trying to push him away, although the poor young man was caught between the chair and the window wall and she was blocking with all the strength of frenzy any attempt at escape. He stood at least a head taller than she. The feeble blows caused such pain I could see the quiver of his lips and the tears welling in his eyes.

"What do you know about it?" she snarled. "What do any of you know about it? What do you care? Don't lie to me anymore!"

And then she turned away, dismissing him with a slashing gesture of her arm, cutting him off before he had found the strength to utter a single word. He covered his face with his hands, and I saw the dejected droop of his head, the slow movement of his body back and forth, the undisguised expression of unfathomable pain and despair.

"Brenda!"

It was Bernice's voice, loud in the room, spoken as the woman brushed past me and stood face-to-face with her daughter. "Brenda," she repeated, gently now, carefully reaching out but not taking her hand, stopping short of that, instead taking the fallen gown and settling it about Brenda's shoulders. The gesture had a sudden quieting effect. Brenda searched her mother's face for some seconds, then ran her hand through her braids, stopping, registering something, perhaps the unexpected disorder, the tangled strands, something not herself.

Bernice said, "It's Steve. And me. We're with you." Then she stepped aside, almost formally, indicating me to her daughter, saying, "This is Dr. Toussaint. She's here now. She knows."

Brenda did not acknowledge me in words, but I caught the change in her face, the flicker of her eye that indicated she was aware of a new presence, an unexpected entity in her shrinking world, but an entity she could still find room for. I took heart at this sign, knowing there was still time, not much, but still perhaps enough to matter.

Instead of speaking to me or to her mother, she again touched her hair, her gestures more purposeful now, moving from one disordered strand to another. She said in an almost normal voice, "Something is wrong, something happened. What happened?"

"Nothing, baby," Bernice began, trying to sound casual, everyday. "Just didn't have time to fix your braids this—"

Before she could finish, if she had the strength to do that, Brenda was in her arms, holding her tight, sobbing, now for a moment let back into the real world and some perception of the disorientation she had suffered for days now, ever since she went home from work feeling she was about to endure a few days of a bad cold, at worst, a mean bout of the flu. At that moment Steve joined them, and the three clung silently together, holding tight against the common danger. Brenda let herself sink into the man's arms as he guided her back to the bed. She clung to him then, sitting with him on the edge of the bed, her head against his shoulder, quiet now, exhausted, possibly falling into what we all prayed would be restful sleep, not stupor, no, not coma, although I knew clinically what they knew in their blood—from sleep Brenda could slip without notice into coma and then possibly into death. They had seen her losing herself in disturbed sleep for days, coming back less and less recognizable. They didn't need a medical degree to know that from such sleep one did not always return safely.

The risk of poisonous levels of ammonia, of severe hepatic encephalopathy, life-threatening cerebral edema—in other words, toxic substances passing from the liver's circulation into the brain, causing it to swell, coursing through the entire body—all these risks made the alarms go off. The conclusion rang clear: Brenda should be on the transplantation list as an emergency candidate, what we call Status 1, the unenviable position that gave the patient only one advantage, being first in the line for the next available donor liver. Since you could not predict when that would happen, you had to make sure you were ready for the chance, the miracle, when it came.

What took a few more moments to sink in should have been the first thing to occur to me. Brenda was still here, in this room, with no signs that she was being considered for a liver transplant. Liver transplant patients are among the most meticulously prepared patients in all of surgery. We subject them to everything we have: Doppler ultrasound of the liver vessels, tests of antimitochondrial antibodies and smooth muscle antibodies, hepatitis profile, head and abdomen CT scans, cardiovascular examination. If there is a technique proven and tested, we want to use it to make sure there are no surprises during the long ordeal of the transplant procedure itself. You do not want surprises in the OR, even though I've had experience with some of them. And always the blood tests; with transplant patients you have to draw so much blood they—and you—come to dread the experience, the painful probing to find yet another usable vein from the fast-diminishing supply that nature gave us.

With just a reassuring pat and a silently mouthed "Be right back," I left Bernice and Steve watching over the now quiet young woman and went to find the chief of gastroenterology. He was not to be found, but I did meet the only African-American Fellow in his service. I had previously met him during one of my presentations to the Medical Grand Round in this hospital. Yes, he said, they were aware of Mrs. Pointer's condition and they had been trying to deal with the . . . outburst . . . the other patients on the floor . . . and yes, they had been waiting for me before making any decision.

"Are you aware that her neurological status is deteriorating?" I asked. He hesitated, then muttered, "I don't think a CT scan was ordered."

I wanted to ask him how a deteriorating neurological status was determined before the CT scan was invented, but I figured he probably wasn't even out of high school in that distant pre–CT scan era when simple observation and patient history had to make do.

"Brenda"—I said the name with some emphasis, probably wanting to make the poor dying woman more real to him than his formal Mrs. Pointer allowed her to be—"Brenda has a weeklong history of lethargy, fatigue, somnolence, confusion, personality change, irritability, stupor . . ." I did not add the next stage, but I could see he knew the probability as well as I.

"We have been trying . . . to make her comfortable. . . ." There was so much hesitation and apology in his voice that I knew he wished he could offer more, something that could snatch this life back from the edge. It wasn't in his power to do any of it, but I knew he would have had the hospital provide liver transplantation services if he could have. I had to thank him for admitting that the real thing was not being done for Brenda.

He put through the call to his chief, several calls, several different places he knew could be tried in an emergency. Without any further pressure from me he realized this was an emergency and took it upon himself to be some part of it, even if the part was basically electronic hound dog, sniffing with beeper, answering machine, voice mail, on the trail until he got his man.

He didn't. I met with the chief not as a competitor, because his hospital did not have a liver transplant unit, but because he was a gastroenterologist and the narrow funnel through which patients might come my way. But he had to release Brenda to me soon, now.

People whose lives are in the hands of trained experts, doctors and surgeons, know that through those gifted, dedicated hands also pass the monetary rewards due them. That's fair. And in thanksgiving for a life improved or saved most people suppress the notion that sometimes the monetary rewards are in excess of the services rendered. Who can put a price on life or the quality of life preserved? We used to think this was an unanswerable question. Brenda was another reminder that answers were being given to the question, and some were not answers I was ready to accept.

Of course Dr. Grasso knew that Brenda was in end-stage liver failure, even though he had no answer as to why this normal, healthy daughter, wife, mother of children should be felled by acute fulminant liver failure. He was doing the best for her, he told me now, by calling me in and seeing if I would agree to take her as a transplant patient. I had to agree that the choice was the correct one, even if late. Brenda was still here, in this posh facility, being treated, for all I could discover, for episodes of peace-and-patient disturbing mania, tasteless displays of hysteria in the hallways, typical of the behavior of some female ethnic types not typically found here.

It was at this point that the descending curve of Brenda's life intersected with the bottom line of modern health care. Yes, her case was recognizable as a liver transplant emergency, but another reality stepped between us, the new medical-economic reality. And this reality had found something excessive in Brenda's present medical predicament and was not going to be responsible for it. Oddly enough, Brenda's insurance did cover her admission to Grasso's hospital as a patient with acute fulminant liver failure; unfortunately, it did not cover what is perhaps the only cure for the condition. Brenda's insurance, in an ironic or perhaps lunatic sense, just guaranteed her a place to die, right along with the 80 percent of Americans who die in health care institutions.

At this point I wanted to disregard the arguments for the new reality, arguments that try to convince me that medicine must be run by business managers with businesslike habits, and that both have a primary fiduciary responsibility to their stockholders. I had always thought and been trained to believe that our primary responsibility was to the patient, first, foremost, regardless, in spite of, no matter what. How else can physicians first do no harm if the patient is not first?

I did not take any joy from watching the fellow's embarrassment, and I guessed that his chief was avoiding similar discomfort, but they had the good grace not to talk to me about fiduciary matters. Brenda was, after all, Grasso's patient, but now he was turning her over to me because his hospital did not provide for liver transplantation, and without adequate insurance coverage or her own money she would be a financial liability to his hospital or any hospital that accepted her, including mine. I was acutely aware how this liability would affect my program and my hospital.

I did not want to use the telephone at the nurses' station, I could not use the one in Brenda's room, and my conversation with my own hospital's medical director was certainly going to be long enough to exhaust all the small change I had, so I just asked the fellow if he would leave me alone in his office because I had some rather delicate business to conduct and needed some privacy. He didn't ask what it was but brought me to his office and shut me in with what seemed to me a mixture of relief and some small degree of pity—he probably guessed what I was going to try to do. And he could sympathize with that.

Relief was not what I had for the next twenty minutes or so as I described Brenda's case to my hospital's medical director. He listened with patience to the clinical details, but then let the line stay dead for a few seconds before he asked the question I knew was coming. "No. No coverage," I said quietly, and sat back to listen to his quietly delivered explanation of why he could not, in conscience, agree to having the hospital assume the financial burden of yet another—he did stress "yet another"—transplant procedure that was not covered either by adequate insurance or private funds. We had had this discussion before, and of course his position remained unchanged.

I ran quickly through everything I could say in defense of Brenda and her family's financial responsibility: She was young, the family was stable, no drugs, no drinking problems, she had a good job as did her husband, had great potential, would in time be able to resume work and honor the accumulated debt to the hospital or more likely pressure the HMO to reconsider payment after her successful liver transplant. I felt as if I were filling out some school report card and giving her straight A's. His replies reflected the position he had taken with my previous requests, my previous uninsured, liability patients.

I was trying the obvious arguments since they were usually the most effective, because they were the most honest arguments. And then I simply put it all before him, saying, "We can't let her die, and she will certainly without us. We cannot abandon her, even though she has been abandoned. It is our moral duty to intervene now that she has been given to us to try to save."

I don't think this conversation was any longer than the last one. My medical director's position did not fail me nor my needy patient. I agreed, as I had before, to do all I could to find adequate reimbursement for the procedure, not immediately but as quickly as possible. After all, we are not a charitable institution, we have responsibilities to all our patients, not just our liver transplant patients. There has to be a limit on what we can provide. He let me go on, letting me explain that yes, she was Status 1 and had to be transferred immediately, readied as quickly as possible. The next available organ would be hers. I had my chance again, and so would Brenda.

I went back to the floor and began making preparations for moving Brenda to my hospital. She would have to be sedated, intubated to keep her airway open, another nasogastric tube inserted. The increasing portal-systemic encephalopathy would bring on more bouts of irrationality, even violence, and I could not risk her tearing out the tubes as she had done earlier. Nor could I risk the chance that she would vomit and with an unprotected airway end up aspirating the vomit. The end result could be pneumonia or choking to death, all of which were possible, even on the short ambulance trip that lay ahead.

I explained each step to Bernice and Steve and hoped they took it all in, getting reassurance from their eager nods and quiet repetitions of the most important words I was saying, quiet echoes of hope. Their looks went back and forth, and some faint hint of relief began to show in their wearied faces. Then came one of those episodes you want to shrink away from in embarrassment, a reminder that the noble practice of medicine is sometimes tripped up, if not bound hand and foot by pettiness. I had clearance from my hospital to do the operation, I had made sure Brenda was listed with the city's Organ Procurement Organization as Status 1, I had prepared her for the move—but I could not convince the ambulance to take her. I was having more difficulty explaining this snag to the disbelieving Bernice and Steve than I had in describing the likely effects of acute, fulminant liver failure. Bernice shook her head several times, then when the issue finally took its proper shape she just about exploded.

"The ambulance doesn't want to take my daughter to your hospital for her operation?"

It was more a challenge than a question, and the social worker who had brought me the ambulance rejection moved instinctively out of the way of this indignant volley.

"The ambulance?" Bernice continued in disbelief.

I began explaining, citing the lame explanation I had just been given, that the insurance coverage did not apply to ambulance transfers, which were considered a separate cost. I wanted to spare her the more cynical explanation that now occurred to me. The insurance company would not pay for the transplantation. They were reinforcing that position by refusing to pay for the transportation of the patient to a hospital where she would receive the transplant. To do so could be interpreted as meaning that the insurance company was agreeing to the transplant surgery.

"Steve," Bernice commanded. "Use your credit card."

Then, to the social worker: "They take credit cards?" And when the social worker looked at her in total disbelief, Bernice asked with some scorn, "How about personal checks? No? If you want cash we have to find a bank or a cash machine, so just tell us what it is you want."

I was not going to let any of that happen, of course, and within a mere three hours had settled with social worker, insurance company, and ambulance personnel. I had managed, at some cost in emotional capital, to drive home the sense of emergency that was now driving me. We finally had our patient in an ambulance and on her way.

Brenda's condition rapidly deteriorated. On the first day the severe cerebral edema kept her comatose and she did not respond to her name or to any commands. As if to damn our hopes irrefutably, the flow scan on the second day indicated that she was brain-dead, although this would have to be confirmed by both neurology and neurosurgery. To do a liver transplant on a comatose patient was extremely risky because the low blood pressure induced by anesthesia would increase the risk of brain death. There was no precedent for performing a liver transplantation on a brain-dead patient. It seemed clearly an unethical use of a valuable and rare resource to give it to a patient who would never awaken to the new life it made possible.

With each hour Brenda's condition continued to worsen in spite of our efforts to stabilize her with drugs that could (and even with Brenda actually did) decrease the dangerously high level of ammonia in her blood. Nothing roused her or lessened the swelling that was causing her deep sleep.

Brenda was admitted to the hospital on late Monday; by early Wednesday we had to face the possibility that she could not be transplanted. And it was at this moment that fate presented us with the gift we had been waiting for—it was not just an organ that could save Brenda, it was the ideal organ, the perfect match. All enthusiasm in organ transplantation is tempered by the knowledge that we receive a gift forged in tragedy. This gift was no exception: The twenty-three-year-old African-American female donor had been killed in a motor vehicle accident, and I knew that nothing could ever make up for the vacancy her death had created in the lives of her loved ones. But each of us at Brenda's bedside, watching her fade away, knew there was hope now. The donor of the liver we would obtain was young, female, closely matched in age and blood type. It was the perfect setting, if only Brenda . . . if only . . .

I again consulted with the radiologist and again he gave his diagnosis: nothing had changed, in his opinion the patient was brain-dead and he expected his conclusion to be supported by the neurologist and the neurosurgeon. He sympathized with the patient's—and my—predicament, but the patient's present condition did not justify use of the available organ. He did not say as much, but I knew I had to relinquish the organ, I had no justifiable claim to it now.

I met Bernice in the intensive care unit. She did not ask me when the operation was to begin, nor what I had learned from the radiologist, nor how long would Brenda and I have before the organ would have to go to someone else. Without any pre-amble she faced me and said simply, "My daughter is not brain-dead."

I muttered something not worthy of a response and she continued with more emotion, clutching my arm and empha-sizing each word. "She knows I am there." I must have looked skeptical because she said the words with more force now. "She knows. Her pulse, her blood pressure, they change when I talk to her. She knows it's me. Something in her knows. That's not death."

She pulled me closer to Brenda's bed and pointed to the monitors that spelled out the young woman's failing struggle for life. "Watch now," she said, and then leaned closer to her daughter. Her voice was clear, calm, charged with more de-mand than request. She said, "It's Mom. I'm talking to you again, and I know you'll hear me, like before. So listen. Tell me you're listening."

What caught my attention first was the unexpected facility with which Bernice had read the monitors, had evidently been reading since Brenda was placed in the ICU. I was surprised, perhaps not altogether pleasantly. We medical people guard our technology with a jealous hand and don't appreciate the uninitiated making free with any of it. Bernice, however, had been reading the monitors accurately and, I had to assume, consistently for many hours now.

Then it happened: Brenda's vital signs changed, as if they had caught her mother's voice rhythms, swelled enough to be seen changing, growing stronger on those rhythms. Bernice watched my reaction, hesitated for a second, then spoke again to her daughter. She stole a quick glance at the monitors, reassuring herself, now certain that she had convinced me. She faced me now with confidence, saying, "You see?"

There wasn't any way I could qualify the nod I involuntarily gave. Yes, I had seen, although what it meant I could not tell for certain. I had seen something, and now I was going to get neurology and neurosurgery to tell me what it was. There were additional tests they could run, more sensitive measures of blood flow to the brain. Maybe Brenda's spirit was now too subtle, too refined to be captured by the crude devices we had been using.

I have many times before been faced by such dilemmas, such contradictions between what my intuition tells me and what my scientific training can allow me to accept. I have tried to give each way of knowing its due because together they make up what is for me the best of all ways of knowing. But it is not always easy to bring them together so that the light they can shed on a problem is in sharp focus, intense and unambiguous. To see my own way clear at such moments I have turned, and I am turning again in this dilemma, to my adviser, my spiritual guide. He is old now, very old, but that has not weakened his voice or his insight. We are far apart now, but that does not diminish the ease and certainty with which he can read me. He does not pretend to see the future or, God forbid, alter its course. He only tries to bring me into line with where the present is headed and then lets me go there, maybe with a little shove. The answers he gives are so simple I sometimes used not to recognize them at once as answers. Maybe that is because his answers to my questions are so obvious I could have discovered them myself had I not been distracted and fragmented by the whirlwind of possibilities and choices and pathways confronting me, with one truth telling me to go one way, another the opposite.

Joe listened to my hasty explanation and said, "Are those the signs that tell you there is life?" And when I said, "Yes, of course," he replied, "Then there is life, and you must bring it on, coax it. Only when there are no signs are you free to let go of your hold on this person."

That was all. I did not want to keep him longer or tire him, even though his voice greeted me as if he had been waiting, happy and waiting, to hear from me. Strengthened by my call, I had a consultation with my colleagues from neurology and neurosurgery. Bernice, surprisingly unintimidated by the credentials and expertise they carried into the ICU like visible badges of distinction, calmly gave them instructions to stand there, no, not there but closer, where there would be an unobstructed view of the monitors. She called on Brenda, and again the signs of life surged on the monitors. Both experts, as if responding to the same cue, pursed their lips, shrugged their shoulders, looked from patient to screen in unison.

Bernice was not about to tolerate their indecision. She said, "She's showing you. That's the best she can do now. You, all of you, and Dr. Toussaint, you have to do it now." And then for the first time I saw her composure fail her for a second, her strength waver. Her voice trembled at the first words, but she rallied by the time she had finished saying, "That's what I can do, now she has to be in your hands."

We left her then and held an impromptu conference. Yes, they agreed, after what they had seen there were signs of life, subtle signs, but enough to justify a more intensive workup, new tests, new evaluations. As long as her condition was stabilizing, the medication to reduce her ammonia level taking effect, the antibiotics still protecting her from infection, there would be time to schedule the necessary tests.

"Time?" I said. "There isn't time. I need a decision now. How quickly can you tell me if she is an acceptable candidate for transplantation?" And when they fixed me with their guarded, professional gaze, I added what they wanted to hear. "Give me your considered evaluation that she is not brain-dead so I can transplant her today, tonight."

Before they could answer I was called to the nurses' station and took the message I had been dreading. It was the organ-procurement coordinator. She had to have my decision now, right now. There was another Status 1 patient whose life depended on the organ reserved so far for Brenda. Was my patient ready? Would the patient be ready within the hour?

I wanted with all my heart to say yes, to follow the intuitive feeling Bernice and my spiritual adviser had strengthened—perhaps awakened is a better word—but most of what I had learned over the past decades said otherwise. Even with my intuitive certainty that Brenda was slowly returning to us, I could not proceed without the promised reevaluation and the new, hopefully more sensitive tests. I needed more than just my intuition, however strong, to do justice to all my years of training and my commitment to medicine. So what I finally said in spite of my misgivings was "No, not ready now. But I want my patient to remain Status 1 until further notice. I want the door kept open."

We rested only fitfully that night and in the morning waited for the results of more sophisticated tests. When Bernice and Steve, who had been keeping watch in the ICU waiting lounge, met me, I told them the news that now, with the donor liver no longer available, was so painfully ironic. Yes, Bernice had been right all along. There was life, still fueled by significant blood flow to Brenda's brain. I could not say aloud what I now blamed myself for. I could not remind them that I could have operated yesterday. There was no sign that they, who had to be sharing my feelings, felt any hostility or reproached me for that decision. They smiled, and Bernice said, "We'll have another chance soon. It will be in time."

Whatever time would be granted us, it would not include

leisure to think in terms of days of tiding Brenda over. Each hour saw her drop deeper into the comatose state from which soon not even Bernice's faith would retrieve her. We clung to the few positive results of all our efforts: the absence of infection; the slow, painfully slow decrease in the swelling in her brain; the continuing decline in ammonia levels from the disastrously high figure of 283 when she was admitted to the more manageable 86 on this, her third day. But I was not fooled— temporary gains in such small pitched battles could be wiped clean away in one crisis.

We waited as we had to, counting the hours, thinking that certainly another sixty minutes could not pass without the longed-for call. Fortunately, Stan was progressing extremely well after his liver and kidney transplants, so I would be ready to remove the organ myself if the donor was close enough to make that feasible. In larger transplantation centers than mine other surgeons are available to perform this shorter but still demanding procedure. I did not have enough hands to go around at all times, but, in any case, retrieving the donor organ followed by my implanting it into my patient, the recipient, was really for me the dream complete. When I was learning this skill I was entrusted only with the simpler part, consigned to watching my superiors perform the lifesaving phase of the operation. I felt cheated somehow of the ultimate gift a surgeon can give a patient, and, to be honest, also cheated of the ultimate satisfaction surgery can offer.

Bernice's intuition was right again; we did not have to wait more than that one interminable day before our Organ Procurement Organization (commonly referred throughout the world as OPO) called to say they had a liver if my patient was still . . . alive. One cannot expect all miracles to be of the same degree of polish and excellence, so I did my best to defuse the disappointment I felt as soon as the coordinator began to describe the donor and the waiting liver. Disappointment turned soon enough into dismay.

To begin with, the liver was that of a fifty-six-year-old male, not in itself a problem, but I knew that even gross physical examination would reveal the inevitable effect of aging. The man had died of a sudden and in no way anticipated cerebral vascular accident. He had been in generally good health—and that in spite of his long-term addiction to moonshine liquor. The moonshine had not yet reduced his liver to the state of cellular and architectural collapse we call cirrhosis, as given enough time it would, but unfortunately for us (and no doubt for him) moonshine is concocted in iron pots and the iron from the pots leaches into the brew and the man drinks the brew and the liver absorbs the iron and a liver packed with iron is not the kind of liver you'd have as your first choice. But, of course, I could not turn down this organ, not even when the coordinator gave me yet another reason for doing so—his blood type and Brenda's were not compatible. So when all the reasons for turning down this gift were added up, I still said yes. Yes, anyway, because of one reason that overrode all the others: Without transplantation now, Brenda would die. I could not say exactly when, but I knew it would be soon. Even the compromised liver was better than the one she was dying with, dying of.

I think back with a kind of awe on the days, then weeks, and now years since the operation that I have known Brenda and her family, for Brenda has survived in spite of all the dangers she faced. It's a feeling that comes not just because of who they are and how they faced the terrible ordeal given them, and not only because I have come to love and appreciate them. From moment to moment Brenda's case grabbed me by the throat as much as by the heart; it was one of those true cliff-hangers packed with totally unexpected twists and turns, dead ends suddenly leading into spectacular openings, a situation where much was taken but much remained. It was enough to make you think, Thank God surgery isn't always like this—but then you remember that it often is.

When I had secured the donor liver and made up my mind that it would work because it had to, when Brenda was fully prepped, then I had time to think about the coming marathon of the operation itself. Because my transplantation unit was new and small, responsibility for the surgical procedure itself, the hours of cutting and binding, maintaining hemostasis, sewing and stapling, all these were my primary responsibilities. For the trained assistants I needed I had relied on the staff, my teachers and friends in the great center where I had learned. But just a few days ago I had called for help and Dave came and worked with me through both the aborted attempt to transplant Mr. Grand and then the long and successful effort that gave Stan both a liver and kidney. How could I call for help again, especially when I had the impression that Dave and the others were thinking it was time I stood on my own two feet? This would mean that I would now be pushing general surgeons in my hospital into more senior positions and thus begin to create my own expert team. Better yet, I could hire one of the African-Americans who had followed in my steps and was in training as a fellow where I had studied. I knew that everyone at that great center for transplant surgery, especially its chief, was most interested in getting me to realize that I could do it. I had already been pushed off the raft and into the water, was already swimming. They wanted me to stop a moment and feel the strength in the strokes I was taking for granted. I appreciated the sentiment, but I wanted the help anyway. From a more practical point of view, it would be at least another year, or another two or three paying patients, before I could afford to recruit a promising surgeon for my own hospital.

I did not have to debate with myself about placing the call for help, help now and at once because Brenda's operation was scheduled for that very evening. I got the help I needed.

Although we began as fellows learning liver transplantation together, Brad had already spent two years during his general surgical residency doing research into the body's immunological responses, research that makes our cutting and stitching possible. He was ahead of me, way ahead, and I knew this and gave him all the credit he deserved. When I asked for help, he called me to say that he would be in town to deliver a speech at an early-morning convention. I knew he had been, in a manner, delivered to my doorstep and I had to take full advantage of the circumstance.

It did not take too much persuasion to get Brad to see the wisdom in using the free hours between arrival and speech-making to better advantage than sleeping. I could always find time later to develop more self-reliance, but now I was going to rely on Brad to help me do the best possible for Brenda.

The operation itself was surprisingly uneventful. But then, Brenda's case was one of acute liver failure, not chronic, long-term degeneration that brought with it portal hypertension and the danger of inadvertently tearing weakened veins. The consequence of this would be lethal bleeding with the patient in sudden shock on the table. I knew there would be no scarring, no massive bleeding from damaged, easily traumatized, thumb-sized vessels. Her liver had shrunk, looking tiny and dead, but it was actually an easy thing to remove. I can just pluck this out, I remember thinking, rid her of this problem once and for all. Irrationally, I thought of the thing as the enemy that I had come to defeat, but then, twelve hours of surgery, not including the hours spent securing the donor liver, can give rise to strange thoughts. Some critics might even say

that surgeons are prone to think of themselves in such mes-
sianic imagery, dragon slayers, magicians. Our failures, however, teach us otherwise, as mine have.

Brenda would not be one of my failures. Her new, or rather
old-new, liver functioned immediately, as if determined to
contradict all my earlier misgivings. I could not go home yet,
for although I had proof that the operation was a success, there
was still the lingering fear that she would not wake up, that
if not technically brain-dead, she would remain, as it were,
disconnected, not beyond our reach, as Bernice had proven,
but beyond reaching us in any purposeful, intentional way. The
hours went by, and it seemed that Bernice and Steve, full of
confidence, were taking over my role, ministering to my doubts
and giving me support. They urged me to go home or at least
to my office and stretch out on the sofa. They offered me coffee, tea, a snack, they treated me like family, which we had
pretty much by this time become.

Then Brenda woke, moved, tried to reach out for Steve but
was too encumbered by tubes and drains, all the life-support
devices we had draped her with. She called his name, then her
mother's. She was still groggy from the long sleep we had induced, but she had finally come out of the sleep we had feared
would last for many days. She was back and knew it so fully
she could let herself slip off again, a faint smile on her lips, the
best she could manage, enough for all of us.

A stay in the ICU of only three days and then transfer to
a regular hospital floor, an uneventful recovery, with little to
record or worry about—it's true, what the history books say,
happy reigns are those that have no history. Brenda had come
back to herself, and the only thing Steve or Bernice could remark on was that she seemed quieter than her old self, as if
preoccupied with something, some memory perhaps she had
not yet been able to get clear. That was understandable, and I
would have left it at that except for something that happened

on the seventh day after the operation (she would remain another six days in recovery).

I came to her room to check on her progress and mentioned that her doctor from the other hospital had called and wanted to know how she was doing after the transplant. Well, Brenda did not even let me get that far but sat up in bed, interrupting me with an unexpectedly sharp tone, and said, "Don't tell him anything. He shouldn't know. He isn't my doctor. He never was."

I assumed that her memory of most of that period was still vague, so I tried to prompt her, saying, "That's why you're here. He was the one who referred you. Without that call you would not have been here. You would . . . could have died."

Now she definitely cut me short with "That man tried to kill me."

"Brenda," I began, quietly, reasonably, "a lot of what happened you probably still don't remember clearly."

"I can see his face right now. That's clear enough. He's not my doctor. I don't want you to tell him anything about me. I specifically remember him trying to kill me."

I had to dig in my heels. "You were not conscious most of the time. How could you remember such a thing?"

"I know his face. I can see him. Don't refer to him as my doctor!"

Bernice and Steve arrived at this moment, in time to hear Brenda's last angry words. I turned to them with a look of astonishment that immediately prompted Bernice to say, "She's right. That's what happened."

"What happened?" I asked.

And then Bernice told me the full story. Yes, Brenda had been rightly diagnosed as end-stage liver failure and an appropriate liver transplant patient, and she had been referred by Sal Grasso to the far-off suburban center, which had sent the transplant surgeon to evaluate her. She was an ideal candidate for emergency liver transplantation, thus categorized as a Status 1. It was the straw she and Steve clutched, it was the news they wished in vain Brenda could hear and understand, it was the hope they lived on for hours, their only nourishment in days of anguish.

Bernice paused as if almost too embarrassed by what happened next to say it out loud, too ashamed at the behavior of—what? I thought. Her betters? But she was determined to have her say and finished. Yes, the transplant surgeon had brought them hope and in the same day smashed it in front of them. Yes, they sent back word that now Brenda was too sick to be transplanted, too far gone for any help. And, oh yes, this too—too sick, too poor. No insurance to cover her life.

Bernice looked me straight in the eye, as if I stood as the representative of the entire profession, and asked in no gentle tone, "How come us not having money makes her life not worth saving? And why couldn't they have the guts to say it that way if that was the way it was going to be? Why lie that she was too sick when we have her right here now, with us, alive?"

I did not even begin to explain that Sal Grasso had been doing his best, in the patient's best interest. But since his hospital did not do transplants, the final decision about transplanting Brenda's was not his to make.

The final piece in this puzzle did not fall into place until more than a year later. I had continued to see Brenda, to check on her progress and get to know her better. I asked her about her experience at that hospital, what if anything she recalled, because I wondered about her vehement response to the inquiry, her assertion that someone had attempted to kill her. I asked what she could have been aware of then as she drifted deeper and deeper into the stupor and the comatose state from which she had been rescued.

But her memory was vivid about the young transplant surgeon who came to evaluate her. She remembered the entire gastroenterology and ICU teams coming into her room, speaking at her bedside as if she were already gone or close to it. She told me they spoke in medical terms she could not comprehend, but then they spoke freely, thinking she was too far gone to hear, saying that she would die without a transplant but that she did not have insurance coverage and so the transplant was being canceled. As she would be. And she remembered one voice saying that in a few days she would be dead and they wished they could make her comfortable but she was so difficult to control. And she remembered the voice and that face, all the faces, all the strange white faces, the professionals deciding her fate. She then said she could only think, Now they are all going to let me die, be at my killing, and let me go.

It took her months to put all this together, and I of course had no way of knowing what was real, what imagined. So I did not know how I could reconcile her with all those she believed had failed her. They could not see their way to her side, and that was the burden they would have to live with. If I came and worked for her benefit, it was because that was what I was appointed, chosen to do. When Brenda and her family tell me I saved her life, I tell them this: I did not save her life, *we* did, all of us together, including her donor's family. I tell them something else, too, when they say I saved her life. I tell them this happened only because I was chosen to do so, doing the work of the One who had appointed me to such tasks many years ago.

My instinct, my intuition, had served me right again, as with Stan, as, unfortunately, with Mr. Grand. In her delirious state, I could not communicate with Brenda as I would have normally done with a transplant patient. But there was Bernice and Steve, and so closely knit were they as a family, so at one with one another, that I could communicate with her through them. They spoke with one voice, and I could hear it clearly.

They vouched for her, they were her surrogates and gave me their word for her desire to live, to take every risk, to follow every painful and tedious step to full recovery.

And that was what happened. During the initial weeks after her release from the hospital, Bernice and Steve were always at her side when she came back for the days of tests and clinical checkups and counseling. Their support and their enthusiasm for her renewed life never wavered. In their darkest moments I knew they clung to hope as they clung to her, pulling her back from death as Bernice's vigil at her bedside had almost literally done. My intuition told me that such love and support would carry us through. I also believe that anyone seeing this family would have believed as I did.

CHAPTER 3

A surgeon's daily life must have been the first scientific proof of that old maxim Nature abhors a vacuum. Abhors? Better, won't tolerate the condition for a second. It may seem that every hour of the past few days had been totally consumed by Brenda's crisis and its twists and turns, but there were in fact gaps of time between the peaks of anxiety and the pits of frustration. Those were hours when I would gladly have let my mind sink into the blissful state of a vacuum, emptied of thought, vacuous. And not be in a transplant unit. For one thing, there was Mr. Grand and his family, the pressing matter I had to attend to while waiting for the next liver to become available for Brenda or, to put it more accurately, waiting to see if Brenda would be available, back with us again and ready to be transplanted when the next liver became available.

I found Mr. Grand's wife and daughter in the waiting area outside the ICU, where we had returned him. Since last I saw them the look on their faces had changed only to reflect greater pain and despair and something new and as unsettling to me—bewilderment, sheer and total bewilderment. And although I had long ago been taught the need to distance myself from my patients and the pain of their loved ones, I could not distance myself from this. They voiced no accusation, I saw none in the desperate eyes they fixed on me, yet I was in no small measure the source of that bewilderment and could not escape the pain that came with it.

For months and months I had been telling them that in my considered judgment a transplant was his only chance for survival. I had been treating symptoms of his liver failure, admitting him, doing stopgap measures, sending him home, hoping to build his strength and, as important, his confidence in me and in the operation itself. Above all, I had tried to instill in him a desire for the surgery because I needed his cooperation. I knew the effort had not paid off 100 percent, no way near that, not even 10 percent, with him. But it had with them. They had believed, they had fed and cared for him and his daily needs for months, trying to bring him along, regardless. They were proof that transplantation is a psychological trauma not just for the patient but the patient's entire family and circle of loved ones. All feel the full weight of this emotional impact during months of anticipation and then the months post-operation, watching for warning signs of rejection, counting each day as a milestone passed.

And I had canceled the procedure at the very last moment.

To them it must have seemed that I had taken the paper on which a sacred pledge had been written and torn it into shreds, tossed it aside, sent him back to them as proof that the promise could be broken as easily as made.

I began to explain, citing all the reasons why, in my considered opinion, in the opinion of my assistant, a surgeon of great skill and experience, their husband and father would in all probability not have survived the burden of surgery. They listened without a word, taking all or none of it in because none of it applied or was relevant to the question they could not ask me.

"We will do everything possible to keep him as comfortable as possible," I said, if only to break the silence. "We will have to wait and see. We will give him round-the-clock care. He may be able to go home when he is sufficiently stabilized . . . his temperature . . ."

By the time Mr. Grand died, three days later in the ICU from which we were never able to move him, I think they had come to accept the inevitability of his going. They thanked me and the staff for the concern we had shown, they knew we had done our best, they were grateful, they would remember us, we would always have their prayers. They seemed resigned, but their faces remained as stricken as on that earlier day. They left me with the doubt I had not yet been able to resolve. In my enthusiasm for transplantation, in my unshaken conviction in its practicality and feasibility and effectiveness, had I grown blind to its limitations? Was I becoming unrealistic in not always accepting that there were situations—rather, patients—where this miracle could not be expected? But then, would it be a miracle if one knew where to expect it?

*   *   *

There was certainly one place where I had expected it, and I was not disappointed. The door to Stan's room was closed, so I knocked softly and walked in.

"How am I doing, Doc?" Stan asked.

I began indirectly, a tease, by telling him what my assistant during the surgery, Dave, had said after meeting him in those frantic preop minutes: "Wow!" Dave had exclaimed just out of Stan's hearing. "This is the one we've got to do!"

I was right in expecting that Stan would appreciate the compliment and be pleased by what it said about his attitude before the operation. I also had to tell him that Dave had reason to temper some of his enthusiasm by the time we were hours into the procedure and had about the same number of hours ahead of us. Not that we were holding him personally responsible, I hastened to reassure Stan, for the long-standing portal hypertension that posed a risk to his life every moment of the long operation, nor did we hold him responsible for the copious bleeding from every possible vessel, bleeding that repeatedly obscured our operating field and had my assistants suctioning at a dizzying pace. We did hold him somewhat responsible for the shape of his liver, a tiny shriveled thing that yet clung to him tenaciously, forcing us to pare it away from the adjacent tissue with the most delicate, tediously executed maneuvers.

I guess I was releasing tension, giving words to some of the pent-up emotions I always experience during a transplant procedure but never allow myself to put down in my official post-operation summary. I felt Stan had a right to know, but I also felt he already knew how we all were affected by the emotional strain of those long hours.

I examined him carefully and reassured myself again—he was going to break some kind of record for discharge after surgery. He didn't need me anymore, except for routine checkups and, I felt sure, just friendly drop-ins. I tidied his gown, drawing it closed over his scar. He would have to have it photographed if he wanted to show it off. I suggested as much, and he pondered this in silence, the silence he had kept for some moments. Stan could tell I had not been reciting a list of grievances but of challenges met and overcome.

"Sorry to have been so much trouble, Doc. But you knew I wasn't going to be a piece of cake. Now what are you going to do for me?"

"Send you home. Soon."

"Soon? Am I going to break a record, walking out of here so soon?"

"I'll check it out in my data bank, but offhand I'd say yes. Must be a question of attitude."

"Attitude?" he said with a laugh. "You know I got attitude."

"You came in with a good one. Hang on to it. You'll need it."

His look was puzzled, then he broke into a smile, not very convincing because my unintentionally brusque tone had taken him by surprise. He could not read me, and I felt I had made a mistake I did not want to rectify then and there.

"Ready for the verdict?"

"Well, seein' you're not likely to discharge me this red-hot moment and there's no backdoor to this room I yet discovered, and I felt a little squeamish taking out these tubes by myself, you know, without anesthesia or anything, but could that have hurt all that much?"

Stan would need that positive I've-got-my-rights-too attitude to see him through the inevitable coming wrangle over money, the money that my hospital had, as it was now doing with Brenda, advanced him to let him exercise that right to life.

Stan wasn't being paranoid when at our first encounter he told me he had been given a death sentence. He had been told his insurance covered only kidney transplants, and he certainly needed one of those and got it. But nobody with liver and kidney failure gets a kidney transplant without also getting a new liver. Stan's insurance was willing to pay for the kidney, a gesture that was not just irrelevant but would more than likely have proved deadly as well. Stan intuited this without any knowledge of the simple reason why: His liver disease inhibited his body's normal blood-clotting mechanism. If he were to be opened up for a kidney transplant he would simply bleed to death, and no transplant surgeon would be able to avoid this fatality.

In the long run, and it was a very long and tedious run for all of us, Stan's attitude was tested time and again as he, either on his own or working with the hospital, tried to get the insurance claim accepted, the bills paid, the advance reimbursed. I think the only time Stan lost his composure was when the argument he thought irrefutably convincing met with no more success than any of the others. Before the kidney transplant Stan had been on dialysis three times a week for more than a year for his nephrotic syndrome; without transplantation he would have had to continue that regimen until his death. The transplant, a one-time-only expense, saved all that. Stan lost his composure over that, but there is just so much attitude you can put into a letter, and Stan never mentioned that he visited the insurance company office in person. But then, I don't recall asking him in so many words.

The battle of words and letters, appeals and rejections, counter-appeals and more rejections raged on, a war of attrition in which

I had as much clout as an ordinary foot soldier. No point complaining that this—what shall I call it, fiduciary warfare?—was not what I had signed up for. Just another example of life drafting us and forcing us to march under foreign standards. But I was learning to fight for my patients, for my hospital, for myself. We all needed it because if we didn't fight we'd all go under. After a year or so, after many a pitched battle with so-called providers who provided selectively, the facts were not to be refuted: The patients referred to me were by and large African-American. Black like me, but different. They had little if any adequate insurance coverage. Insured patients were referred to other transplant centers. Moreover, my patients tended to be the ones other centers did not usually want to take a chance on, patients like Stan, with a history of abusing his body, patients too sick or too far gone to benefit from transplantation, cancer patients with no insurance, patients not likely to be offered a second chance. My transplant service had become the last-ditch effort for those who would certainly wind up in the deep ditch without it. The excuse is usually that resources are limited, not enough to go around. But in honesty, the fact is that when scarce things go around, they don't go around to most of my patients first.

In the long run, my hospital was paid for only the kidney transplant, about one sixth of Stan's huge bill, a true loss for my hospital. Ironies abound in this situation. In spite of his errant ways, Stan had worked steadily for two decades and had paid his HMO medical insurance premiums faithfully. But the HMO insurer simply called his attention to the fine print in his twenty-year-old, twenty-page medical coverage document. The print cautioned him that only kidney transplantation would be covered, not liver or heart or bone marrow transplantation. But twenty years ago liver, heart, and bone marrow transplants were done only in laboratories. By the time Stan needed a liver transplant, the procedure was no longer experimental but had become the standard medical practice and a lifesaving procedure for thousands around the world. Fine print, however, does not yield to such obvious reasoning.

CHAPTER 4

I always remind myself not to give one of those data-driven speeches when I'm asked, as I often am, to talk to school-children about a career in medicine. I'll remind myself again this afternoon when I'm standing up in the assembly room, listening to myself trying to cram all the encouraging new facts and statistics into their eager and open minds. I'll try for a scientifically balanced presentation. I'll try to sketch in some of the still-dark facts children such as these will face: continuing if more subtle discrimination because of gender or color or economic status, goals not met by a long shot, a still immovable and apparently not movable ceiling on moving up through the ranks. I know it was different when I started my journey, years ago, different and more difficult in many ways, but I don't know if they want to hear about that, my life and hard times.

Always when I stand in front of a class of youngsters, many with as limited prospects as mine were, I wish I had a tongue of fire to ignite in them a passion for this great calling. I try not to have my enthusiasm chilled by my knowledge that the road is still strewn with obstacles they more than others will have to overcome.

Today I'm to talk at another inner-city school, so most if not all of the youngsters will be black children of limited prospects but not potential. They probably have already had some experience with black doctors, less with women doctors, probably little if any experience with female surgeons of any color, let alone black. So I'll begin by letting them know that as a woman I'm not all that much of a freak in the medical world. I'll tell them that the number of female doctors in the United States has more than quadrupled since the 1970s and now women make up more than 40 percent of medical school students. We were less than 10 percent in the 1960s and 1970s. I'll tell them that, as a group, minority members—I'll say, "people like you and me"—are better represented in the profession (here comes more hard data, am I beginning to lose them?), with an increase of almost twenty thousand working physicians in the last decade alone. And if, with luck, the numbers grow and there are some thirty thousand or so black physicians practicing in the next decade, with equal luck some 40 percent of them will be women. We started far behind, but we're in the running. At this point I usually drop in my favorite historic anecdote to validate that sporty image. I tell the kids that the first black woman to become a doctor in this country graduated in 1864, only fifteen years behind the first white female medical school graduate. But they should keep in mind that in a nearby major city, 65 percent of the population is black but only 6 percent of the physicians are black. As individuals, as a people, we need to do our utmost to improve such statistics because in so doing we are really improving the lives of all our brothers and sisters.

All along I know they want to ask me the kinds of questions kids eventually get up the courage to ask: What's it like to cut somebody up? Did it make you sick once? Did you ever have a patient die right there on the operating table after you cut him up, and what did you feel like when that happened, and why did he die, and did you feel something you did made it happen? They're never satisfied with something as dismissive as "Yes, all of the above. Next question." Kids know the truth is in the details.

They'll hang on to every word in the question-and-answer session but for the moment are polite and patient, listening to my exhortations to study hard, not try to skip by with easy courses, be judicious in the time allotted to television watching, have confidence you can make it. What I want to tell each one is what I learned—before any miracle can happen you have to believe it can happen. It doesn't just happen, you have to coax it along. You have to imagine yourself sharing the miracle before it can happen to you.

My own journey, the one whose destination rather than origin I try to share with schoolchildren, began on an ordinary day in the place where I was born. As I remember ordinary days of growing up in Haiti, I remember sun and warmth, a sky so blue and without streaks or smudges it seemed freshly painted every morning, distant green hills with this sky behind them, the scent coming to me of far-off fields and flowers in pots in front of the house where I lived and in front of the other small houses that formed a semicircle, somewhat elevated, a vantage point that let us look down from our front yard onto the huge playing field where there was always some kind of activity, something to sit and watch even without understanding. I was seven years old and knew that my future had been discussed and argued over, if not altogether decided, but that was too far off to concern me greatly.

The old man sat under a tree, leaning against its ancient bark comfortably, as if it were not rough and hard at all. Children, my playmates, surrounded him, but at some distance, respectful but not fearful, knowing he was an *oungan*, a priest, but knowing as well that he was a gentle and familiar old man who had to hold your hand in his for only a second to see everything, all the rest of your life. He would share this great news freely, casually, letting us children in on the secrets of his priestly wisdom as easily as we wandered in and out of all the other festivals and celebrations in honor of the spirits of the voodoo religion, in remembrance of departed souls, homage to friendly and not so friendly beings of the other world. The old man and others younger and, surprising, even older, and women, too, presided over these celebrations, so we accepted him and his special place in the world. Such events, just big, happy parties to us children, were a part of our ordinary life and had their place in the year's calendar. We never confused these voodoo festivals with our other religious life, the one that was official at school, the one that really governed our daily life and observances.

Going to church on Sunday with your best dress and behavior on display was definitely not like staying up all hours at a festival, eating until you fell asleep, then waking to the sound of more music and merrymaking. Children were accepted, expected to behave like children, praised and blessed as children. Sometimes someone, a parent or relative or even friend, would ask of a priest a special blessing on a child, but even that was not considered unusual or cause for alarm among the rest of us not so singled out.

*   *   *

So there was nothing at all to hold one back from going up to the old priest when one's turn came, except perhaps for a little shyness at having everyone's eyes riveted on you alone and knowing you were honor-bound to repeat all you had been given to tell. I felt perhaps a slight qualm in taking my turn, for I had already been told what my future would be and so might be accused of wasting his time and gifts.

He took my hand but did not look into my palm. He said, "What do you want your future to be?"

"I am supposed to become a nun," I said.

He laughed very softly, gently, then turned my hand around and showed me my own palm. "But no," he said, "you cannot be a nun this time. It is not necessary to discuss that further."

I looked at him in disbelief. Would this really be the end of the endless arguments between my mother and father? Would I be able to run the risk of taking such a message to the one who had lost and the one who had won this battle about my future?

He closed my hand, curling it for a second in his. I looked into his eyes and saw something I could not understand or even find words for. It was as if his eyes held all history in them and from them went a line opening into the entire universe. He could reach into the universe even while he was sitting against this tree near my own house.

"But," I began suddenly, on an impulse taking away my hand and trying to explain why my future had been decided. "But my two aunts are nuns. They are holy persons. So is my grandfather, my father's father. Everyone says it."

He laughed outright at this, letting go my hand to clap his together in delight, saying, "Good. They will be there to protect and pray for you. Enough. We don't need you a nun when there are three such holy persons. A triangle of divine protection." Then his eyes narrowed craftily, as if he would catch me out: "Everyone says so. You told me. Isn't it so?"

I could not deny it, and my quick nod brought one in exchange. "So," he went on energetically, reclaiming my hand, "your future is yours. For you, now." He paused, searching my hand, nodded to himself as if in confirmation of what he had concluded on his own, then relinquished me with a gesture that ended the consultation.

"You will be a physician. You will be a physician and a surgeon. You will often have to remember it was told to you, but greatness lies that way."

I moved away and let the next child take my place, happy to retreat to the back of the crowd, not willing to answer any questions about my reading. A physician? A surgeon? I thought. What did this mean to me except the remembered pain of my only serious encounter with medicine when I was taken to have my tonsils removed? I remembered only that I had been given pain and kept that memory. To me this meant that something, some other kind of healing, had been left out. I am certain now that I had been told that the pain was only temporary, would quickly pass, but from the day of my prophecy I began to think differently about healing and healers.

Starting from the painful memory of my minor surgery, the idea of becoming a physician and then a surgeon combined with what I knew of the common folk medicine I saw around me daily. I began to see things in a new light, one that would intensify over the years. Somehow, in a way my childish mind could not yet fully comprehend, the idea of a doctor as more than and not just a physical healer began to shape itself. The good doctor would have to doctor the spirit as well as the body, learn the necessary physical skills but let them be guided by the patient's spiritual needs.

I never questioned that the old voodoo priest had the authority to speak to me of physicians and surgeons and healing.

Healing was the ancient heart of this man's practice; he had spent a life listening and responding to the pain of most individuals in the world around him. Much of this pain was too deep for cures that worked only on the physical level. Little he could do on that level alone would bring comfort to the spirit—and without that comfort the body languishes. I would in time learn to hail such ministers to a troubled people as colleagues, ones who possessed few of the resources I would have at my disposal yet whom I believed in with a conviction many of us have failed to instill in those who turn to us in their need.

My future was not the only point of contention between my mother and father, although I had the typical child's feeling that somehow I was the cause of all the arguments, the nagging and name-calling. And because most of the verbal brickbats were hurled by my mother, I felt guilty on that score as well, thinking that as women, my mother and me, we were giving him, the man, a hard time and must not. I should have spared myself the anguish. Most of the brickbats, like most other adverse criticism, seemed to bounce off my father, leaving him as placid, happy-go-lucky, accessible (when present) as ever. I think his persistent calm in the face of so much verbal abuse, his seeming imperturbability in the face of all my mother's justifiable, excusable rancor made his abrupt departure all the more stunning to me and my brothers and sister.

I think back on my early years, the ones that are supposed to be so formative, and it's as though I were listening to a tape from which segments had been erased by error, perhaps by intention, or maybe those memories had been transcribed somewhere else and might possibly be retrieved someday. Everything I experienced must have contributed to my life and therefore must be living within me somehow, and this knowledge makes the sometimes painful task of reconstruction of the past necessary. Not just reconstruction, but sifting through, looking for meaning, connections, the place where some life lived by someone else connected with mine still reflects on mine and perhaps gave mine the direction it took.

My mother's mother, I recall, was the last of some ten children. And when her mother died in childbirth my grandmother was, for some inexplicable reason, perhaps as an expiation for being so abandoned, left all the considerable land the family owned, acres and acres of rich farmland such as could be found throughout Haiti in those days before overuse, abuse, and political and financial ruin overtook the island. I recall my grandmother, by then looking ancient but probably not so, working, working through the day and into the night, hour after hour, running the farm, the big house, the many workers, even presiding over and taking on herself the concerns of the smaller houses scattered throughout the acres, cottages in which her more lackadaisical, less-driven brothers and sisters, even cousins, aunts, uncles, lived. They lived comfortably, casually, off the farm. They lived off her labor.

Of course she never complained, but like her daughter, my mother, she paid not just with her body but also with a deep-rooted sense of anger that the gift of taking life easy, as it comes, was denied her. Like my mother, she did not seem to know the meaning of laughter and smiled only rarely. When she did, it was a beautiful smile, but it was never enough to take you through to the next time. You remembered her strength and admired it; you remembered she never seemed to tire and wondered how it was possible for her to go on hour after hour, dawn to dark; you remembered her rigor and somehow knew she was justified in being as she was. You wondered if you would ever have the strength to wage the daily battles she did. Being a child, wanting your bed and comfort, you thought about the simplest thing—you worried if you would ever have to be up with the first sun and then not lie down until everything was night again. Would you, too, forget how to laugh, smile only as an afterthought?

Although the worlds they lived in were totally different, my mother became like my grandmother, the two making a continuum of hard and almost endless work, care, concern, strength, rigor, unbending, unbent. But my mother's world was compressed, without the freedom of rich acres yielding enough to live off and live well. Hers was a life in a small city, in a small house, caught in a lower-middle-class socio-economic stratum that was narrow, precarious, yet more secure for the moment than the poverty-devastated masses. There was the small family over which she presided and, somehow mir-roring it, her other domain, the classes of primary-school chil-dren over which she ruled and taught with competence and often noted firmness. I cannot say she would have been more open to us, easier, given a larger space in which to live and move. Her mother had, I knew, hundreds of acres and still grew harder with the years.

Nothing my father did should have come as a surprise to my mother, except for one thing—his remaining always the same in spite of everything she did. She must have expected him to become different and married him on that expectation. The sounds of her disappointment rang through the house and my early years. My brothers and sisters and I would sleep with heads under pillows, just as we did to keep out the music of the all-night-long bands and revelers celebrating a voodoo spirit. The singers and dancers swirled through the town, swept along with sheer delight in the music and rhythm, the closeness of the spirit cajoled by their songs. But, trembling under our pil-lows, we were terrified that all our transgressions would now have to be paid for. The voodoo spirit surely had to know each of our private dark deeds. And the other sin, the one we shared, the discord in the home, was to our anxious minds another such transgression, as bewilderingly unearned as the stain of original sin but, like that first wrong, something we could not escape. Some part of it had to be our share and fault.

She had expected him to change, but he did not. We never

wanted that. Who would want his smile to change, or the gentle way he came to you and learned what you needed and
brought it for you, or, later, helped you make your own way
toward it. Perhaps we feel guilty because we did not want him
to be different, anything other than easy and loving. We must
have feared that if we did not have his nurturing to support us
we would be unable to bear or ever learn from her hard determination and discipline.

I learned this story much later but grew up with its bitter after-
math, unknowing. As a young man courting my mother, my father worked for a rich man who needed his accounting skills to
increase his wealth further. There was a beautiful young mulatto woman who also worked for the man as his maid, and she
and my father became lovers. In time she gave birth to a son,
the first child for each of them. But she was too young and
could not care for the child, and in time it languished, no matter what my father did to support them. He never thought of
abandoning them.

A year later he met my mother and began to court her. A
few months later he brought the child to her, and because
it was still languishing he asked if she would care for it. She
consented even before the promised marriage, even though
the child was not hers nor had anything to do with the life
she had imagined for them. After the marriage they lived on
his parents' large farm. The child began to thrive with my
mother's care.

The story has another, an unhappy, ending. My mother's
first pregnancy was not successful, and she suffered an early
miscarriage. She grieved, but she knew she had to go on, seek
divine help, hope that the next time it would bring better
luck. On the day she came home from the hospital after this
terrible thing the maid announced a visitor with a letter for

my father. She agreed to give him the letter, but with trepidation she read what was not meant for her to see. His mulatto sweetheart, the mother of his first son, was telling him that they had a second child, conceived before his marriage to my mother, a girl, as light-skinned as she was. My mother felt the blow: She was dark-skinned. The light-skinned mistress went on to tell him that it had been an easy birth, as it is for the lucky ones.

My mother was not lucky, not in her love, not in the color of her skin, which was as dark as mine, too black in a land such as ours where the color of one's skin was used against you. This prejudice is ever-present in most countries where blacks were enslaved, a device to keep the spirit down, self-doubting and then self-hating. I imagined my mother felt my father loved the other woman simply because she had lighter skin. My mother automatically assumed the woman was far happier than she herself could ever be, and the reason was that she was luckier in the color of her skin.

Later I could not understand why she was always surprised by what he did, even though more and more I found I was taking her part, blaming him, but only in silence. I hated the discord and the angry words, but now I know I took delight in the words she laid as traps for him. Even though I would never use any of them against him, I was storing them up for the future. I was promising myself that if I ever was, by some mistake, in her position, which I would never be, I would have suitable weapons of defense or, as good, offense. But I promised myself I would not be in her position.

Now, looking back from a different vantage point, I see this life in what my education would call its broader, culturally determined aspects. Traditionally, women had their domain, the home, the children, the responsibilities, all of which they controlled tightly. Men, particularly those men who had the resources, moved from one such place to another, back and forth over years sometimes, or now here and then there, fathering and sometimes coming back to nurture, taking as much as they gave, gathering responsibilities along the way. Some men took these seriously, some not so seriously. It was a traditional pattern, something Haitian men probably inherited along with other customs of their African ancestors. In that long-lost African past a man would take as many wives as he could afford to keep. The entire family lived and interacted positively. That pedigree clearly did nothing to recommend the practice to women such as my mother. And yet she accepted some of it—did she have any choice? Perhaps she never gave up the idea that she could change the path he was on, not take it as something separate from her. Eventually, he was the one who saw things more clearly.

Children make do in spite of the confusion around them. And when there are enough in a family they draw support from one another unconsciously. So I leaned on my older sister, who was more outgoing, owning more of the self-confidence and self-reliance my mother had, easier to confide in or use as an intermediary when I had reason to fear a reprimand. With my two younger brothers I had the occasional joy of seeing my role reversed as I became the confident one, calming, sometimes mocking their fears.

But most of all I found solace in school, the place where all questions had answers and most, sometimes all, could be understood and explained to others. I would overcome my shyness to do that. I think of my growing appreciation of elementary, rudimentary science, of numbers and signs and calculations. I marveled at the way the confusing demands of a mathematics problem, at first like noisy tangled voices in an argument, soon sorted themselves out, accepted the way you calmed and managed them, let you finally help them all contribute to the one answer, something you were sure would be the same the next day you explored it. I wore down my pencils and blackened the pages of my exercise book in this reassuring pursuit of the reassuring certainty of numbers.

I don't think I yet understood that what I was doing was laying the foundation for a life study of science. I don't think I understood the relationship between the problems I studied and the life of a doctor of medicine that I had been promised. I wasn't told that what I was doing was "goal-oriented" work. I could not very well tell the nuns who taught me that I was inspired by a voodoo priest's reading of my palm. Most important, I probably had not yet fully realized that becoming a doctor would involve work, hard, unrelenting, disciplined, often body- and soul-consuming work, from dawn to night and then some. The full knowledge of that would come later— and take me by surprise. I think I assumed that because the prophecy had been made, the career in medicine would simply be waiting for me when I was ready, like a party dress that had been ordered and all I had to do was step into it, shake it down around me, checking the fit, admiring how perfectly it had been made to fit.

Like everything you anticipate but never let yourself imagine, my father's sudden leaving struck us all as something unthinkable. We shouted and screamed at my mother, in our anguish finding the courage to call her a liar, deceiving us, threatening us. We were too overwrought to notice that she took this unprecedented abuse without a word of reprimand, not lifting a threatening hand. She did not even tell us to be quiet, quieter, to think of what the neighborhood would think hearing our cries at such an hour. And indeed it was the dead of night we found when we ran to the front door and saw the deepest indigo blue sky above, the stars hung there, the faintly visible distant hills, and the empty, silent street down which he could easily have come walking but never would again. Then we crept back to our own beds, too stricken to hope for any comfort, beginning to grieve in earnest and knowing it would be useless to hope anymore for his presence, knowing that if he could leave in such a way, without a word or touch, then the break was final. I do not think any one of us asked why. This was pain that could not be changed in any way by such knowledge.

CHAPTER 5

The argument this time was different, about a pencil, but the screams and the angry pulls and tugs, the sharp blows were the same as ever. Maybe my mother's explosive temper was no worse after than before my father left. But her temper was harder for me to bear because he was no longer there to comfort me and to make excuses for her anger. I know I had tried to explain to my mother that the nun had let me have the pencil even though I did not have money to pay for it that morning. She knew I could take it now and pay for it later because we always did pay for what we needed in school. This was a private school, and only families that could pay sent their children there. I did not think I would not have the money next morning. I did not yet fully understand all that my father's absence would mean.

My mother kept insisting I had stolen this pencil from school and she would beat me until I confessed. And she did continue to beat me until the pain was near unbearable. Then I lied, acknowledging a theft I had not committed. Whenever I remember this incident I could cry again, in exasperation. Why doesn't the woman listen? I remember thinking. Why would I steal from one of the sisters when I didn't even have to ask for the pencil?

But then, somewhere amid all the sobs and slaps, I began to have some little understanding. My mother could not bear what had happened to us since he left. She could not bear the thought that we were becoming objects of charity like the growing numbers of the hard-pressed and near destitute increasingly visible around us. We were slipping down from our previous position, and nothing she had been able to do so far was holding us fast to the small security we once had. Then I gave in and confessed to a crime I did not commit, wondering if I would have to confess to the priest that I had confessed to a sin I had not committed and was that a sin, even though I had not committed the sin I had confessed to in the first place. It would take years to get my mind and soul free of such rigid spiritual calculations.

The whole experience saddened me, not just the smarting blows, not the image of my near frantic, angry, and insistent mother, not the thought that I had to deny the kindness of the good nun who did not want me to fall behind for even one day. I now knew our life was changing, and I was afraid because I could not imagine what the changes would mean. For the first time I saw the certain, brilliant future predicted for me, my life as a physician and surgeon, as a burden to be cared for and carried through this and possibly other times of trouble. For the first time I saw my predicted future as something I would be held responsible for.

The next morning I had the money I needed and was very careful to repeat to the nun precisely as I had memorized them

my mother's words of thanks for the temporary, much appreciated, but not necessarily to be repeated loan of the items necessary for my continuing progress in school. The temporary
loan showed that my hard work was being recognized.

Then we had to experience the most shattering repercus-
sion of my father's departure, something that all children unconsciously dread and anticipate when one parent is gone. My
mother announced abruptly that she was leaving as well. We
did not cry as we had done months before, perhaps because
her leaving seemed so foreordained, but we listened without
comprehension to her explanation. Later I understood that she
was merely part of what would become a vast wave of hard-
pressed Haitians leaving for America, seeking better chances, a
few seeking a life at least as good as what they had enjoyed,
most seeking just something more tolerable, less deprived and
hopeless than what they had endured. I did not then know
enough to suffer with her as she, alone, joined the numbers of
the least appreciated, least desired, least tolerated of any of the
millions who had so journeyed before her.

She told us that there had been word of my father, that
he had taken various jobs, found work on a cruise ship, found
that his skill with numbers and his knowledge of accounting
were not of use to him where there were different systems in
place, then had found work in some port cities, working with
trucks, a delivery van, would risk going to Miami as an illegal
alien, would send what he could as soon as he could. We
did not ask her how long she had kept this news from us,
we did not ask why her own plans were to go to New York and
not where he would be, we did not ask how we could be
united as a family if they lived so far apart. She knew she could
find work in New York, not as a grade school teacher, that
would have to be put aside, but work using other skills, because
she still had her hands as well as her head and a seamstress
could find work without questions being asked about her legal
right to work or her ability to support her own children. She

would not debate her right to support her children with any authority. In any case, she would enjoy the break from the "intellectual" life, especially knowing she was turning that field over to her smart children to till.

The young cousin who came to make a home for us brought her own young children, whose father we never met. We fought with them and they with us, everyone giving vent in the loudest possible way to the emotional distress of the recent or recurring separations and the hastily patched together household. Due in large measure to our constant kicking and pulling at it, this flimsy structure soon collapsed and our cousin departed, to be succeeded by an old aunt of my mother's, one who at times had even presided over her upbringing, none too gently, as my mother had us understand.

This one was not so easily dislodged, and as she stayed from month to month she gave us our first exposure to real tyranny and abuse. Our mother's blows, physical or emotional, were always subject to the restraint imposed by her unquestioned love and concern for us. The old aunt was under no such restraint.

My memory may color these months, soon turning into years, too highly, and the sense of abandonment that lay heavy on all of us may have left exaggerated scars from the blows we suffered. Not that the blows and the verbal abuse that went with them were not real enough, and perhaps in part deserved because we had become an unruly lot and knew it. Then one day, as I again submitted to my aunt's hand or hairbrush, longing for my mother's lighter touch, it came to me that my mother, too, had endured this, as guilty or not as I for whatever offense had provoked the onslaught.

First there came flooding through me a feeling of sympathy for that unknown young girl who became my mother and then a feeling to which I thought I had no right—a desire to forgive her all her uncontrolled anger at my real or imagined transgressions. The tyranny of another troubled woman had given me my first sense of true identification with my mother and her life. It was not the birth of love, for I had always loved my mother. It was rather the birth of the conviction that I was her daughter and would know that as long as I was able to know myself.

We were at last to be delivered from the old aunt. Not that we had worn her down; her heavy hands were falling on us as freely on the last day as on the one following her arrival (she had, I recall, given us one day of grace, or perhaps we had simply been stunned into momentary good behavior by her appearance). We had been summoned, my father had sent word that we were now to join him in America, in the vast city of Miami that we had read about and heard about and now saw in the travel folder he sent with our tickets. There it was, the fabulous place, its great expensive white buildings arrayed like defensive walls holding back the blue waters of the same sea that washed our impoverished shore. Staring at those pictures, we children could hardly believe the same sea touched that enchanted land as well as ours, now so torn and depleted, seeming to have shriveled and lessened as we grew older.

For practical reasons we were to go in small parcels, first my older sister and my older half brother, then I and my two younger full brothers, to be followed by my half sister. I would have preferred to have us packed all in one box for delivery to him, everyone around me offering protection from the flight and the anticipated arrival in a strange land where we would most certainly become immediately lost underfoot. Even though we had heard that now my father drove with great skill and knowledge all over America, commanding the highways in huge trucks and vans, I was convinced he would never find his way through the traffic that packed the roads to the airport solid and we would languish forever on the airport runway.

At the small airport the planes were like color paintings,

not expected to take off into the air. We waved good-bye to friends and family, taking in a last, loving glimpse of the vast landscape, distant hills under the intense Haitian sun. What I remember of the flight itself was the uncontrolled rush down the runway, the incessant roar of the engine, the loss of my stomach when we pointed up and into the sun and left all safety behind, the loss of hearing, the bursting in my head. I had to face all of this and the ridicule of my brothers, who had already seized with a grip that would never weaken this first true proof that America would be theirs if only they held tight.

The flight was to me an eternity of punishment, made worse by the realization that it was all over so quickly and I had made such an infantile fuss. We were soon bustling along with hundreds of others through a chamber of inexplicable purpose along a corridor that ended abruptly at another mystery. I saw the heads, the bodies moving up in regular rows, one head lower than the next, all moving smoothly along, but saw nothing else moving but heads and bodies. The people weren't moving, the stairs were, and that was something difficult to accept, impossible to subject myself to. Somehow this harmless, commonplace, necessary convenience, the run-of-the-mill escalator, was the new land itself to me, a place where you could be swept up and away, carried off regardless of your own movement or will. I was pushed forward and on, taking hold of the handrail, which offered little comfort because it, too, was moving under my trembling hand, being driven forward and up as I was.

At the top of the moving stairs the crowd dispersed, seeming to fade off to the sides, leaving an opening into which he stepped, exactly as he was the last time I saw him, two years ago, kept in the flesh even more faithfully than in any of my dreams of him. He made for us all a joyful homecoming in a foreign land, and he welcomed us as easily and calmly as if it was the easiest thing in the world to do and had taken him just a day or two, not the years we lived without him.

*   *   *

Revelations in the new world came hard and fast. For one thing, my mother was not with my father. I suppose we had just assumed our family life with the two of them would automatically pick up that way, even though we had had no word at all from either of them that it would be so. In reality, a surprise he had kept for our first day, my father had married again, and it was into this new household that we settled, uncomfortably, with a feeling that it could only be a temporary measure. We at once recognized his old married style. He would be home every night for sure, but for sure late. He filled his off-work hours with an even broader range of activities than he had found time for in Haiti. We knew without being told that the new wife did not share with him the time he spent away from home, involved in such things as the local Masonic order, the Roman Catholic Church, the Rosicrucians, what have you, societies and cults mystical and practical, partaking indiscriminately in the rites of all, undisturbed by any contradictions among these different systems of belief.

We had arrived in early April; from then until June I was enrolled in the ninth grade. We had been told that it would have to be an all-African-American school. Coming from Haiti, the notion of an all-black school was nothing that had to be spelled out, not unusual, the norm. I didn't give it a second thought. Besides, I had a real problem to solve. What I had assumed was my easy grasp of English quickly proved as illusory as some of my other ideas about the new life in America.

We had been taught English by French-speaking nuns from Canada who had been living for years in Haiti. English by way of French, Canadian French, Haitian French was not the kind of English you normally ran into on the streets of Miami in the early 1970s. I tried out my school English in various stores, clutching the groceries for easy reference in case my questions about price could not be understood. The answers were unin-telligible to me, nothing ever heard before. They were worse than unintelligible, coming at me so fast that the few full stops or pauses ended not a sentence but a single word, spewed out as if the entire thing was one hot potato that had to be gotten rid of as quickly as humanly possible. It seemed to me that all my diligent study of English had given me was just enough knowledge to recognize when I was being ridiculed.

I did what many people do in times of great stress—I turned on the television. And left it on all summer. My father was on the road daily, my stepmother was busy working long hours sewing, my sister was in New York with my mother, my brothers easily fell into the rough-and-tumble of boy street life where the nec-essary words were few, repetitive, and unambiguous. I sank into daytime soaps, games, commercials, news, nonsense. I memorized every jingle and tag, I became a walking, talking encyclopedia of American commercialism. I rode the emotional roller coaster of every melodrama, taking all the roles, repeating every declaration of love, denunciations of infidelity, protestations of innocence, of indignation, affirmation, denigration. I mimicked emotions I had never heard of and laughed at jokes I did not understand. I played all the roles, and by the end of the summer I had my own repertoire of hot potatoes to spout.

I needed all the verbal skills I could muster. Relations with the young African-Americans who made up the majority in the inner-city junior school I attended were not easy. I had a rude awakening from my perhaps unconscious assumption that we would all be brothers and sisters because of our shared color. We shared little else, however. To most of my schoolmates I was foreign enough to be dubbed the French Fry. There was some justification in this because no matter how hard I tried, exotic traces of Haitian Creole lingered in my voice. To these Americans there was no distinction between French and

Creole—all outsiders, all fair game for ridicule. I consoled myself with thinking that all they knew of Haiti was probably de-
rived from movies about voodoo priests, the walking dead,
zombies. More recently, they had probably heard of the trick-
les, then waves, of immigrants poorer even than they. I knew I
would never have the courage to wave my former country's
flag, tell them that not even Napoleon's troops could conquer
Haiti when it rebelled in 1791, freed itself, and became in
1804 the first black-ruled nation in the world, and the second,
after the United States, to become completely independent. I
knew that if I told them this I was also bound in conscience to
tell them of the betrayals and broken promises that had undermined those achievements ever since. And even if I committed
the sin of omission and never spoke of Haiti's fall from grace,
its present tragic condition, I doubt if I could have convinced
many that, in spite of all our differences, all of us of color shared
a common African heritage and ancestry.

To me, my Miami schoolmates were more American than
African, in my eyes indistinguishable except for color from
anyone else in that still strange city. If I had expected to find a
welcome I was disappointed. I had to understand that for now
at least I was in a kind of double exile, away from my own land
and language, not yet accepted in my new country, not yet
fully at ease in its language and ways. Even my name was taken
from me. I was no longer Rose-Marie, as I was back there and
back then. In typical hurried American style, I was cut down to
simply Rose. All this would one day change; I was determined
to make it change. I wasn't going back. I had been given my future and had to start moving toward it.

Algebra was a start, as were calculus, biology, introduction to
physics, chemistry. I was good at these, having had a head start
in Haiti and having had a nun drill Latin into my head. Latin
might be a dead language for ordinary conversation, but it

was a good guide to the meaning of most of the words in which science is tied up. Not many of my schoolmates had this advantage, but then, not many took the science courses I worked at except under duress. I was having my first lesson in the America enigma: Why did the children of the most technologically, scientifically advanced nation in the world show such indifference to science and the mathematical basis of the technology they grew up with and took for granted? I did not have the answer then, but I truly understand the problem now. If a child's personality is formed by the age of six, then all too many African-American children have been left with the burden of forming themselves in the absence of parental guidance, taking whatever role models they can find from television or, worse, from the streets. With their real parents absent or in only partial attendance, the children are not nurtured or groomed to take their place in an advanced, technological society. Much of the world remains closed to them.

Within the year, predictably, Father's marriage fell apart. Unpredictably, my mother returned from New York and began to attend school to learn what was then an advanced skill, data processing, and Father continued in the role of provider. Mother and Father became reconciled and brought us together as a family. The same one, unfortunately.

Only the words and accents were different, for we had all determined to cleanse our speech of all traces of Haitian French and Haitian Creole. The angry arguments, accusations, taunts, jibes, and ridicule were all about the same thing. It did little good for me to say to both my mother and now-grown sister, "If you don't watch, he will leave again." I meant that if you do not give him his freedom, he will take it. I saw that Miami had not remade him and that America could not do the job. They had different expectations. Father left a second time, and my mother went back to work, but her job as a data processor was not adequate to sustain us without the help of food stamps.

* * *

It might have been just one of those accidents of history or it might have been foreordained, but in any case by the time I was ready for full-fledged high school, desegregation was in force in Miami, and schools were opened to all of us, not just white Americans, but African-Americans, Haitian Americans, any Americans. But the irony of the situation was that I suddenly found myself transported from an all-black school to an almost all-white one, and a predominantly Jewish one at that. As usual, I was destined to be odd girl out.

Everyone was very nice, everyone was polite, everyone was (I thought) glad I was Haitian rather than otherwise and fresh enough in this country not to have taken up any bad habits, attitudes. But as I became more at ease I began to work harder and harder, and this in turn began to draw the attention of my teachers, who took up the challenge of this odd, lonely little black girl who was never late for class, never forgot an assignment, never missed a paper or examination. The more I worked, the more work they had ready for me. They knew of my ambition to become a physician, and they supported and encouraged me, keeping to themselves whatever fears they had on the chances I would succeed in reaching that goal. For the time being, they set the tasks, harder and harder ones, and they were ready with praise when I met the challenges.

I was the only black female in calculus, which was not as strange as being the only black female in the Premed Club. I risked that because it gave me the opportunity to do volunteer work at a city hospital, one that still had an all-white medical staff and patients. On certain days and on some weekend days I did things like wheel a cart with magazines and books and snacks through the corridors or help transport patients. Unless something called attention to my special uniform or my youth, I was probably taken for one of the help.

But something else must have stuck out, because I found

that one or two of the nurses would call me over when they needed help dealing with a patient and I was the nearest volunteer. I would be asked to get a certain kind of bandage (I would memorize the name and how it was used immediately). I would be asked to hold something, some precious piece of medical equipment, and I did so trembling, wondering if my hands were clean enough or if I was guilty of a break in sterile technique, a phrase I had recently picked up.

I eventually became so familiar, or perhaps had made such a pest of myself, that I was once or twice given the extraordinary privilege of tagging along when the doctor and the residents made rounds. I was so grateful I did not then think it strange that the doctor more or less lectured the others, using the patient as a convenient illustration, something three-dimensional and hence more useful than the standard text provided, but not someone to be communicated with. In my imagination I saw the doctor using a pointer to indicate the malfunctioning parts, as if the patient had been sketched on a blackboard and had as much reality as a sketch. I knew otherwise. I saw the look of fear and awe and apprehension with which patients fixed the man in the spotless white coat, not daring to utter anything except quick answers to short questions, as if they were no longer certain it was their life being discussed, certain at any rate that it would be discourteous to interrupt. I was picking up a lot of useful information about medicine—and a lot I would have to unlearn.

The high school career counselor had her own room and saw upper-class men and women only by appointments, made long in advance. On certain days and between certain hours when no one was scheduled for an interview, she arranged to have the room unlocked. You were allowed to enter and browse through the shelves and shelves of college catalogs and brochures, books on career opportunities, guides for writing letters of application. You could even find books on what to do when you were turned down by your college of choice, but these were the less-consulted volumes. You could not remove anything from Ms. Diamond's shelves. We were certain she would have the fingerprints of anyone who dared the sacrilege of tearing out a page too long to copy. You could and did use the pencil sharpener screwed to one of the shelves. You brought your own notepaper and made sure you had enough. You read and read, took note after note, imagining those distant, hallowed shrines of higher learning, trying without success to imagine yourself within such, any such. It was a very emotional experience, even without Ms. Devra Diamond.

I was sure I had the time for my appointment right, but I checked the paper anyway before I knocked, held back by the voices I heard. Someone else had either stayed too long or come too early, although I could not imagine Ms. Diamond countenancing either breach of protocol. She half rose from the desk and smiled nicely, muttering my name with a slight question mark after it. I knew she was not doubting the explicitness of her appointment schedule or the timeliness of my arrival. I had to suppress the thought that she had some doubt about why I was there.

Ms. Diamond exchanged handshakes only with men students, and usually just smiled and nodded to young ladies. The desk was covered with catalogs and books, notepaper and form letters. They had been at work for some time and had not yet gotten to the tidying-up stage. It must be a difficult decision, I thought. Too many options—or too few. She waved me more or less in the direction of the reference shelves, saying something about running late, immediately adding in correction something about the importance of making the right choice, making the perfect match, maximizing one's strengths. We all knew she never let a didactic opportunity slip past. We always said she would find something useful to add to a conversation even if she were falling into a volcano or being throttled.

I fiddled among the catalogs I had already consulted over the last year, hearing bits and pieces of the hushed yet excited conversation, things about the advantage of this engineering course over that, the world recognition of that professor as opposed to the mere national reputation of the other, the number of Nobel laureates coaxed from that institution to the other. It was the kind of conversation I longed to have with Ms. Diamond and would have waited an age for.

I waited not an age but close to an hour before the student was perfectly fitted into his future life and work. When he left with many blessings on his head I was invited to sit down in the chair now restored to its familiar place across from the desk. Ms. Diamond folded her hands over the mess on her desk and smiled at me, waiting for me to tell her what plans I had made or dreams I had. As I spoke my short sentence the smile faded, the hands opened and then closed and held. The long interview must have tired her.

"A small college?" she repeated, thinking, I suppose, that was the safest place to begin.

"I would feel more comfortable."

"And also Catholic?"

I nodded, and she added, "For the same reason," without a question mark.

"I grew up a—" I began, but she seemed not to be listening.

There was a short pause. She opened her hands wide and spread them over the litter on her desk. There was nothing left now but the third part of my opening request and so, reluctantly, she had to address this.

"Premed?"

"Yes," I said quickly, hoping she would not make too much of it, almost wanting to hide the idea.

"But," she began, then backtracked, tried another opening: "You're intelligent," she said. I might have sighed; she sees my point. Then she went on, gathering herself, becoming Ms. Diamond. "You should use your intelligence."

I muttered something, indicating my general agreement with this.

"Where it can be most useful," she continued, finishing her sentence as if there had been no interruption at all.

I said something about believing that would be in medicine.

She looked at me more closely, then dropped her eyes and said, "The technical skills are also useful."

"Oh, yes!" I agreed at once. A slight pursing of her lips suggested I had not gotten the point, not at all.

"I would like information on a small Catholic college with a good premedical program," I heard someone in the room say and had to assume that I was repeating myself.

She was all business now, sweeping the booklets in a neat pile with one gesture, then up from her desk, to the appropriate shelf without hesitation, back to me with a small handful of undistinguished pamphlets, not a soaring spire in Technicolor on the limp cover of any one.

"We are fortunate in having right here in Miami or environs a good number of excellent technical schools where you can learn an appropriate medical assistant skill in a relatively short time and at an affordable cost, with the possibility of study-work assistance and government-guaranteed loans. If you haven't studied any of this literature, you've done yourself an injustice. But applications can be filed late at most of the better schools. There are always openings."

I did not offer to take any of the material she was holding across the desk; my resistance was entirely nonverbal. I was speechless, feeling all conviction draining out of me.

Even with downcast eyes I could see her withdraw the pamphlets, letting them drop on the desk. Her voice was very kind and now almost reflecting the weariness on her face. "Do you really want to go to medical school?"

"But I must," I said, with a sudden intensity that took her by surprise.

"Do you have any idea of how difficult it will be?"

"Oh, yes," I exclaimed at once. "I have read many books where doctors complain about how difficult it was and how much they had to do and everything. They all say it's why they charge so much when they get their degrees and why—"

"None of that has anything to do with your case," she broke in, and then did not stop until my own doubts and fears and disbelief in my own destiny began to speak to me in her voice, with her words.

"No, no," I moaned to myself, "you're not going to make it. Why should you, you just barely learned English, you won't be able to keep up, you can't afford all those years, how can you work and study, how will you be able to pay off the loans, find a place to live, find time to study, how will you get into residency after medical school, there's no place in this system for someone like you, just go back to Haiti, there are black doctors there, maybe even black women doctors, you won't stand out, you will fit in there, where black women may have a chance. . . ."

She had been writing furiously, consulting one after the other of the booklets, jotting down words and figures. When I raised my head she was smiling. She held out the pages she had filled. She offered me the final inducement, saying, "Look, there is even a bus near your neighborhood that goes close to one of the better technical schools."

Ms. Diamond took me to the door herself, her hand lightly on my shoulder. She had come through again, arranged another career, matched up my potential with the real possibilities out there, spared another young soul the disappointment that comes inevitably from clinging against the odds to an unrealistic goal in life. At the door she did not smile, but I could feel the warm and lingering hold of her hand on my shoulder.

I left in tears. Why was I brought to this country where a dream could be ignored or denied because of the color of a person's skin? If I had stayed in Haiti I would not have been denied. In Haiti my doctors, my teachers, my counselors were black, even the president of the nation was black.

My mother did not read what Ms. Diamond had written. When I explained the advice I had received, she simply took the pages from me, glanced at them, then crumpled them in her fist, and as she spoke continued to manipulate them into a tighter and tighter ball, releasing her anger unconsciously so that her words would be clear and exact.

All she said was "Go back to the woman and tell her we are not interested in technical schools. Tell her she misunderstood. Make it clear to her this time. Remind her she is supposed to do her job right."

I got my appointment with Ms. Diamond sooner than I had expected. She asked if I had made up my mind. I hesitated, not trusting my own words to convince her that I did in truth know where I wanted to go. I decided I would have to risk offending her, so I simply told her about my conversation with my mother. I think I tidied things up a bit. I did not exactly say, "We are not interested in technical schools," but rather something like "My daughter's talents would be better used in a more challenging field such as a premedical program." I tidied it all up, and then I mentioned some of my science teachers and some of the things they had said about my work over the years.

Ms. Diamond listened, then asked me to repeat over again for her my reasons for wanting to try to get accepted into a premedical program. She questioned me closely about my grades and my classwork. She let me talk until I think I had said it all over for her several times and even I was beginning to doubt if all of it, any of it, was really true. Then she got up and seemed to bring the conversation to a conclusion.

"Then I guess that's the way things will be," she said. "We

should get to work now. I wasted some days that could have been put to good use."

We spent a long time going through catalog after catalog, weighing and balancing possibilities. I did not think it strange that no other student came to interrupt us or remind Ms. Diamond that she was running late. Together we found what I— and by now she—had been looking for. Playing a part in such miracles was, after all, what she had been doing all her life. I might have been in some ways a first for her, but I know I am not the last.

CHAPTER 6

It was the first big step, except that I saw myself at the bottom of a huge flight of steps, an epic movie set, each riser seeming taller than any stretch of mine could manage at once. There would be no taking these steps two at a time, no easy, exhilarating rush to the top. But at least I was there, enrolled in the college of my choice, beginning the longed-for premed program, anxious, lonely, afraid, timid, yet drawing some immediate relief from the realization that I had four full years to prove myself worthy of the faith—and the loans and part scholarship and work-study opportunities—placed in me. I would certainly get the hang of it somewhere along the way. It couldn't be any worse than high school . . . or could it?

One part about this new experience was going to be different, I felt at once. For the first time in my life I had an enormous sense of how costly my dream would be. I was committed to four years at a place where every breath I drew could be reckoned in dollars and cents, none of them contributed by me. I had settled on a university in New Orleans because it was small, Catholic, and had an excellent premedical program. Getting me in the door was a minor miracle of shoestring financial manipulation. A small scholarship, student loans, loans from family members, promises of further loans—it was a patchwork put together by my father and mother and my relatives. For the next four years they would continue to work to hold the sustaining fabric together, and even when great rents would suddenly appear, some hoped-for loan fail to materialize, they managed to grab the frayed ends and hold them closer until the next saving money appeared. It was a labor of love and a labor of their hands.

Ask me today how I first grasped the basic medical science that makes up the foundation of my daily practice today and I don't think I could answer. That would be something like asking a child who has learned to speak well, rapidly, inventively, "How did you learn? What was it like to put the first sentence together?" It didn't happen that way. The process was more hit-and-miss, trial and error, than intentional, guided probably by some instinctive feel for the way sentences had to go. I had from my primary school days a sense of how mathematics and science went, had an aptitude for them. I had to convince myself in those first few weeks of feeling my way around that there would be more hits than misses. And I suppose that if I looked back through my old college texts I would feel a surge of superiority, not just that I now have a more polished vocabulary, speak in more complex sentences, have learned so much more since then that I forgot where I began, but that science and medicine had advanced so fast in the ensuing years that much that I studied has necessarily been changed. Probably the only thing that has not become obsolete is the human body itself; you can still trust basic anatomy to bide with you over the long haul.

Premeds were distinguished by the books they carried, big books, heavy books, many books. We carried them around in sacks slung over our shoulders or clutched them tightly to our chests, as if hoping to absorb something by such intimate contact. Maybe that is what ultimately happened, accumulated knowledge filtering not just into my brain (from where it some-times unexpectedly leaked out) but into my bloodstream as well. Facts becoming flesh, or at least second nature. The facts had to become that, for how could you be thinking of the defi-nitions of hemohistioblast, thrombocyte, and erythrocyte when you had a patient bleeding to death in the emergency room on a Saturday night? I somehow always saw myself in the emergency room facing knife wounds and sirens.

But that assimilation did not happen at once and, I must confess, for some kinds of facts, some branches of science, it happened late and haphazardly. You plugged away, course after course, semester after semester—calculus, biochemistry, physical chemistry, physics, anatomy, biology—hoping you had plugged every memorized term in so tight it could not es-cape. You were amazed at what wasn't there when you looked for it again; you were amazed at what was retained. You had assumed that you would learn every subject with an equal de-gree of proficiency so that at the end your brain would resem-ble a neat card catalog. You didn't march steadily forward. You set out with the other troops but sometimes got ambushed, had to take cover, lost your way, spent days in the wilderness trying to catch up, and then you did, only to find the van-guard was off on yet another forced march. The metaphor is military, but you did feel you were in the trenches for the dura-tion. You had to remind yourself that this was only premed, a skirmish where your high school skills gave you some cover. It was not the real thing, not medical school itself. That was still four years off, but you could hear the big guns in the distance, sounding closer with each semester.

I was not the only woman in premed that year. I was the only black woman, an unwanted distinction that was becoming more or less routine. The 10 percent or so of the premed student body that was female proved in however small measure that women did study science. The 1 percent that was female and black (just me, you know) proved that the opportunity or the inclination to study science was not commonplace among the people to whom I belonged. Finding my solitary black face amid the uniform white ones might even lead you to suspect that there was something genetic about it. That is to say, blacks don't study science because they can't. Indeed, I eventually came across weighty, well-received academic tomes that spent hundreds of thousands of words proving that very point. Some such notions were even packaged as best-selling "scientific" studies, making the authors rich and again showing that a lot of people are uncomfortable with their prejudices unless someone offers them proof that they're justified in hanging on to them. Sort of like saying, "Sure, we treat 'em like part of the human family, but we don't go so far as to believe they can think." I had seen a different reality. In my former country I had seen black scientists, physicians, engineers, mathematicians. They were as naturally a part of our intellectual landscape as the landscape itself.

A number of others were black like me and highly motivated to do well in different programs. My roommate, for instance, was determined to get honors as a business major because she knew that educated black women with college degrees were going places in business. Even though we were roommates and on good terms, we never did become close. Maybe that's because premeds tend to stick, or rather cling, together out of shared interests and concerns, or maybe just because misery needs company—and where else can you go after midnight when your calculus problems defy all efforts at calculation? In any case, my roommate had an instinctive self-assurance that, had it ever been met with in a premed, would have been excised root and branch. We were told and then subsequently supposed to feel that the amount of science to be learned exceeded by light-years our meager ability to absorb it. (You immediately tried to remember just how long a light-year was—or was that supposed to be how far?) We never stopped to examine the contradiction in each class we attended. If it was so impossibly difficult to learn this stuff, why were those guys (never, as is still generally true today, women) standing up there telling us they had in fact learned enough of it to be comfortable in their jobs? You can be sure they didn't get their doctorates in self-doubt.

"What is the sound of one hand clapping? Meditate, don't doze off! Back straight, thumbs barely touching. Think of the sound of silence. Find your inner teacher, inner guide, protector, your inner Christ and omniscient one."

The shouted exhortations were in keeping with the man's appearance, typical 1960s hippie beard-and-beads, baggy-pants-and-sandals, a bit dated now in the late seventies but nice on his lean, rangy form. Neither the words nor the look were in keeping with his position in this narrow academic world. He was a professor, a priest, and a teacher in a solidly Catholic institution. He was there because he was an acknowledged authority on religions, including those with little in common with Christianity. Maybe being part Asian himself gave him an additional authority in our eyes. I was there taking a humanities elective because meditation, Zen Buddhism, and Eastern spirituality were in the air, as I found out when I sometimes came up for gulps of it at a rare Saturday-night party or dance. I even had a date once who asked me about my karma and didn't know what to do with my made-up answer, so he dropped the subject of karma at once and then dropped me.

I wanted to see if any of these teachings would hold any meaning for me, me with my set beliefs and growing doubts about how those beliefs related to my present life. I knew without knowing that I was slowly losing the peace within I once had. I knew it because inner peace was something I once felt without question. It had to be slipping away if there was room for questions. I took the course that would in large measure change the course of my life.

Bill Chu, Father Chu, William Albert Chu, Chu-Chu—he accepted any form of address benignly, as if none caught the essential Chu—was talking to a mixed bag of students, many of them brought up as Catholics or in some other equally regimented religion, some of them toiling to learn scientific objectivity. The last thing these systems welcomed was the "not-knowing mind," the leisure of doubting the fixed notions of things as set forth in church dogma or biology textbook. Nevertheless, some of the spiritual teaching I now heard could fit into my increasingly pragmatic and practical head, provided I gave them the necessary premed twist. I found it easy to believe with the Buddhists in the transitory, unsatisfactory condition of life, especially life as a premed. It was more difficult to believe that I could be released from this unsatisfactory condition by changing my perception. I found myself agreeing completely with the notion that the causes of suffering can themselves be the means of release from suffering. After all, as a physician I would often be a cause of suffering to patients, or at least have to do things that hurt the patient. That suffering, however, would bring release from suffering. I had managed to stuff Zen into my preconceptions and felt proud to have done it so logically. Not bad for a beginner! I congratulated myself on my first flight into Zen, not realizing that as far as true inner understanding was concerned I had done about as well as Orville Wright's twelve-second first airplane attempt at Kitty Hawk. History was made, a new era begun, but as with most beginnings, you had to have faith.

The church was cavernous, its tapering walls and windows so overwhelming that they always made the Sunday congregation, no matter how densely packed, seem insignificant. Even when played softly, the organ notes boomed and echoed over my head, a distraction rather than inducement to prayer. I kept my eyes down throughout most of the mass, not just out of devotion but to avoid a reminder of the obvious. As usual, I was the only black face in the congregation. But the moment I dreaded came regardless and I stood with the rest, waiting for my fellow worshiper on one side to turn to me, bend over, come as close as reasonable to my cheek, mutter the kiss-of-peace words, releasing me to turn to the person on the other side. And then I would be placed in the uncomfortable position my first neighbor was now freed from. I reached up, sought the offered cheek, mouthed into the space between us the words of peace, let that one go in relief to the white face waiting. I felt my own discomfort acutely, I could feel that of my neighbors. I felt more pity and sorrow than anger, but I wanted to be angry that such feeling came to intrude on my need for peace and consolation.

I had first gone to the big church because I needed something to separate Sunday from all the other weekdays. During the week the small chapel on campus was adequate for my increasingly desperate pleas for divine help in my studies, a little boost in physics, another insight into the puzzles of histology. I brought nothing but the very practical to the divine throne. If I had gone to Sunday services in the chapel with the rest I would not stand out with my cheap and casual clothing, blouse and jeans, no pocketbook, an unembroidered handkerchief making due for a proper hat. I would not have stood out with my skin, for I was not the only black practicing Catholic on campus.

If I had gone to the chapel I would not have to hasten out of that cold cavern with a feeling of emptiness, no spiritual enrichment, no contentment, avoiding those I felt wanted to avoid me.

I had in the past tried to rationalize my growing resentment at the official church, zeroing in on its history, the role it played, however passive, in the coercion, conversion, and exploitation of peoples of color around the world. I thought of the motto that greeted my African ancestors as they waited in apprehension for the loaded ships to land their soldiers and guns and horses and priests: We bring you civilization and faith. We'll take all the rest you have, gold, land, you yourselves. Thank you. Now line up for civilization.

I wasn't being fair, I knew, not to history, not to those who struggle against the abuses of colonialism, finally not to those kindly souls who went to Sunday mass in the big church. I was certainly projecting my social uneasiness onto them, assuming that they felt uncomfortable coming that close, close enough for touch, even though that was deftly avoided. I wanted to be fair, objective. I had history on my side, history written in the blood of people like me. And even though we had been brought to this world against our will, I was the intruder in their midst.

I didn't realize how angry I was beneath this false objectivity until Bill Chu turned me around to face my anger. It wasn't there at first. I couldn't let it be. Nor could I let show the other negatives, the very personal fear of rejection, the resentment at this possible humiliation, the sense of superiority to such mundane souls as those I cowered before. I wasn't going to accept any of these feelings as mine, until Bill simply turned me around and showed me all of it. He showed the self I had been making out of my extreme shyness, my anger and fear—and my denial of these unacceptable emotions. The first sustained heavier-than-air flight I took, with Bill my copilot, exposed a part of myself I did not know existed, had denied, had never brought inside. I had left the unacceptable Rose-Marie at the church steps, so to speak. But she was there waiting for me. All I had to do was acknowledge the family resemblance. Bill brought me to see that by embracing all of my selves, even the unaccepted ones, I no longer had to spend my energy creating a false self. And then I could release that energy as concern and compassion. I could begin to imagine the conflicts within the person whose lips I could almost feel hesitating so close to my face those Sunday mornings.

To move very far ahead in my story, I would from this beginning eventually learn to listen for signs of the conflicts and fears and resentments and denials in my patients clearly. I would learn that they and their loved ones could not often express these feelings directly, certainly not to me, the doctor in charge of their lives. I had to learn to show them that I understood such feelings myself, had my share of them. I had to let them know that it was all right with me if they let it all out, even taking me as the target, if necessary. If making me the target was the first step in communication, let it be. It was not the neatest way to begin communicating, but it was effective in its own messy way. I struggled not to let either my own or their unreal selves get in the way of our understanding. Nothing should ever get in the way of this mutual and loving exchange: my concern for their well-being, their need for that assurance. It continues to surprise me that I learned the first important lesson about being wholly with my patients not from a science course but from a slightly middle-aged hippie priest, still into beads and beards, not worried for a moment that history would ever pass his truth by—my only textbook that has never become obsolete.

I met him at Mardi Gras and always felt there was something especially fitting about that. His name was Larry, and he was an automobile salesman downtown but was at this party masquerading as a pirate, and he seemed to me both dangerous and harmless, like the fake but still realistically edged and pointed knife he would clutch between his dazzlingly white teeth while waiting for my stumbling replies to his questions. I was stumbling a lot, tongue-tied, trying to hide my delight—well, sheer ecstasy—that the most handsome man in the entire room was talking to me, had actually pushed through the crowd to the corner where I stood alone to say he admired my costume. Not what you'd expect, not predictable, he said. I had to take a quick, guilty look to see what it was I was wearing as I accepted the compliment. I might not have been wearing one at all. I probably hadn't wanted to come, had probably been dragged from the library as I was, in work clothes. I saw that the earring was actually his own, but no doubt kept for occasions like this. He was the kind of man who could slip in and out of disguises without much effort. But there was always some evidence, the minute, nearly invisible indent in an earlobe, he couldn't disguise or didn't think to.

It was inevitable that I should have wanted it to last forever. It was stupidity that I should have thought it would. It was my first love.

He was a used car salesman, but that did me no good because I didn't know how to drive and had to turn down his offers of a car that could get me to his apartment quickly, easily. I was always rushed for time, always guilty about the time I was spending with him in his small, almost barren apartment downtown that took a long wait for a trolley, a long trolley ride, a long walk to get to. I tried to deal with my guilt by dragging along my heavy sack of books and reading, furiously highlighting passages, terms, definitions I knew simply were not registering on me then. I would have to learn it all over at some later, less-pressured time. I finally discovered that the books had lost much of their meaning for me when I went off early one Monday morning without them, forgot them in the corner where they had been dropped, discarded two nights before. And I didn't even understand why I felt so light, so unburdened, light-headed, light-footed, until I walked through the campus gate and discovered I had left my burden behind.

He would say he kept the apartment bare, down to the barest essentials, because he believed in traveling light, concentrating on the essentials. He told me I was an essential and so fitted in easily with his life, which had space already held waiting for me. I don't want him to sound solemn, because he wasn't and didn't make pronouncements. He was jovial, joking, happy-go-lucky, a comfort after days and hours of cramming, memorizing, rationalizing, and always being graded and evaluated and as often as not found wanting. He was my first love. I was infatuated, in love.

He helped me turn off my mind. He showed me that as a woman I could be secure and certain with him, a man. He never made me feel there were things I had to be taught. He made me secure in the feeling I already knew. He was the best of teachers, the one who lets you believe you've always known what has to be learned. You just knew it differently. I was being nurtured in a way I had never been before. When I lay half dreaming in his arms and felt my head lifting and falling with the tide of his breathing, I dreamed myself back to my early days, my remembrances of my father cradling me in his arms and rocking me, us, both of us together into peace and safety, rocking away all the insecurities of my life and possibly his as well.

The apartment was so small and neat that anything out of place registered immediately. That morning I had wakened before him, for not even these weekend flights from reality could break me of the necessary habit of early rising. I was lying still, watching the first morning light bring things back into place. There were no city sounds yet, and I was conscious only of his breathing, not mine. I saw the small bundle of envelopes, bound with a rubber band, on the floor where they must have fallen. I supposed he had gone through them and was ready to file them away somewhere. They were far under the table where he did his paperwork, so it was logical for me to think they were too far for him to have noticed. I slipped quietly out of bed and put the letters back on the desk, where he would expect them to be.

At first I thought they were addressed to his mother and father, although he had never mentioned them nor had he spoken about dealing with their affairs. Yet why would he have so much of their correspondence if he were not doing so? And even if he had never mentioned them, there had to be a Mr. and Mrs. Lawrence Jefferson because all these letters had been addressed to the couple and were proof that they existed, at least in the mind of the senders. Not one of the letters had an urgent Please Forward scribbled on it. They had been correctly addressed. Nevertheless, Mr. and Mrs. Jefferson did not exist in my mind in those first seconds. I was not going to give that thought any reality for as long as I could fight it off.

He woke up, although I had done nothing to disturb him while I sat on the edge of the bed, the letters in my hand. He smiled and reached out to take me closer, but I held him off and said, "You are Mr. Lawrence Jefferson, aren't you?"

He looked around in mock dismay. "If I'm not, you have been the victim of an intruder and an impersonator."

"You aren't impersonating Mr. Jefferson?"

He crossed his hands across his bare chest and intoned, "I cannot tell a lie."

"Washington," I corrected.

"What's that?" he asked.

"I said Washington said I cannot tell a lie."

"Jefferson didn't? I mean, Jefferson didn't have occasion to say it, too?"

"What does Jefferson say about Mrs. Jefferson?"

We both let the silence fall over us then. He pulled the covers close and did not move toward me. After a while he said in a quiet voice, no joking now, "I cannot tell a lie."

"But you have," I said, probably without any gentleness at all.

He propped himself up and began with "You'd understand if I told you what kind of a life I lived with her."

"Live with her," I said, correcting him once again and not to his pleasure.

"Okay! I see her sometimes, for the kid's sake."

"That must be convenient for you, if not them."

"What does that mean?"

I had begun to dress, making sure I did it carefully enough so that nothing would be left behind. My silence irritated him into repeating his question.

"What does that mean?"

"It's a convenience to be able to do exactly as you want to do, especially if you can say you're doing it for them."

"You don't know anything about it," he shot back with an unmistakable tone of contempt in his voice.

"I know everything about it," I began, but stopped myself at once. I had to finish dressing, make sure I had all my things, not leave a book or a note or a pencil behind. He was saying something that sounded like mimicry of my own words, but not even this slowed me. I knew what I was thinking, but I wasn't going to share any of it with him. Maybe it was pride, or maybe a fear of humiliation, but I was not going to let him know that I was intimately acquainted with such misery as this. The difference between the past and this present was that what I had once known as a spectator I was now feeling in my blood, my beating pulse and burning face. I always knew I was my father's child, but now more than ever in my life I felt what it was to be my mother's daughter.

*   *   *

As Bill Chu would say the Buddha had said, I had been taken for a spin on the Wheel of Life, animal realm division, characterized by stupidity, maybe even sensuality. What better way to spend your college years, provided you weren't premed? But to be led to discover why and how I had been really stupid was agony. To realize that I had hoped to find in his bed (one that belonged to another woman, I almost screamed) the security and self-confidence I had never found on my own—that was altogether too much! I had lost not just Larry—and good riddance to him and all other married men—but an illusion about myself. I had fallen in love, stupidly, unknowingly, with a married man. I had lost my virginity to an unfaithful husband.

I had wanted a quick fix for the gnawing doubts I had about myself, and rather than risk going deeper within to find the source of the doubt and maybe in the process find the self that doubted, I had avoided the issue, assuming I was okay because he made me feel okay another way. He was good at that, but it was the wrong medicine, even if at the time it was the only thing that could be done to help a patient like me. Larry used the only medicine he had, but as far as opening me up to life, he was just practicing without a license.

Hard thoughts to contend with under any circumstances, but thoughts most incompatible with, say, Professor Dobson's advanced biology lectures and labs. By general agreement he was the most brilliant teacher in the entire premed program, brilliant always being meant to include the title of most difficult. Undergraduates used to ask: If life is really as difficult as Dobson's course makes it seem, how did it possibly evolve at all? If he weren't a Jesuit and hence denied such heretical thoughts and practices, we earnestly believed that he would set about making life more complex than God had, more or less improving on basically immature work. After all, the world was God's first attempt, and Dobson had the advantage of hindsight.

The really smart ones among us made a try at concocting the ideal life-form such as Dobson would have created. I don't think anyone brought the model to the professor for his comment. In our eyes he made only two concessions to ordinary life, and these only involuntarily. He had the misfortune of having been christened Robin, and he had the worse misfortune of having developed, late in life, a slight but incessant bobbing of his head. It was mesmerizing, should get you caught up in its regular rhythms, but no one dared nod off in his presence. And no one was allowed to say "Bobbin' Robin" except with affection or awe.

We premeds hung together more and more as the last year and the final, most difficult courses approached. Individually, we had our own by then well-worked-out techniques for coping. I was studying meditation, having learned to my relief that this did not involve simply emptying the mind. I could not afford that, obviously, since it had been so difficult to cram my mind so full of scientific bits and pieces, none of which I could afford to lose track of. I was trying to learn to focus on the simple awareness of things, trying to keep in touch with what was in front of my face at any single moment, every moment. I was trying to keep in front of me all that was present and then remember how I responded to all that. It was enough for the moment, really all I could do, although I knew there was much more to it than this preliminary step.

Others had other methods, including the forbidden but common-as-dirt stimulants and stay-up-all-the-time pills and magic potions. We may have been small, Catholic, traditional, regimented, disciplined, but in these things we were definitely mainstream. Daniel did it with pot. He always seemed to have enough money and connections to buy as much as he needed, which seemed a large amount to me. He came from a good, no, a best family. He was also at the top of the class, a seeming contradiction that I did not want to resolve. If he was so dissolute he should have been dumb, or at least careless enough to get caught and dumped. He was lucky, or clever. Others I was to meet would not be so lucky, but then, they didn't have the advantages.

Daniel was kind and receptive and understanding. Best of all, he always had the correct answer to your problem of the day—or night. His blue eyes looked larger than life, often were larger than life, but his brilliant mind was never similarly out of focus. He played with science the way some people play music by ear, as if he knew how it went before being taught. Nevertheless, how he managed remains one of the unplumbed mysteries, just as how he retained all his bright boyish blond American good looks, his fair unblemished skin, his sturdy lithe body, the whole works on an absolutely rotten diet, self-imposed sleep deprivation, and the much-needed weed. He might have fallen apart the day after graduation, gone to pieces the first semester in medical school (there was never any question that he wouldn't be accepted by any school of his choice). But as it turned out, Daniel settled down, graduated from medical school, got married, became a first-rate urologist in a major hospital.

I hadn't really taken to him at first—he was as much a naked display of his race and background as I was of mine. The difference between us was, as they said, like night and day, black and white. And besides, he was several years into an affair with my best friend. Still, I knew I could always call on him and he would always guide me gently through every step of a problem, spinning out the intricacies of chemistry or biology or whatever as if they were all beautiful variations on a fabulous theme that nature played in his head. Maybe the pot kept him open to the music inherent in all things and made him see the connections to which I was blind and deaf. I came away understanding, luckily, just enough to get the answer down on the next exam.

I was having trouble keeping up with the work, which seemed to be getting more difficult. I was becoming dependent on Daniel to answer the problems I did not seem to have time to do myself. I was staying up all night and forcing myself to keep going without sleep. I was eating as poorly as Daniel, but he was in the top 10 percent in the class and I wasn't. I was being a typical premed student worrying about medical school and would I be going and if not, then what? I tried to concentrate on the moments before me, the facts, letting each one sink in without worrying if I had caught their full meaning or could or ever would. Get myself out of the way.

Daniel and I began to spend more and more time together. I wanted to talk to him about the pot, but didn't. I tried to improve our diet. He would watch me eat, insisting that there was still a lot to be learned about blood-clotting factors, and if I couldn't understand what was now in the books that was okay because then my mind wouldn't be cluttered with notions I would have to discard when the whole story came in. He didn't seem to mind that I was taking up so much of his time.

His real girlfriend, my best friend, Christie, was living off campus in the kind of apartment students can afford, and the neighborhood was the same. You had to be careful, but nothing bad had happened in the year or so she was there. Then her roommate moved out, and, before she could find another, the terrible thing happened to her. The man had probably only wanted to find something to steal, but there wasn't much of value and she was there alone. She went to the school doctor and then had to tell the police, so we knew it had been a black man, but she could not give a good description of him other than that. They would never catch him with just that to go on. Too many possibilities.

I tried to keep away from the thought that Christie somehow wanted me to apologize for what had happened to her. It was someone from my race, even though there had to be rapists everywhere. I felt for her, I felt her pain and outrage and even humiliation. But I became angry when I thought I was expected to apologize. And I didn't want to admit to the anger. That wasn't what I had been taught. But still, Christie had been violated and had a right to blame everyone, anyone, even me. Everyone gets to share in the guilt.

I found I could talk to Daniel about some of this, about the anger I had no place for, about the guilt, about my having to pray for Christie in her pain but also for the terrible person who had done this thing because he didn't know anything, maybe even didn't want to know anything better, and he would have to live with so little sense of the value of people or anything at all. He would never have the chance to know the value of someone like Christie. Or himself. You weren't supposed to pray for the lost because they were beyond help. That person was given up by everyone as lost, but I prayed for him anyway.

Christie broke off her relationship with Daniel right after the terrible thing happened to her. She just didn't want to be involved anymore with him or anyone.

Daniel and I then became lovers. I would lie awake and look at his white—no, flesh-colored, pink-colored, soft-colored body—and compare it with my own ebony skin color. The contrast was startling no matter where I put my hand, my arm. How could the same creation contain us both? I wondered. How did we come about, so different yet, as I knew from all my courses, basically so much the same? Either of us would do perfectly well as, say, a cadaver for a gross anatomy class. If our blood types were the same, either of us . . . But I couldn't solve the problem, nor has anyone.

I don't think he was taking pity on me and on the feeling of responsibility and humiliation I had because of Christie. We never talked about why we were together, maybe because we knew we did not have much time and shouldn't waste it talking over what probably didn't have an easy, if any, explanation except that we were in love.

The final semester was being wrapped up. The hundreds of letters of applications to medical schools, references, personal essays were gone, with everyone's hopes and anxieties sealed up with them—four years in a manila envelope. My mother and sister made plans to stay with me for graduation, even taking an apartment so they could stay weeks in advance. I had not seen my mother in almost two years, and I knew my loss of weight would surprise her. I didn't know she was bringing with her an entire wardrobe for me, unfortunately the old me, the one with the extra thirty pounds. She was more than surprised, was terrified, shocked, appalled. She wanted me admitted to the hospital immediately. When I satisfied her that my health was good enough she turned her frustration on the clothing. Nothing would fit, and she would have to remake it all, furiously, in indignation and worry, bringing everything down to my current size.

Daniel's parents were coming to see him graduate as expected, top of the class. When we met, the reception I received was as expected. They didn't care that I loved him. They didn't have Daniel's reasons for accepting me and saw me only as an impediment.

Each and every surviving premed had to go to Professor Dobson for a final interview in those last weeks. He promised us he would pray for us, be present at the final ceremony, be available for consultation and guidance anytime we needed it in the next phase of our careers. After the interviews we compared notes on how pale and sick he looked, how rapidly deteriorated, how fragile. We did not mention the bobbing head, never still now, painful and pitiful to behold. We could imagine the pain it caused him, even, for once, the embarrassment. We could not speak of it, remembering how lightly we had turned the affliction into a childish joke.

He came to our pregraduation-night celebration and stayed almost to the end, waving weakly at each of us, greeting us by name and with some personal, individual remembrance that took us by surprise, wondering how he had noticed such things in those hurried, crowded years. He saw us through it all, and when it was over he died. It was chance that it happened while we were still together, immediately after graduation and before we had packed and gone off in our separate directions. We could thus pay him tribute and honor as if we were in truth the single group he had molded out of many different men and women, many different talents and possibilities. He died thinking we were now equal, having given to all of us all he was capable of giving. To the best of his great abilities he had sent us all off in the same direction, to the same destiny and greater challenge.

It would not be that way. I watched day after day as the letters arrived bearing the logo of all those many desired destinations, everywhere we had applied with such beating hearts and trembling fingers. I heard the wild shouts of joy as one after another acceptance was torn from the fancy envelopes. I took my first rejections in stride, as the others did, as one had to. I learned to avoid the well-intended embraces of consolation from the luckier—no, more gifted ones. I kept away from the company of those like me who had not yet received a glimmer of hope. I went to my mailbox at night and read the letters by

lamplight. In the end there wasn't any light. It had not happened. It was not going to happen. I had not been accepted.
Not anywhere. The four years behind me lost their meaning in
a wink of an eye, leaving nothing and nothing I could see in
the future. It was as simple as that and not to be questioned. I
had not won against the odds. There would be no miracle.

CHAPTER 7

I went home to my mother and sister in Miami and let them find me something to do. They took me quickly in hand, reasoning that I needed something as quickly as possible. They also knew I needed time to find an alternate route to where I wanted to go, or several alternates if necessary. Or maybe come to decide on another goal altogether. That did not seem an unlikely compromise to them, although they did not suggest that to me directly. To do any of the above, I would need some time to think it out—and something to keep my mind off thinking too much about it.

My sister had always been very practical. Being smart helped. What with practical and smart she had made her way remarkably well, taking her college degree and using it as a lever to get into an accounting firm that managed the affairs of restaurants at Miami International Airport.

The airport catered to travelers' needs and preferences with six full-service restaurants and seven fast-food stands. From a beginner struggling with ledgers to keep track of all this culinary commerce, she soon graduated to office supervisor, then supervisor of the restaurants themselves, then assistant to the president of the company that ran the entire show. She was also smart enough to know that assistant was pretty much where she would remain, given that the president was male and young, white, and affable. Not as well educated as she, but she had picked up enough practical information along the way to know that young, female, black, and educated does not outweigh young, male, white, less educated. She was looking for something better and would eventually find it, but not before retooling herself. She took on law school and slugged her way through with the same determination she had used in college. She wound up not just a lawyer but one of the chief assistants to the state district attorney, and that represents a lot of slugging.

But while she was still assisting, she used her limited clout to get me set up in the accounting office where she had begun. I think she breathed a bit easier knowing that I was then set on the road to success (with luck, from this office to that, from that to the next, from the bottom to, well, almost the top). At least I had a job to keep my mind off medicine for a while.

The thing you don't often realize about food is that it is a commodity like anything else and like anything else has to be counted. Back then, before computers did away with people and paperwork, it was usually counted by people. That's what I did. I counted. Take hot dogs, for instance. Everybody eats hot dogs, but that is only the end of the story (a part that also has to be recorded, however).

This was just the beginning. I had been started on something easy like the hot dog and potato chip account, but there were thirteen restaurants at the airport and somebody had to account for all that food, every last bite and ethnic variation of it. How long would I have to be at this job before I lost my appetite for everything, including the mysterious, pricey items featured on the gourmet menus?

The hot summer weeks were passing slowly by, as slowly as each nine-to-five day passed in my office, where the sheets of now familiar names and repetitive numbers were checked and tabulated and verified and sent off, only to sprout again the next morning. I seemed to be in a state of suspended animation, doing the routine, automatic work in a routine, automatic way.

I went to the local library sometimes, just to "keep my hand in," browsing through the new books, popular guides to home health care, how to lose those ten ugly pounds without cutting off your head, what foods will kill you even if you don't eat them regularly but just keep them in the refrigerator, how to live forever on yogurt and white vinegar. You know the kind. I even ventured into the more serious shelves and marveled—yes, they are still writing books about the heart after all these years! What else could be learned about the human heart and its ways?

I got bold enough to more or less fake my way into the university library where the heavy-duty medical books were available. I began asking for journals whose names I recalled from my premed courses. Once in a while the librarian did a kind of half-suppressed double take, checking the name of the journal and then checking me out. "No, not *Essence*," I wanted to reply. "Just the current issue of the *Journal of the American Medical Woman's Association*. It's the one without the recipes."

One day I came upon an article that seemed written just for me. The research and scholarship that went into the study seemed impeccable: tables, figures, percentages, conceptual model, references. Four authors and enough titles after their names to qualify them for the Nobel Prize in medicine. The article was called "The Rejected Medical School Applicant," and I felt as if I was reading my own obituary. There were some morsels of consolation at the beginning—at least I got through premed and was not among the 40 percent or so that dropped out before the end. And about 20 percent of my class had gotten into medical school. I, of course, was not among them, but as a consolation prize, the article was telling me that us "rejectees" have highly relevant constellations of training, talents, and interests. Nice, but who was interested?

Naturally, I read on. Confronted with her own obituary, who wouldn't be dying to know what happened next? Alas, what happens next to women rejectees, according to the experts, is nothing, little or nothing at all. Only 2 percent persist, reapply, keep the dream alive. There was more: It's not just that we women give up. We think they (mostly males) were right in keeping us out and we were wrong in trying to get in. In the rational words of the experts, females were far more willing to view their rejection as "fair" than men were and less likely to try again. I think it's called the self-fulfilling prophecy, which has the nasty quality of fulfilling only your worst expectations about yourself.

Speaking of prophecy, I discovered something else that day, something that I at least had a sneaking suspicion would surface again. Where did your average female medical school rejectee wind up? I didn't hold my breath waiting for the answer but spoke the words even as I turned the page. There I was, medical laboratory technician, coming around after a slight detour into the land of dreams that could not be filled. I wanted to write to Ms. Diamond and apologize, tell her she had it right the first time. If I had listened to her at the first interview, I would at least have a job as a lab tech. Lab work was hard and honest, and I should be thankful if I ever got it. But then I remembered at the second interview I had converted her to a different point of view, and converts usually believe with greater conviction than those who convert them in the first place. I did not think I could face Ms. Diamond with this new version of the history I had tried to avoid.

The article had been doing a good job of telling me where I had been and where I was and even where I was likely to be. But with the corner of the veil covering the future lifted a bit, I naturally wanted to peek under the tent and see more. What else could I expect for the future—meaning, of course, was there any hope at all? Certainly! I read. A female's predisposition to science is a considerable inducement to reapply to medical school in spite of rejection. There you go! Stay predisposed to science. Keep counting those wieners, sharpen your mathematical skills, devour all the sciences, including the culinary, stay motivated, the way you've been doing. Isn't that how it's done? Playing it safe . . . nine to five . . . licking your wounds. It's only fair, isn't it? Of course you recognized the lady in the obituary. Could have written it yourself.

I told my sister I would give two weeks' notice, but she said I did not have to stand on ceremony with her. In any case, there were any number of competent accountants who would be more than willing to have the job, even if it meant counting wieners from nine to five to prove one's competence. The chance of working on the account of one of the airport's luxury restaurants was always a good lure—some people like reading about dinners they would never consider paying such outrageous prices for. So I was not leaving her in the lurch, although I had made up my mind in an instant and was ready to leave as quickly as possible. I did not fool her, however, for in spite of what seemed like determination, she knew I really had no idea of where I should be headed or why. She caught the essential point: I had to get my life back on track, and almost any point could be considered a starting point for someone as lost as I was.

I did not decide on California because it was the land of the lost or the point from which anything would lead off to something better. At the end of the 1970s and the beginning of the new decade, California was the land of dreams realized, not dreams deferred. I might have been thinking that I could get a boost from geography. I was not being a solitary pioneer, however, but was again retreating into the bosom of my family, taking strength from the stronger until I had gathered enough of my own. I called my full brother, who, at the end of his second year studying electrical engineering, had taken an internship to get practical experience working with a computer company in San Jose. I knew he had an apartment and asked if I could stay with him until I found a place of my own.

It wasn't him but them. He told me his girlfriend had moved in but that would not be a problem, at least for the short term. What were my plans? I did not tell him the odds against me. Maybe embarrassment made me hold back the grim statistic that only 2 percent of us rejectees reapplied to medical school. But I did say I wanted to get back into science, possibly even somehow get back on the track that might, by some miracle, get me into medicine. I told him I was thinking of studying on my own so that I could apply to graduate school, perhaps go on to earn a doctorate in biology or some other science. I did not tell him something else I had learned. Chances of my doing any of the above were not very good, in spite of my intentions. To persevere and get into graduate school and earn my doctorate in science I would have to do better than the almost 80 percent of women who couldn't hack it, turned away from even this dream by the rejection whose crippling emotional impact they could not overcome.

My last paycheck added to what I had saved made the airfare. I wasn't taking much with me, figuring that there would not be much difference between the weather in California and what I was already dressing for. I would pack my books and take them, although I felt they had come to stand for where I had been, not where I was going. Or perhaps I saw them as stepping-stones that hadn't brought me very far, had tripped me up instead.

My mother helped me pack, stuffing some things—new socks, shorts, undershirts—for my brother into the suitcases. Not that he had asked for them, but he certainly needed them. "Besides," she said, "they will fill out your empty suitcases, and the corners will stay firm and not collapse when the ground crew throws them in and out of the plane as they always do, no matter what they say about courteous service."

Then, when she thought I wasn't noticing, she slipped one other book into the suitcase, something I recognized immediately and knew why she wanted it to go with me even if I was leaving others behind. I stopped her before she could go and uncovered the book. I opened it, and in spite of its thick cover it opened to the page to which she must have opened it so often in the past. There I was, my photograph stacked among classmates I had already begun to forget until this moment brought them all back to me. And in all the wide margin spaces were the messages of congratulation and hope, shorthand mementos of those high school years. My teachers sending me off with the best wishes they could cram into my book, love and wishes that were meant to last me through all the ensuing years of work. We had each phrase memorized, my mother and I, and so looked not at the page but into one another's eyes as we held the book between us.

"I admire your determination and love of science. These will see you through no matter what comes."

"Work hard. Keep working hard. It will work for you."

"Never lose your beautiful enthusiasm. It will keep the dream alive."

Then she took the book and closed it, putting it carefully under the protective layer of my few things. I would have to take it with me all across the country. It was part of my inheritance. More had been bestowed on me than all I had lost. I could never reject what I had been promised and so far been given.

CHAPTER 8

It was flat, all very flat. I had never been in a landscape that was so devoid of contours. The land was flat, the buildings were flat, there were no tall buildings, no towers, nothing between the dry earth and the hot sky once you left the small clusters of houses that made up each neighborhood. Every morning right at dawn I put on my running gear and crept out of my brother's apartment and tried still another arrow-straight road out of town. For the first few days I kept hoping I'd feel the tug of an incline in my muscles as my legs adjusted to the strain of running uphill. Even a small hill, a bump in the road, would have produced some strain after so much zero incline. I would have appreciated even a small hill, and not only for the slight breeze in my face I could anticipate on returning. No ups, no downs, no change.

* * *

I had years ago trained myself not to look down when I was running, which is why I kept waiting for the signals of a change in terrain from the nerves and muscles in my legs. Not looking down allows you to take into consciousness the entire field of vision, folding yourself into it, losing yourself in it. Running frees you for a time from yourself yet lets you feel in control, wholly responsible for your actions. You alone set the goal and are responsible for getting yourself there. I used to think there was something symbolic or mystical about this feeling, and surely there is. But on the other hand, it's as much practical as mystical. In what other form of, well, transportation, are you so completely in charge? You have only yourself to praise or blame for your progress and, naturally, any lack thereof.

Fortunately, plain exhaustion and the growing heat of the California morning usually put an end to such speculations. That and the urgency I always felt to get back to the small apartment I was sharing with my brother and Patty, his girl-friend. I was made welcome, I was made to feel confident they were happy to have me share this place with them. But I was still the body on the sofa bed in the living room they would have to encounter and, perhaps startled by the presence, have to recall where the body had come from and who was inhabiting it and their small space.

Lovers always make their own space, and even the most welcome guest is an intrusion. So I always got up and out before any chance of their awakening, then back and showered and ready to greet them when they awoke and made their own preparations for their own busy day.

After the first weeks they did not ask how I would be spending my day. Perhaps the sight of the newspapers, folded to the classified pages, red boxes carefully drawn around the most promising want ads, continued to tell the story. It was the same story, with the same beginning, middle, and end. Sort of like a television soap opera that went on from day to day, always with slightly new incidents, slight variations in settings, maybe a new character or two, but still basically just a beginning, middle, and end. Everything different, yet everything predictable. That's a comfortable, even comforting way to tell a story, but not if you have to live it.

I was looking for a job. I was taken by surprise to discover how quickly "a" job became "any" job. I was looking for any job at all. So were a lot of other people. I imagined they were all better qualified than I. They had that look. Or maybe they had been at it longer. But most had the look, and that was why it was such a shock to hear myself being told that I was the one who was too qualified, even overqualified for most jobs I applied for. I had to restrain myself from arguing, saying, "But I'm not overqualified. I'm barely qualified. You'll see. All I really know is biochemistry and counting hot dogs and chips. Believe me, I'm not too smart for this job. If I were, I wouldn't be asking for it, would I?"

I never said any such thing, no matter how much the logic behind my words seemed to me irrefutable. Most people who interviewed me did not seem to have the time for irrefutable argumentation. They still had to find the person who had only the right amount of qualification and no superfluities that would cause a problem.

Weeks went by. I was not wearing out my welcome, but I felt I was wearing a hole in the living room carpet with my midnight pacing. I had run myself below my ideal body weight in my college years. And premed study I found to be the as yet undiscovered instant diet formula. I was mostly skin and bones, but I still feared my body imprint would remain on the sofa indelibly after I was gone. Maybe that was why I never slept for long, waking at what seemed regular intervals, sitting up, getting up, smoothing out the sofa bed, erasing the evidence of my dependence. Even though they never made me feel unwanted or dependent, I still didn't want this to be the impression I would leave with my brother and his girl.

Then the telephone company answered my call. I dressed well, quietly, as demurely as possible and went to the interview with my heart in my throat. That might have carried certain liabilities, considering that the job opening was for a telephone operator. But I did manage to answer the interviewer's questions in an audible voice. In the end he appeared to be sufficiently impressed, whether by my careful grooming and modest demeanor or by my voice I could not tell. I would have certain weeks of training, and then I would be able to get off the streets of San Jose, stop buying all the newspapers in town, understand and accept my level of qualification, have a real, honest-to-goodness career, begin to look for my own place, my own carpet to wear a hole in, my own future to begin to construct. I thought, however erroneously, as time would tell, that I was beginning to get my life under control.

I was the voice at the end of dial 0. When you dialed me and told me your complaints and travails with the telephone company, the petty indignities you had suffered, I listened sympathetically and then told you the number you had to call to tell the story all over again. I always listened to the end of your story. I always assured you that you would find a sympathetic ear no matter how many times you were transferred and had to tell your story over again. I was always glad that I was the first to hear such complaints, while the customer was still in a relatively benign frame of mind. I hoped promotion did not mean I would be further down the line.

I did not envision a lifetime of such empathetic consultations, for I had been told that I would be able to apply for any of the courses the telephone company offered in some of the

more technical aspects of communications. Some of the positions that might be available required the use of finger dex-
terity, something always handy in a physician or surgeon and
something I had always excelled at. In any case, more of a
challenge than dialing numbers all day. Unfortunately, they
had neglected to tell me I could not apply for any course at
all until I had served at least two years as the voice with the
0 personality. Being deprived of a dream is distressing. With
deprivation came knowledge that what I had been doing was
dreaming, wasting time and avoiding the real future. I had by
then found my own small place, my own carpet and sofa. By
doing this I had guaranteed that most of my earnings would go
to supporting me in my present position of earning enough to
support myself in my present position of earning enough. But
enough.

If I had come to California with any idea at all, it was the
idea of beginning again, of trying again for a career in science,
studying and applying for graduate school, working for a degree that would, in time, increase my chances of being accepted by a medical school. Toward that end I had gotten a
job at the telephone company and made nice with a lot of
truly irate, near-the-breaking-point customers. To my credit, I
had also given out a lot of fairly accurate area code numbers
and had put through many long-distance calls for distraught
people who had somehow been given inaccurate or fictitious
area code numbers and were desperately trying to contact
missing or perhaps vanished friends and loved ones.

Such good works aside, I hadn't really done anything for
myself. Perhaps I had become so despondent I unconsciously
thought I didn't owe myself anything anymore. That's the final
despondency, when you don't think you're worth your best
dream anymore. Maybe I took that research paper on the
likely future of a woman rejected by medical school too much
to heart. Perhaps I had good reason. The report did say that
only about 17 percent of rejected females had the determina-

tion to keep at it, get into graduate school, master the grind, graduate a doctor, not the healing kind, a Ph.D., not an M.D., but of some value nonetheless.

These and worse thoughts ran with me daily. They were with me on that bitter, wet morning when my body was soaked as much by the rain as by the sweat of anxiety that I could not wipe away fast enough. For days I had been willing myself into a statistic, ignoring my own chance to make my life what I wanted it to be, ignoring my own individual destiny. I had caught myself in another failure, nothing academic, just personal, but just as deadly. I had reneged on the single most important commandment—to be wholly responsible for every word, action, and thought.

What had gotten me out of my place so early that morning was the memory of a dream from which I had awoken in the middle of the night and had not been able to shake off all the remaining hours, waiting for dawn. The shapes in the dream had simply materialized out of darkness, as if someone had taken handfuls of dark and quickly, with indifference, molded each into some form and tossed it aside, not bothering to look at the end result, just tossing each away, some in my direction, but with no clear intent of sending them all my way. As things do in dreams, each of these vague, unshaped products of darkness changed with threatening suddenness, reappearing as something more frightening. Each was, as I at once knew in my dream it had to be, finally human in form. But each was misshapen, twisted, contorted, deformed—stunted children who used what means they had to reach out, appeal to me, fading in and out of the darkness. At first I felt only disgust, the involuntary upheaval of the stomach at some intolerable stench. I dreamed the taste of bile in my mouth. I imagined my heart bursting with terror, each chamber a ruin.

They did not go away but stood quietly watching me, waiting for me to recover, not pressing toward me as they had done at first. I felt they were giving me time to recover, taking pity. But for all that there was a sense of incompleteness, as if they could not leave or be dismissed until some further act was begun and completed. Whatever this was to be, it would have to happen naturally, spontaneously. The sense of menace evaporated. I felt there was nothing to fear. And when a misshapen form again reached out I was there, or I at least saw myself moving there, close to it, accepting its outreach. I had stepped into the circle of its pity and compassion and was also sharing those feelings. I had accepted this failure of expectation and was taking pity on it, feeling for it, accepting its limitations.

I awoke hearing the rain, the unseasonable cold. I waited in the dark but knew there would not be more light than I already had. I had the message of the dream. All meaningful dreams must be simple to interpret or they have no real meaning. I had taken pity on failure. I had pitied the creatures in my dream. I had called them up to do so. I knew I had not yet done the same thing for myself. But I now had the courage to ask. I would have to pull up stakes again and move on, this time, with luck, moving closer.

At least the want ads for jobs as a lab technician with a chemical company are clustered in the same place in the newspaper. Lets your red pencil do the walking, the checking off, the consigning of false leads to the dustbin of what might have been. A job with a chemical company doing things with chemicals would, I reasoned, be closer to my goal than a job with the telephone company. Certainly closer than my old job counting hot dogs, although considering what really goes into some of those things, maybe the two have more in common. . . . Nevertheless, I had begun my search for work closer to my chosen field of science, hoping that the job would play into the study program I was beginning to work out. With luck, I would be learning on my own more about the theory of chemistry while

I applied the theory in practice at a daily job. Growing ever more practical with each passing day, I began to calculate just how much I could be putting aside to make graduate work possible.

What I left out of this equation was the utter indifference to such well-laid plans exhibited by every chemical manufacturer I approached. When I was finally forced to factor in that indifference, I realized I had about three weeks of solvency left and then it was back to the telephone company, irate dialers and all.

If the moguls of commerce did not want me, I reasoned, then perhaps the mandarins of academia might. I toyed with the letter, almost caressing the expensive paper, running my finger back and forth on the envelope's sharp edge. I read the name and title and department, trying to convince myself that no one would waste stationery and postage just for the pleasure of killing my hopes. It could be done more efficiently with a telephone call. But then, some people, even people with titles and positions in departments of biology at prestigious institutions, are cowards when it comes to actually slipping the knife in between the ribs of a dream.

I tore through the envelope, almost shredding it and the enclosed letter, holding the page together well enough to read that she, Dr. Helen Redman, laboratory supervisor, giver of lucrative employment to the penniless and near hopeless, sole dispenser of sundry largesse, would be pleased to have me call and discuss a possible position in her department. This paragon among women, this heavenly angel in academic disguise, then went on to caution me that a decision on suitable applicants would have to be made quickly in view of the impending semester, which I might perhaps understand, given my background. I would have to take that unavoidable time constraint into consideration in making my own decision. . . .

In brief, I was actually being asked to forgive the rush, the pressure of time that would not allow me all the luxury I would need to make my decision. Someone was actually apologizing for riding to my rescue, for hurrying my dream into reality. In her innocence, Dr. Redman was assuming that someone in my position had an alternative.

By the end of the first interview I understood that Helen had no allusions about my alternatives—or hers, for that matter. That was the overall impression I had from our meeting, although I must admit I was not able to concentrate for the first minutes, or perhaps longer. I had taken the bus to the university campus, in my nervous anxiety leaving myself more time than any single interview could possibly require. A lucky move, for I had the hour to wander across those lawns and dells of tree and flowering shrubbery. It was all more beautiful than any pat phrase like "ivory tower" could convey. These were towers of green, an oasis of tranquility, a landscape where the mind could blossom along with the flowers. I had to repeatedly remind myself that if you listened real close you would hear more than the grass growing. You would hear the real sighs and groans of students such as I once was. I had no doubt that even in this idyllic place most of the young people I saw were still struggling to learn at least enough to justify being in such a refuge at all.

Of course I came close to being late. I had drifted off to a remote area of the campus from which I could not even see the building I had at first carefully identified as the one where Dr. Redman held interviews. I asked at least three separate students for directions, accepting with profuse thanks each brief instruction, yet too anxious not to have each confirmed by the next student I encountered. So they handed me more or less in relay down to the building I sought and its cool, empty corridors.

Only the name and title on the door, but somehow they seemed to offer hope after long absence: Helen Redman, Ph.D., Biology Laboratories Supervisor. I knocked, thought I heard a welcome, and entered. I did not turn at once to leave, but I did wonder into what kind of world I had stepped. It was an office, no doubt about that, but an office that had gone into some kind of disguise, an office that was also doing duty as a home away from home. I hesitated, feeling I should have a definite welcome before I stepped across that threshold.

"Just make room for yourself," she said, waving toward a chair already occupied. "Louisa May is movable," she added, catching my hesitation.

I looked down and saw the black cat; when I did not reach for it it jumped to the desk and settled down for the interview. Most of the objects about the room, outside of the piles of textbooks, workbooks, papers, pamphlets, and similar academic debris, were personal things—little ceramic objects, souvenirs, figurines, pictures in fancy picture frames, small notes written on flower-edged notepaper pinned to corkboards of various sizes that also held what seemed to be schedules of classes, entire semesters laid out for inspection, work accomplished or still to be done. I had the feeling I was in someone's kitchen with all the kitchen cabinet doors missing, in a one-room apartment without space enough to separate private from professional life.

"The work isn't very challenging," she said. "A trained monkey can do it." She must have taken my look of anxiety— did she mean to suggest that I was overqualified?—for one of skepticism because she went on: "No, I haven't tried. To train a monkey, that is. I've trained many like you, however."

"I think I am qualified for the job," I heard myself say.

"Not overqualified?" she asked. I could not believe she was setting a trap, she looked too kindly at me in saying it. But I had nothing to answer.

She rose to her feet and swept the cat up in her arms in one gesture. Then I saw how large a woman she was, large as a colorful flowering tree in her voluminous but shapeless sack of a dress, like some tropical vista brought close, very close. She floated back to the desk, pushing the chair back to give her room for the cat on her lap. The cat took the drastic change in terrain—I was about one-quarter Dr. Redman's size and offered practically nothing in the way of padded lap—completely in stride.

"It was the grades," she said, again making me feel I had drifted off and missed all the conversational links that would have given this remark its proper context. "Of course, you're also a woman and black, and they would have known that, too. That would have made a difference in some cases. But it was the grades, a point or two. I have the paper somewhere."

Whatever the paper was, I hoped she would not stop then and there to search for it in all that rubble. I had come for the interview. I had come for a job. I didn't care about the paper, whatever it said.

"Anyway," she said, a complete sentence. She fell silent, moving a few tiny figures on her desk into different relationships to one another. As if she were playing chess, I thought, but I knew it wasn't chess.

Something had disturbed her, but as I had no clue to its cause or meaning, I remained silent until she again turned her full attention to me. Her eyes held mine, and I was immediately, completely, and from then always convinced how simple and straightforward was her concern, not only for me, even though I was the immediate object of that concern now, but for all who had sat there in confusion and hurt before me, for all who would.

She moved the figures again, perhaps back to their original positions, although I could not tell, and began again, more gently than ever, quieter. "They don't want it known, but most rely on grades. Not on all you are. And most make their decision on the tiniest margin. They tell you it's the whole person they're looking at, but if you have a grade point average of 3.9 you're in and if you have just a 3.8 you're not. And if you have anything below that, God forbid it should be as low as, say, 3.5 . . ."

She stopped and smiled with that look some people have when they don't actually want to shed tears in front of you.

"Mind you, I think a 3.5 grade point average is neat work. But if that's all you came to the med school admissions officer with, then that's why you came to me."

I did not speak and knew I did not have to. Something had already told me we shared a common sorrow, common loss. But I figured she had been 3.8 and I had just about managed the neat work she would have accepted had she been in a position of authority. "One bad semester could have done it," she was going on, lifting her hand from its gentle massage of the cat's back as if to stop the confession she assumed I was about to make. "Even a single course, an important one, not the history of Western thought or the absence thereof. One serious science thing you fudged because your mind wasn't on it.

"Need the job," she said, not making any effort to disguise it as a polite question, not waiting for a polite, even a slightly self-serving and evasive, answer. "Of course," she added with what seemed to me some twinge of embarrassment, as if she could not bear to have me confess to my need, not just yet.

Then she coaxed Louisa May off her lap and onto the floor and got up and extended her hand over the cluttered desk to me. I took it and also rose, not knowing if we had actually come to a decision and I had let that part of the conversation also drift past me. "Monkey work," she said. "Nothing you're used to."

I was at once struck with guilt. I had deliberately hidden the hot dogs and chips from her, not mentioned the lady with the 0 voice in my brief résumé. I had disguised the monkeys in my past and called them "junior clerk position," "company representative." I would have to confess, but I was already deciding that she had seen enough of such euphemisms to translate them automatically, without thinking, translating everything into her native tongue of honesty and candor.

Still holding my hand in hers, sealing the deal, she came

around the desk and led me to the door, the brilliantly painted fabric not disturbing a single one of all the fragile things she had gathered under her protection. "You'll have the schedule as soon as I know it . . . or, more exactly, as soon as I write it up."

At the opened door she stood aside and let me pass. I muttered a good-bye, still slightly stunned by the entire proceeding. Louisa May had come to the door as well and, casting a doubtful glance up and down the empty, unadorned corridor, sat apart, waiting for the door to remove it all from her sight.

It was a way of getting rid of the world I would come to rely on myself in the next months.

CHAPTER 9

Louisa May was all cat, bold, curious, no doubt fearless, but she drew the line at frogs' legs, or at least those I had to deal with, preserved as they were in formaldehyde and giving off that unmistakable odor. On rare occasions when I could coax Louisa out of Helen's office (I don't think I ever called her Dr. Redman) just for her companionship on my early-morning rounds, she kept a good distance between me, my frogs, and her acute olfactory apparatus. Sometimes she came with me right up to the biology laboratory door, looked into the vast room with some mild degree of interest, then turned and retraced her steps unerringly through the corridors back to the warm safety of her office home. I never doubted Louisa May's navigational skills, for she had been wandering those corridors at least as long as Helen and had as much right to call them her own as anyone had.

I had the frogs, and I had the packs of dissecting instruments. I had my white lab coat and my assignment worksheets. I had twenty dissecting stations to cover with frogs and instruments. I went from station to station, making sure everything was in order for the first class of eager biology students whose early breakfast would soon be competing in their stomachs with essence of frog à la formaldehyde. I did not envy them the experience, remembering my own high school and premed labs. When such reminiscences were especially vivid I took care to have the frog pinned most accurately on the dissecting board, took care that the instruments were fresh and sharp. Perhaps the poor budding scientist would appreciate these little gestures, provided the waves of discomfort permitted such thoughts.

If it was monkey work it was no worse than some jobs I had already survived, and at least I had the sense and feel of being a part again of a huge, humming beehive of academic interest. I was only on the edge of all this intellectual activity, but every friendly nod of recognition I received (the nods came within a day or two of my appearing in my white coat at a regular hour, looking as if I had some place to be in a hurry) brought an undeniable, even if unjustified and unearned, thrill to my heart.

See, I told myself, you fit in . . . or at least these nice people are giving you the benefit of the doubt and are assuming you fit in because, well, just because you are here right along with them and they certainly don't doubt that they fit in. And if you had somehow gotten here without any right to be here, they would feel that would in some way reflect on them. I usually had to get a grip on myself at that point and settle for the obvious conclusion. A monkey wouldn't get even the casual recognition I was getting, no matter how much better it could be doing my job.

I was under no illusions about my job, however, and Helen certainly never encouraged me to entertain any. It was not to be a learning experience. I already knew how to dissect a frog. It was to be just a dull, mind-lulling, soul-sapping nine-to-five routine, such as most people have to endure to get by in the world with some degree of self-respect and a halfway decent credit rating. To say nothing of paying the rent on time. Maybe it was trading the future for some comfort and peace of mind in the present. Sometimes you are grateful for the opportunity to strike even that bad a bargain.

After a few weeks I had the day's routine down pat and could get the frogs and their paraphernalia distributed in no time at all. I found that my heart was hardening toward the biology students and I was not wasting too much emotional energy worrying about their ability to cope. Sink or swim, I challenged them in imaginary confrontations: Sharpen your own knives! Tighten your belts! Don't eat breakfast. Get used to the grind.

I didn't mean any of it and would never have said any such thing in an encounter with a real student. I suppose I was just visualizing myself in the role of a hard-nosed science professor, like some I had encountered in my own schooling. But if it ever transpired that I did become a teacher of science, how would I deal with students? I hadn't thought about that possibility before, but I had to now.

I believed I had won Helen's confidence, so I risked asking if I could help with some of the simpler paperwork in her office. I did not tell her that becoming involved in her routine work was a welcome relief from the deadening routine of my own. But of course she knew that and accepted my offer eagerly.

The time was well spent, not just those hours in her office but also the many others we were able to share in the few months before the job came to its anticipated end with the conclusion of the school year. The first thing I learned was not to trust the stereotype. At first glance Helen fitted into at least one category—the big, jovial, carefree lady of a certain age, with a cat or two (there was another cat at home who did not fancy office work). Big and caring, to expand the category. And mothering. All these might be expected. What I also came to appreciate was her practicality and realism, an unblinking appraisal of the possibilities that confronted someone in my position—and in hers.

She let me know right off that I was marking time. She let me know that marking time was not, however, controlling time. Even if I was standing still, time was not, and if I thought I could march in place for much longer, events were certain to prove me wrong. She said she was convinced of the truth of all this for a simple reason: She had been there, marking time, marching in place. And that was pretty much where I found her. She did not take time to describe for me her own dreams. Perhaps they were too faded by then to be recalled with any accuracy or conviction or with enough of those qualities to inspire believability. I doubted that, and I could have supplied what was missing, but I did not press her. Not because she intimidated me in any way. Although she was almost my mentor from the beginning, she always somehow conveyed the feeling that she was more a companion along the way, not just one to whom the way was familiar.

I was never to learn what had distracted Helen early on from fulfilling her dream—we never got to that level of intimacy where such questions could be answered without having to be asked. But from the way she responded to me in my most depressed, give-it-all-up moods, the way she just took my half-empty glass of tepid iced tea and filled it again, waiting for me to drink some quietly, becoming calmer under her gaze, I knew she was not just ministering to me in my need but remembering her own. I did not ask if there had ever been someone like her, for her, in her days of worry and pain and frustration. Perhaps. She had come through, so that suggests some help and comfort along the way. But she had not come through to where she wanted to be, and that said something else.

She was good at scheduling, so scheduling is what she did for me. Schedules are time-driven, and time-driven was what I was. We had the unmentioned but ever-present force driving us to the end of the school year and the end of my employment. In our endless talks, the vague plans I had contemplated began to take definite shape. I would begin to prepare myself for graduate school. I would begin studying for entrance examinations to various advanced programs that would lead to a master's degree in biology. I would look into how such a career could be financed. If I found a school that would accept me, and if I could swing the finances, and if I could complete the program with acceptable grades (no, not just acceptable but superior grades, as Helen had convinced me that only superior grades made any impression), and if I had another title to tack onto my name, then perhaps if I were not immediately seduced into some convenient, safe, relatively well paying position that I could easily manage on my recently gathered knowledge . . . If any or all of the above actually happened, if I avoided the pitfalls and leaped over the roadblocks, then perhaps somewhere I might gather my courage and reapply to medical school.

And if, after all this, I could not storm those heights, I would make another strategic retreat. I would begin again. I would apply to graduate school for a doctorate in biology. I would examine sources of financing those additional years. I would find the whole process easier this time because I had already done it before. Persistence breeds familiarity, to say nothing of sheer boredom. With yet another title to add to my name, I would feel more confident that I had the right to reapply (make that, by this time, re-reapply) to the medical school of my choice.

Would any of these labors make me the medical school applicant of their choice? I had no more certainty of this than Helen had, but on this point she allowed herself the only

trace of wishful thinking I had detected in her during all
these weeks, actually months now, since my future began to
take shape.

Ever the practical one, Helen secured for me library privileges that extended pretty much throughout all the medical
buildings. In this way I could find at more or less any time of
the day or evening someplace where I could consult the science books I needed to refresh the content of my old college
courses.

Some of the smaller reading rooms and special medical
collections were a good distance away from the corridors
where I usually made my rounds, checking on the labs and the
needs of students. But I found my way to these special enclaves
and even got to be known there. None of the other readers,
most of them medical students, interns, residents, sometimes
even an attending physician, took me for anything other than
one of them. Just someone too small, too insignificant to have
attracted attention on any personal level. Or so I assumed. I
poured over articles in the medical journals with as much
desperate concentration as the others did. I scribbled notes
as assiduously. I compared texts with as keen a critical eye. I
allowed a slight skeptical smile to modulate my seriousness.
I even let my head drop onto my opened hands and closed my
eyes with as much a look of exhaustion as any of the others
did. Not as frequently, of course, for I did not have the reason
they did.

I had a white coat. I had an identification tag with my picture on it. I had someone in an important position who could
vouch for me. I had library privileges. I could venture afield. I
grew bolder and bolder. In time I had the maze of buildings
memorized, especially those dedicated to the medical school
and its laboratories and libraries. Then the clinics, then the
hospital itself.

My passing did not provoke much interest, although I
would have been hard-pressed to explain my presence if I had

been challenged. I don't know what I would have answered if asked. I could not have told anyone that apparently I had begun to take my scheduled future for real. Or that by now, to feed my impoverished imagination I might have simply jumped ahead a few years and was savoring my first days after acceptance, my first time as a bona fide medical student, a postgraduate, an intern, a resident, legitimately passing through on the way to some lifesaving mission. I guess I was aware of how quickly my fantasies could escalate, but I wasn't deterred by that. I just wanted to get close for a few minutes, and who would not have recognized, even honored, that need?

The small group outside the patient's room did not block my way, but I still hesitated to pass by, simply out of curiosity to hear more clearly the dialogue that had been going on for some moments as I approached. Not exactly a dialogue. The senior member of the group was easily distinguished by his gray hair, stooped shoulders, and careworn face from the young males, who were mostly strong and well set up, before him. He had been pausing after each question, as if eager to spark some kind of exchange. But as the pauses lengthened, the questions began to rain down more rapidly.

He had a sheaf of papers in his hand, and he began to read off words and phrases, shooting them into the group like so much ammunition he did not mind expending. I recognized some of the terms from my premed textbooks. He was quoting the hematologic values and blood chemical values, diagnostic findings. I could not tell their import, but the numbers seemed to increase the gloom that now had the men in its grip.

"What should we be looking for?" he almost shouted in conclusion.

The bodies in their white coats seemed to shift and flinch, but few coherent phrases rose to fill the increasingly limited opportunity to answer. The older man's mood seemed to move in one smooth curve from disappointment to frustration to anger. I came closer, not wanting to, but drawn by the emotions that were so easy to read in the scene. He was being let down, and he did not like it one bit. The young people in the group before him were too intimidated to do anything more than retreat into self-protective silence.

"The patient's pneumonia is worsening, and his blood pressure is decreasing," the man began, and the others shifted again, as if the statement were an accusation. "What's happening? Do we have a clue to what's happening to this patient?"

Silence for a brief moment, and then, with a return to his former brusque tone, he added, "I saw the findings of the catheterization study. Told me a lot. Mainly that the patient's blood pressure was decreasing. Too bad you didn't have a chance to examine it. Maybe next time when a study is done you, some one of you, will take the time to find it and review it. Could have provided a clue. Maybe give you something to go on. Here's a hint. It's pneumonia, granted, but what if the catheterization study indicates congestive heart failure? Is that imposed on the initial pulmonary infection, or is it just mimicking signs of acute respiratory distress syndrome? What are the possibilities in this case? Any takers? I'll take anything at all as an answer! Does anybody know what I'm talking about?"

I was suddenly aware that they were all turned facing me, and I looked at them dumbfounded. I knew he had spoken directly to me, but the shock of that exposure had for the moment completely obliterated what he had said. In fact, facing the young men, seeing their involuntary looks of relief as the attention—and the heat—was suddenly shifted to me, I realized I did not remember being spoken to at all.

"Will you please tell these gentlemen what the findings of the heart function study are. You might, if you please, tell them what these findings suggest."

The requests were delivered with somewhat exaggerated formality and what he must have assumed would be taken for old-world courtesy. All of which meant that I would be given several more seconds to answer than the others had. I am sure my mouth opened, possibly closed as well. I saw him lean toward me, expectantly, his chin lifted, urging me to speak. I must have repeated my efforts to speak, for now he raised a hand as if to prevent the others from offering any interference, an unlikely event.

He turned to face the men and said in a suddenly gentle, impossibly artificial, and ultimately infuriating tone of voice, "Her voice was ever soft, gentle, and low, an excellent thing in a woman."

In spite of the phony performance, I recognized the lines as poetry, but could not identify them, so annoyed was I with the way they were being used. Later Helen told me the lines were indeed poetry, and from Shakespeare. She then looked them up in her book of poetry quotations and said they were King Lear talking to one of his daughters, but she was dead at the time and he did not know it.

I don't know if the examining doctor intended sarcasm or if the words were something he always said at such opportunities. But as I heard him speak I was angry enough to speak up and be heard. "I am not a doctor," I said. I did not add, "Sorry."

He offered an understanding half shrug of his shoulder, easily buying the denial. The gesture was meant to suggest that he was not deceived in the first place. I felt I had to go on, so I said, "I am not a nurse." And of course I did not add "either."

"Not a nurse," he echoed, clearly disappointed, his body, inclining slightly toward me, asking for further clarification.

"I work with . . ." I began, but did not think he would care to know with what I worked, so I amended this to "I am a lab technician."

He took it easily, in stride. "Very good," he said. "A useful trade. More young women like you should avail themselves of the opportunity. Stick with it. Don't get in over your head." At this point he actually resisted indicating the entire group to me, but I felt it was a gesture just barely suppressed. I knew he would add, as he did, "Like some do."

And he topped this with "And live to regret it. Yes, even if the patients don't."

With that he dismissed me, walking away from the group in disgust, or maybe just in frustration, leaving them to trail behind him. Leaving me to wonder if I would ever really come to regret getting in where it might be over my head, if I would ever come that far. I might also have begun to wonder if, assuming what I had witnessed was a typical "day in the life of," I would want to test the waters at all.

I did not think too much about this, however. The schedule Helen and I had been working on left medical school and its conflicts, confrontations, challenges . . . humiliations . . . off in the future, at some near vanishing point after studious application to science and diligent applications to graduate schools, admissions, degrees, reapplication. The eternal cycles of the academic life. With me bound upon the wheel of fortune. There were degrees to go before I would have a chance to participate honestly in a scene such as I had just blundered into in my innocence. I had a feeling then, however, that innocence was something that did not enjoy much longevity in medical school.

The job with Helen was drawing to its end, and I had made some, but not sufficient, progress toward the next phase of my career, if not life. I had applied myself with the requisite discipline, brushing off the cobwebs that had formed, rather faster than I expected, about my recollection of my earlier scientific studies. I had to admit that I was finding it difficult to divorce abstract scientific study from the application I had always longed to be a part of. I did not want to see chemistry or biology as just things in themselves. I really wanted science in

the service of a patient whose blood chemistries and hematologic values might contain a clue to a diagnosis, a clue to therapy
and recovery. That's what every doctor wants. You'd go in over
your head to get there. I would, given the chance.

The chance I would now have, however, was different. It
would have to be approached the long way around. Helen had
another Shakespeare quote ready for me when I talked this
way for the first time. It went something like "By indirections
find directions out." From *Hamlet*, she said. I did not have the
heart to tell her that the only thing I really remembered about
Hamlet was that he could never make up his mind.

The line cautioned patience, advised patience, even praised
patience (indirectly). But did you ever look out a car window
and see other drivers forced to take the same detour you were
taking? They're all taking the indirect route, the detour, finding their true direction that way. But there's not a happy face to
be seen for many a mile. I told myself, I even told Helen, that I
supposed I would gradually get used to the indirect path. That
was probably only because no other seemed to be open.

But I might have been premature in assuming that even so
diminished a fate would be mine. It gradually became clear to
me that I had nowhere near the financial wherewithal to sustain myself through a graduate school career, especially when
that was not an end in itself but only a stepping-stone. A very
expensive stone, it might well turn out to be. If the graduate
detour did not get me into medical school, it might wind up a
stone around my neck, each pound of that stone representing
one of the many loans I would have taken to finance the project in the beginning. You could really sink deep with that kind
of burden to carry.

Without actually telling Helen in so many words, I began
to prepare for a more realistic future. With grim practicality
I began to compose letters of application, this time not for
institutions of higher learning but for labs, labs pathological,
labs hematological, labs of any sort. And for manufacturers

of chemicals toxic or not and for whatever technological outfits that were in the area, regardless of what they produced. Anything short of chemical warfare. I drew the line at that, hoping I would not be asked to step over it. Perhaps someone receiving one of my poignant letters might, in an odd moment of concern for struggling humanity, consider giving me a position.

This time, however, I would have something more than stark necessity to plead my cause. I would have letters of recommendation from Helen. I assumed she thought they were meant for graduate schools. She didn't really ask how they should be addressed. She just wrote, "To whom it may concern." Her letterhead would guarantee authenticity.

I had copies of the letters made. I wrote each potential employer that I had references, available immediately upon request. I mentioned that they were from a most prestigious institution. I took my letters to the post office. I mailed them and waited. I prayed that human kindness and compassion had not dried up since the last time I mailed a letter of application. I prayed that there were still people willing to gamble on the unknowns out there. I prayed I would not have to suffer in this state of unknowing for long, not for too much longer. It had been a year, and I think I needed some certainty in my life again. I wished that promised miracles came with at least a tentative schedule, even a hint, a clue. I needed some clue as to when or even if my miracle would ever come due.

CHAPTER 10

I waited. I passed the time, constructively, I hoped, construct-
ing in my imagination a positive future. I saw myself going
through it step by step. First I would be receiving, say by letter,
better by phone call, a possible, just possible, job offer. Then I
saw myself coming through the interview at the company
headquarters (I would have to find the bus route to get there)
with my composure more or less intact. I would have to take
the bus back home, then wait a few eons longer, only a few,
for a decision to be made. I would take up knitting to make
the time pass meaningfully. I would not call them. I would
keep both of my hands busy with my knitting, and that would
keep me from using the telephone.

No, I later decided, it will not be a letter. The final decision
will be made in a hurry, the way of the marketplace. And I

must be prepared to keep my voice level and controlled answering the call, saying, "Yes, I can begin next week, tomorrow,
now"—imagining myself doing all of this. Not really believing
any of it.

Entire weeks ticked by interminably, with nothing to set
one apart from another. Nothing could, except word that I
would have some small future to hang on to. Actually, I had no
illusions about what a job in industry would mean. It would
mean pouring one chemical into another, waiting, calculating,
consulting, tabulating, then the same again, with maybe a different calculation to do. It would be as routine as frogs, but I
would do the work conscientiously, diligently. I promised. If
only someone out there could hear how desperately I promised myself that. I began to believe that it didn't matter what
you promised. The thing you promised didn't matter in itself.
It was only the intensity with which you made the promise. I
promised I would learn the routine and learn to love it.

I debated sending out still more letters of application. I had
twinges of uncertainty, guilt. Perhaps I had already flooded the
market with my letters. I had dreadful imaginings. At meetings
and industry conventions personnel managers were producing
copies of my letter, the same letter, scores of copies, identical.
"Oh," I heard each one say to the other, "you got one, too. She
may not be good, but she sure is persistent."

And as I waited, I struggled against depression. I struggled
to find some way to understand myself. I wrote in my diary: "I
have been reading the books of ancient Eastern wisdom my
mother gave me as a parting gift, and I have begun to think of
a path to some better understanding of myself. I am letting
these newly found insights find their place along with those I
already have some notions of, even if I have not fully absorbed
them. I won't force anything but will wait patiently until these
different voices speak with the same voice. Or until I find my

own voice. In the meantime, I will try to hear what others are hearing, see what they see."

The voices of the celebrants could be heard a block away, which was where I was, and probably beyond that. The sound was not in the least muffled by the building from which it came. I saw a simple structure, even up close more like a toy miniature of a church, a sketch of a church, than a building in its own right. It had all the traditional lines of a place of worship, however, right up from the white clapboard-siding walls with tall slender windows set into them to the slim steeple with its single bell clearly visible under its own little peaked roof.

The man at the head of the congregation wore a loose-fitting white vestment and was holding a leather-bound book. But these signs of authority appeared to mean little to the others, the sea of black faces that moved and flowed like waves that obeyed their own natural law. They did not defer to him but for the most part were leading the worship on their own. After a few minutes I caught the overall rhythm of the sound and the movements.

The preacher continued to read phrases out of the Bible, phrases familiar enough so that I could complete them even when the shouted approval of the congregation drowned out his voice. The chorus of amens was interrupted at times by individuals who not only repeated the phrases but went on to embellish the sacred words with personal observations, fragments of personal history, testimonials, tribulations. Several of these solo performances would be going on simultaneously, casually overlapping, not competing but simply adding to the store of truth. Then, either by general consent or by the sheer conviction with which an individual had infused his or her own response, the surrounding crowd parted, leaving a breath of space and a void of hushed expectancy. Someone had been, was in the very process of being, visited by the Spirit. The moment and the entire volume of the church were then instantaneously filled with the rapturous voice of the one transfixed and transformed by a vision. The vision was private, and so in part the language in which it was being made public had to be. The selected one was now speaking in tongues, words never heard before. But to that congregation the message was not meaningless. Each man and woman knew that the message was too packed with meaning to be carried to them by the common, worn, one-dimensional words of everyday use. New vision, new words—the logic was irrefutable.

I did not stay. No matter how I might have longed for such a transporting experience, I knew I did not have the strength (or was it the grace?) to give myself so completely to any voice or impulse whose dimensions I had not sufficiently explored and explained. I did not for a moment deny the reality of such abandonment to an inner experience as I had just witnessed. But I knew I was outside such experience, not a witness in the religious sense but rather a spectator. I blushed with embarrassment to think that I might have been described more accurately as just a tourist.

I visited the great formal churches that offered worship at prescribed times and in prescribed ceremonies. These at least offered the consolation of predictability. Private illumination would have to take its turn in line, with any luck keeping its flame alive until everyone's candle had been dutifully offered and lit from the authorized source. The places I visited smelled mostly of gutted candles. The sounds I heard were formulas, generic pleas tried and true, but still to me mostly too rigid to be bent to accommodate an individual passion. It seemed that they demanded that I first go outside myself in order to return within, an indirection I did not want to add to those I had already consented to take. My worldly career was on a detour. I did not want that kind of worldly compromise mirrored in my spiritual quest.

True to form and training, I called logic to my aid. I persuaded myself that I could never have enough time to concentrate on my inner experiences if I had to spend so much time outside of them. It was not a question of losing one's faith but rather of having to keep listening for the words that most accurately spoke to you about your faith in yourself. At that moment in my life, whatever voice might have been speaking was pitched too low for me to hear. And in thinking this, in recalling and writing this, I see that at least I still believed in a voice and a calling. If the voice were low and distant, then I knew what I could do or all I could do. I would be quiet and listen, quiet myself and my anger and anxiety and demands. I would try to silence discord. Perhaps voices are clear and loud or soft and weak only in relation to the degree of noise they must contend with.

Helen had my library privileges extended, even though I no longer had even my previous and tenuous affiliation with the university to justify my roaming the open shelves of scientific journals. I liked Saturdays in the library, the places mostly empty or taken by old scholars oblivious of time or season, surrounded by stacks of books, a protective barrier behind which they would pass that day as they had thousands before. I liked being ignored, except for the rare glance, the slight nod of recognition at the high seriousness of the journals stacked at my seat. I always stacked more than I was likely to have time to consult. But then, I had always curried favor with my teachers. Didn't I have their testimonials, scrawled like ribbons around my graduation picture, to prove it?

I was trying hard to concentrate on the challenge ahead. Not immediately ahead, but around the bend, after the letters had struck a responsive chord somewhere in the marketplace.

One striking a single note would have been encouragement enough. I could improvise anything if given just a single note to work with.

I was concentrating on learning all I could to pass my graduate school examinations whenever I would have the chance to sit for them. Whenever was, well, whenever. I was into long-term storage of facts and theories and theorems. Cold storage. I was, as a change from my academic past, not having to learn under pressure, no exam looming up a few hours away while I was already full of aches and pains, a cramp in my neck and my butt dead. And, worst of all, the coffee and whatever pills someone gave me to keep the adrenaline alive at least until dawn, always put me to sleep instead of charging my batteries. All of that in the past and not to be duplicated.

I woke with a start. My head had been lying on my note-paper, something like a cushion. The old professor had the ingrained, never-to-be-lost courtesy not to notice. The reading room had not filled, but there were a few more occupied places. From a great distance I caught the smell of cooking stale in the air. It was past noon, into the afternoon. I had missed lunch in the cafeteria. I could smell food past eating. I could have slept at home and dealt with the guilt of not using the time more profitably by going to the library. And sleeping guilt-free.

I gathered up all I had intended to read and took the books back to the desk for reshelving. I could have done this myself, would have as a kind of act of contrition, but I did not want to violate library regulations, in violation as I already was. I hugged my unused notebooks and pencils and left.

I walked through the long empty passageway, my shoes making sharp sounds on the stone floor. From the narrow bands of window high up in the stone walls, flat beams of faded light angled down. I would pass through some of these as I had done many times before at this time of day. Usually the slanting rays of light were constantly being scattered by

hurrying students and faculty, or people like me, using any opportunity to relieve the monotony of the day's routine. The
passageway was a kind of aboveground tunnel that was meant
to let you in at one end and out the other as quickly as possible. You had business elsewhere, you didn't linger there. If you
weren't going in, you were going out. Nobody hung out in the
tunnel. Its stone walls and echoes discouraged conversation. It
always seemed damp, although it was not underground. Everybody had a better place to be.

Maybe his clothes were as gray as the stone floor on which
he sat, his legs drawn up and held tight by bare arms. Maybe
the color of his face and arms blended into the gray of the
walls. I was almost upon him before I caught his eyes, not gray
but charged with anger and not moving from mine for an instant. He had to have heard the sound of my shoes approaching on the stone floor. But he had not used the time to stand up
and pull himself together. I knew that I wanted him to have
used the time to get out of there, to run away because he
should not have been there at all. He did not have any reason
to be there; he had no affiliations, no credentials.

I stopped. I looked away. I did not want to see his eyes,
even when he began to speak. At first I could not register what
he was saying. The sound of his voice, unlike the fierce look
spilling from his eyes, was peaceful, carefully pitched to carry
to me and not beyond in that place where every sound echoed.
"You look good," he said. He repeated it, the first time as if it
had only been something to say and the second time as if
something had just struck him. "You look good."

I could not look at him, but I knew he had not moved at all
nor had his angry eyes left off staring at me. He should not
be here at all, I thought. I had the sudden, inexplicable conviction that this was the place he picked to be after being kept
closed up for years. It did not matter if he had escaped and
somehow found his way to confront me here. He had been kept
closed up for years and that had ravaged him, and whether he

had escaped or had been finally released did not matter. Nothing could ever change what had already been done to him. Freedom came too late for him.

"Sure you hear me," he said.

I would either have to turn and go back the way I came or I would have to go past him and continue on the way I was going before this interruption.

He had stood up, just pushing himself up against the wall but not moving away from it. I thought I wanted to ask him, "How did you come to lose your freedom?" but I said nothing. I knew I wanted to know what would have been worth that price. He had paid for something with his freedom, that I could tell from his eyes. But what was worth that? I wanted to know if he remembered what he thought was worth that, but it was not a thing to be asked. How could he have remembered after so much time?

All he remembers is that something has been lost, I thought. I said to him, "Thank you." He moved his head back as if taken off guard, questioning. "Thank you for the compliment," I said. "That's all?" he finally said.

It had to be done now. I lifted my face and made him look into my eyes. I tried to see not him but only the loss of freedom, something that could happen to any of us, to me as well as him. I tried to see myself struggling to hold on to something as important as that and not letting go, fighting with everything I had, fighting beyond my own strength. I imagined how I would fight to keep my freedom.

I said, "I am going there. That way." He did not have to move out of my way. He was still holding close against the wall. But I wanted him to withdraw totally from me so I could pass. I had already resolved to pass. I had already taken myself past him and was through the door I had always meant to pass through. He could not prevent me in any way. I had already gone through.

*   *   *

My mother first and then Helen got the news. I had already taken some time, a few seconds, to absorb it, so I had gotten somewhat used to it. Nevertheless, I was still surprised by the casualness with which they both responded. It was mostly a matter of "Of course" and "See, I told you so."

I was happy to join in, not feeling any anticlimax at all. If this was to be a detour, it was a road paved almost with gold. Not just a job, an answered prayer, an answered letter, but a job at what must have been the very top of all starting salaries for the simple lab technician I was and would be. "Think of the freedom, think of the freedom." The words rang in my head, although I don't remember who said them first. Perhaps both, perhaps neither. Perhaps just imagined on my part.

My mother congratulated me, began to tell me what I would need in order to look my best, put my best foot forward in such a position. She did not want to waste my money on a long-distance telephone call across the country, but she prom-ised a long letter with detailed instructions. Or suggestions. I think she quickly corrected herself and said she would make some suggestions in a letter and I could think about them in the time I had. I told her I had some time to make up my mind. She said having some time was good when difficult decisions had to be made. She was being careful not to put any unneces-sary difficulties in my way now. I would have much to think about. She said I should take some time to be quiet and listen. I would hear what was necessary for me to hear about this new experience.

I do not have an adequate definition of a miracle. But to add my own to the list of inadequacies, I would say that a miracle is a condensed moment of pure reality, a condensation of all the possibilities inherent in all possible desires, allowed to come together, gather, become real.

It was the end of July of my first year of exile from my desired future, my delayed desires. I had worked through the worst of the pain that had come with rejection. I had turned inward and was beginning to still the voices of regret and anger. I was gathering strength. I had, with never-to-be-forgotten help, found a door that was open to me. I would go through. I would pick up on the other side as quickly as I could find the strength for that further change. I had achieved some measure of safety. I felt it would cost only a small measure of freedom.

Miracles, however, always unravel the expected.

CHAPTER 11

I was flying high above the city, the usual terror I felt at the experience of flying intensified by fear of what would be waiting for me when the plane finally descended. The monuments familiar from postcards and travel books were vaguely in view, indistinct, wrapped in a haze of heat. Even the distant surrounding belt of green seemed tinted down by the late summer-morning mist. I had read that Washington was always soaked in this summer haze. The humid bath would make breathing even more difficult than it had been ever since I left California. No, I hadn't drawn a normal breath since I left, and probably not for days before that.

Was I really here, up here suspended above the world, waiting for it to come into focus? Would I in moments be dropped

down out of the sky and into reality the way my dreams sometimes suddenly left me falling from a height, waking on the
floor? But how could I doubt the obvious? There had been too
many steps involved in getting me here, buckled into this seat
next to the narrow window-framing green trees, white buildings, with the sound of the airplane engines filling my head.
There had been too many steps for me now to doubt that I had
taken each one. Even in my most distracted moments I could
not have been so out of it as to have just stumbled accidentally
into this. I had to have made some simple, practical decisions,
made a reservation, decided on the quickest, cheapest way to
get to the airport, set the alarm, packed a bag, decided on
something to wear. I certainly had to have made all those decisions along the way. I had the evidence, if only in my throb-
bing head. What was still missing after all the hours that
separated me from my daily California routine was a real conviction that any of it was happening to me. I kept telling myself, "No, they can't mean me, not me. Some mistake. Not me."

But if I didn't believe, if some part of me wasn't clinging
to some hope, then why was I here? What splendid, highly
commendable, completely uncharacteristic altruism was com-
pelling me thousands of miles across the country to set right
an error I had not committed in the first place? I could have
made a phone call. I could have just returned the letter, scribbled on it Addressee Unknown, or Opened in Error, or Please
Do Not Forward Again, even Do Not Disturb. I could have
added any phrase of my choice to those already on the envelope. I could have sent it directly to the dead letter office.

I thought back through several days to when it all began. I was
just back from another shopping spree. My hands were full
when I struggled with the letter-box key, found the slot, turned
and tugged, and had the small door open and was rewarded
with the usual catalogs and flyers, nothing to hold my atten-

tion at the moment. In the apartment I tossed it all on the bed and got down to the more important task of going through my day's purchases. Even though I had not made my acceptance of the lab job final, I thought a few additions to my meager wardrobe would ease me along to that decision. I would not bother to get all dressed up if I did not plan on having someplace to go. Every day. So I set aside my studies for a while and joined the other bargain hunters. I felt a bit out of practice for the first few expeditions, but shopping probably has a genetic basis and the dominant genes quickly asserted themselves.

I did not have any qualms of conscience about spending money on clothing even when I knew that my job specs insisted on a uniform. Some bits of feminine finery would always be visible in spite of the white lab coat. In any case, I would know I was wearing something new and attractive, maybe something different every day.

I had the wrappings and tags off, had hung up things that could be trusted to lose their creases without ironing, separated out those that would not, not even after being hung in the bathroom through several hot showers. I was relaxing, sitting with my feet up, reading the "how to care for this garment" labels. I was eagerly anticipating the time I would have for such gentle washing and drying. I would even have the time to make sure the iron was cool, my touch in applying it to hem and pleat considerate, competent. I was imagining that with my new daily job so routine in nature and with graduate school entrance examinations somewhere off in the still unscheduled future, then perhaps I would concentrate on acquiring these skills. No longer just the science student, the scholarly drudge, the bookworm. All that was now transformed into the complete woman. Yet I had to concede that a woman needs time to learn the skills that go into making herself feel the complete woman. I would have enough to begin with right here, memorizing instructions on how to care for these garments.

* * *

It was unmistakably my father's handwriting. The size of the envelope confused me, for it was larger than usual, not the same kind of stationery he had always used in writing to me. I had not expected to find his hand on the oversized envelope when I turned it over and recognized his writing and the return address.

He had not enclosed a letter or even a note. I thought how much like him that was. He never overexplained, hardly ever explained. He always believed you understood or did not and overexplaining was not a way to bring someone around to an understanding that was being resisted.

The smaller standard-business-size envelope he had placed in the larger one had a Please Forward notice on its front. The letter had gone originally to me at my college address. I did not look closely at the postmark date, although it was still visible. The address had been crossed out and the new destination, where presumably the letter would find me, had been written in, certainly by someone in the college post office. By looking carefully at the second postmark, I could have calculated the days or perhaps even weeks between the letter's first arrival and its subsequent dispatch. I did not. The pace of a college summer session probably slowed the letter, but this was only a vague thought, quickly dismissed. The postal clerk's appointed rounds, I had learned back in the days of my first attempts to memorize American myths, are not stayed by storm or sleet, so summer could not be a deterrent.

Nevertheless, I visualized the letter languishing under piles of unfinished business in the small college post office. It had once almost been noticed at the last minute before the wrap-up of daily business but left for the first thing in the morning. It was then swept under more urgent matters, again frustrated in its destination. It languished in dusty far-off corners of the office, got moved about, lost, found. Once, by accident, it even got into the hands of a clerk, whose Please Forward rubber stamp was inked, raised, ready to descend and dispatch the letter across state lines. What minor catastrophe held back the hand that would have sent the letter, what distraction? Nothing you would have read about in the newspapers, but sufficient for the day, and the next. Eventually, because even fate tires of its own fickleness, the rubber stamp descended and the letter's destination was sealed.

I opened the letter carefully, imagining I had recently been studying something about the care of this kind of thing, thinking all things should be treated with care, especially those that defy the odds and wind up in your hands after many detours. My hands were steady unfolding the stiff paper. It took a long gaze at the letterhead to drive home what I had not registered from the same return address printed on the envelope itself. Yes, this was official. This was an official letter from a medical school. This was a letter from the admissions office of a college of medicine, Washington, D.C. This letter was addressed to me.

I read but did not grasp what the letter said. How could I? The words I was superimposing on those actually on the page sent back to me the two conflicting messages I had created. I was convincing myself that I was reading a message that said simultaneously "Yes, your application to this medical school has been studied carefully" and "No, your application has been rejected." I was not even aware of the contradiction, assuming that I was reading the opposite, "Yes, your application has been, etc.," and "Yes, your application has been accepted."

But the letter's real message was none of the above, as it used to say at the end of those multiple-choice questions that left you dizzy with all the many possibilities you had never considered. None of the above is something you always have to take into consideration, even when you realize that it does leave the main question unanswered.

The letter from the admissions office did not open the doors wide to me. It invited me to come for an interview, leaving unexpressed the possibility that if the interview went well, I might be invited to enter that door. The letter invited me with all due courtesy, but it was clearly not an invitation I was allowed to consider at leisure. I could paraphrase the polite language thus: "School's on in three weeks. If you're interested, haul yourself out this way and let's see if we're as interested. In any case, we are not delaying opening of the school year for truants. We assume you've been using the last year making up your mind. How much more time do you think you need?"

With at least this much clear in my head—that is to say, with their intentions and parameters and limits to patience clear to me, and postponing for the moment consideration of my own feelings—I did what most people would do. I called my mother. I read her the letter. There was a pause. I could hear the open line ticking off the coins the call was costing me. She was waiting for me to fill the space. You do not attempt to wait out your mother. I had to speak up—or pay. I said, "I don't know what to do."

"You don't know what to do about what?" she asked. I hesitated. She had caught me in the trap, and her maneuver was simplicity itself. All she did was ask the obvious question. Of course I did not ask her to clarify. I knew what she meant. She was asking me to tell her, and myself, where I really was. I muttered something that sounded like, "The job . . ."

"You don't have a job," she said.

You also don't bristle at your mother. I tried to qualify what I had said. I didn't mention the letters, the interview, the qualifications I now proudly wore. I didn't dare mention the new wardrobe, which now revealed itself to me as the final, however premature, commitment to take the job and put the rest of life and its unrealized goals on hold.

"They gave me two weeks," I offered in full explanation. "You need that much time," she said. The inflection that would have softened it, made it a question, must have gotten lost in telephonic transmission. I hesitated again.

"The school is giving you time," she said, but immediately took away whatever comfort there was in this with "but not enough time."

"But I waited a whole year for this job!" It was the wrong move. I gave her the opening she would have found eventually. She did not actually begin with the voodoo priest and me a little girl of preteen years, but she certainly included that scene somewhere along the way, with all the family's hopes and expectations, her own labor and confidence in me, and so on and so forth. The conclusion was something I could have said right with her. In one year I was going to give up what I had spent the past decade or so working for.

It wasn't just stupid. In her opinion it bordered on the blasphemous. I did not try to get my mother's sympathy by describing more precisely the dilemma I felt myself in. After a year of struggle I had a splendid (for me at least) job offer, solid as stone, gleaming with undeniable reality. And right on the heels of that a vague hint of a possibility or perhaps a chance at a theoretical opening in medical school. She would not be impressed by talk of dilemma because to her there was only one reality, the other a figment of my imagination. We might have been looking at the same thing through different ends of a telescope.

Somewhere along the way she played her trump card. Not at the end of the conversation, because that is when she simply told me she would have the money for the fare, the overnight stay, the return, in the mail for me tomorrow. But somewhere before this she slipped quietly into the conversation, making it sound like one more justifiable complaint the older generation had about the younger—the clincher.

"You have too many questions and problems and opinions for someone with a miracle in her hands."

I did not answer, so she concluded, "It is so, isn't it?" She left me wondering if she meant the questions and problems or the reality of the miraculous that had found at last a direct route into my life.

Everything about the man was larger than life, the way I had always imagined all persons, places, and events connected with medical school would have to be. Large and loud. His voice seemed to occupy as much volume in the room as his body. Not by any means hostile or abrasive, just there and inescapable. This was at last the head of the medical school admissions committee. This was Perry Norwood, M.D., Ph.D. He was one of those "doctor doctors" we used to mock in college, more than half in awe of such persistence, but also with an innate awareness of how endless the grind, how relentless and ultimately boring the hours spent in lectures, over books, and in labs to achieve one degree and then go on to tackle another. I doubt if anyone dared refer to Perry Norwood as "doctor doctor," even in the privacy of his or her own mind.

"We're not all black here, so don't think you'll get cushioned," he said. "We're not all men here, either," he then went on, but did not at once correct what erroneous conclusion I might be drawing from that fact.

He was certainly black himself. A man from the islands, he told me, perhaps trying to set me at ease. But educated in Europe, he added, setting the boundaries. In France and Germany. He even dropped in and out of French, not Haitian Creole but the polished French of Paris, also I suppose to set me at ease. He told me he had to learn German in order to follow the lectures at the medical school where he obtained his degree. Both the written and oral examinations were in that language. He did not engage me in German and quickly reverted to English when he detected how hesitant were my replies to his rapid-fire French. I was, in fact, by now much more comfortable in English.

In spite of this display of his credentials, I did not feel he was trying to impress me. Dr. Norwood did not often have to make any special effort to impress. That more or less came with the territory. What also came with his particular territory was the faint but lingering scent of male cologne, no doubt French, a delicate touch in the cool air of the room. How did he know just how much to use? I wondered. How did he gauge how long it would last? I knew my thoughts were drifting, a way I had of calming anxiety. The scent of a male's cologne can do it as well as music can. But he brought me back.

"You're part of the new wave," he boomed at me as if in congratulation. "Young female medical school student rushing forbidden territory. Tossing gauntlets left and right. Courageous, but also dangerous. People are going to be waiting to chew you up. What are you going to do about that?"

He leaned across the desk at me, waiting for a reply as though I should have already given thought to the prospect of being chewed up by people of as-yet-undisclosed identity.

"I don't think I'd be to everyone's taste," I heard myself say. He leaned back, cocking his head and eyeing me for a moment. He did not laugh. Not a trace of a smile creased his face. "Some won't mind. They'll do it just to get you out of their way."

The moment passed. I have been let in somewhere, I felt. He gave me something I would need to remember. He would not have given it if I had not been let in.

But he was going on so rapidly now, English, not French or German, that I missed a few beats and had to concentrate to catch up. "Data are coming in. More will get here as we take in more of you." He flipped open a folder he had on the desk before him and waved a photostat of an article at me. "You females will all have more potentially serious problems than male students. The male students are likely to be your worst problem; try to find a way to navigate around them and negotiate with them. Many won't want to. Many won't thank you for trying." He threw the paper aside, then picked it up and carefully replaced it in the folder. He closed it and held his hand over it for a moment.

"We'd like to promise you'll get through a skilled doctor and a well-adjusted, flexible, adaptable, creative person. We can't be responsible for everything. When the chips are down, we have to choose. We're here to make skilled doctors. It's what we do. You have to do that, too. And the other as well."

There had to be the standard interview, and he asked the standard questions about what I had already learned and why I wanted to persist and what my goals were. Because I am a woman he asked if I thought I would want to marry and how soon and, if so, if I would have children and how many and when. I did not ask him if he also asked male applicants the same questions. I wanted to believe he did. He could not be one of those who automatically assume that marriage is a distraction in a woman's career but a take-it-or-leave-it proposition in a man's.

He had already prepared packets of papers for me to complete and send back. He more or less assumed without even asking that I would send them back and that I would be back, in the time allotted, not asking for any extension, ready to begin with the class of students that had already been selected and had been taking the last few months to relax before the doors shut on them for the next four years and then beyond that. He asked if I had any idea of how difficult it would be, and I said yes, I had. I did not have to tell him my ideas were purely theoretical and that I had not the slightest clue to what it would really be like. I knew he had been through enough such meetings to take all that for granted.

He got up and led me to the door, inquiring about my accommodations, my flight back, the weather in California, of which he had heard. At the door he said, out of nowhere, something that could have fit in somewhere earlier in our con-versation: "In medical school in Germany I often longed for the chance to spend the night in a hot tub. Not the whole night, but several significant hours doing nothing in a hot bath. That never happened. Most of the time there was just time enough for a quick shower. I think that is where I picked up the cologne habit."

I could not help but smile, embarrassed as I was, feeling caught out for acknowledging what was inescapable in the room.

"You noticed," he said, returning my smile. He held open the door but kept me another moment. "When you have to try to think in another language there is a temptation to believe you've caught the full meaning of a concept just because you recall the words it is cloaked in. You have to get past the words." He let me go. I wanted to believe that it was done, I had been accepted, that was why he was so gracious and ac-cepting. But then I knew he would have to confer with the other members of the admissions committee, and then they would deliberate, and then I would be told, by telephone call, mercifully quick, by letter, which I would tremble to open. All that did happen, and within a few days. But saying good-bye that moment I did not know what my future would be. It did not reside in this man's hands alone. But his manner, his spirit, gave me hope, and I knew I needed that for the coming days and hours. Then it came, first the call, then the letter, every-thing saying yes, now, at last, starting now again.

CHAPTER 12

It helped if you imagined the worst, but given the general state of paranoia rampant among medical students, you had already imagined the worst. Now the printed pages from the school's catalog laid it out, boldface. It was the official blueprint for your life over the next four years, the medical school curriculum, the straitjacket you had wanted to tie yourself into for lo those many past years. Here it was, tying straps dangling, empty arms waiting to embrace you.

Your first year, aptly depersonalized as the first academic period, would last thirty-eight weeks. What with lectures, labs, and conferences you were committed to—had committed yourself to—one thousand hours of such things as anatomy, gross and otherwise, biochemistry, psychiatry, microbiology, neuro-

science, patient care. "Don't despair," you told yourself. In small print was the reminder that you would have each week something termed "unscheduled hours." There did not seem to be a trace of irony here. There were six such hours. Would this mean time for yourself, things like a guilt-ridden visit to the beauty salon or a movie . . . part of a movie . . . coming attractions? Best not to think about it. Also best not to look beyond the first academic period into the second year. Yet a sneaked glance revealed that the period would be only thirty-six weeks long, only 975 hours of required courses, labs, and so forth, and, no doubt as a bonus for surviving the first academic period, an extra one-half unscheduled hour each week. By that time, you concluded, you would have forgotten the meaning of free time and how such a luxury might be used. And beyond the first two years there were two more, and beyond those . . .

It was work such as I had been told about many times before, but now it was work laid out to be performed by me, hour by hour, week by week, period by period. And just to remind you that none of this was going to be a pure and unadulterated pursuit of knowledge for its own good, there was first to be resolved the issue of paying for all the hours in all those coming academic periods. Funny that my first introduction to high finance should have consisted of sessions in which institutes of high finance arranged for me to go into debt for a good number of years after my education was complete, carrying with me a reminder of those carefree days in the monthly payments I would be making. Paying for my future on the installment plan with, as usual, help from those closest to me. My father agreed to more or less put his future into hock for mine by acting as cosigner on the major loans that would be extended to me over the next four years. Nothing like Payment Due notices looming up in the future to keep your nose to the grindstone in the present. As an indebted student you would try to put the financial worries off in a separate compartment, not let them add to the pressure of learning, say, gross anatomy I and II and psychiatry. It never did work that way. Somehow the indebtedness, the practical sign of all the faith invested in you and your ability to progress through medical school and beyond, became as palpable and as relentless a concern as the daily demands of lectures, labs, conferences.

In those first weeks of my first year I did not have the time to notice the romance of a brilliant career in medicine, the romance that was pretty much the story of my life to date, fading away. I set off to classes and labs with an eager bounce to my step. I even bounced up the steps to the gross anatomy lab, and the bounce left for good.

The gross anatomy laboratory did not offer a conducive ambience for romance of any kind. You were more inclined to hold your nose and put the other hand on your heaving stomach. Except that your hands were already occupied, one with a sharp scalpel, the other with rapidly turning the pages of the guide to the labyrinth opened before you.

Imagine an enormous room, cold, even clammy-damp, a look of scrubbed metal everywhere, every sound reverberating off unyielding surfaces. Usually, before we arrived in the morning, the cadavers had been raised out of the tanks of preserving fluid into which they were resubmerged after each session. I had no trouble imagining what that daily resurrection looked like. The gray forms under their opaque drapery would, at some command, be slowly emerging from the fluid that oozed away and back into the trough. The forms inert on the metal table would rise to a certain height, then the mechanism moving them would stop, leaving them suspended. I imagined the bodies all rising at once, stopping at once, some kind of grotesque but carefully choreographed routine. In the next instant the covering would be snatched aside in one gesture. Multiple nightmares. Worse than a movie. I had trouble keeping the imagined scene out of my head when I tried to sleep at night.

It wasn't a movie set, however. It was gross anatomy, and

we had that year more than three hundred hours in which to master it. After a few days that became "What, only three hundred hours! They must be kidding! You cannot learn all there is to learn about anatomy in that many years."

But it was the smell and not the visual imagery that made the greatest impact and will be remembered long after all the other impressions are gone. At first you tried to ignore it, then you caught yourself involuntarily tilting your head away, holding yourself back until you felt the strain in every muscle. Then you were unconsciously brushing your hand across your face as if that would remove the reeking cowl in which you felt enveloped. It was the inescapable, heavy odor of formaldehyde, as indelibly in the atmosphere of the laboratory room as it was actually present in the cadaver now under your knife. There was no escaping it. And while at the end of the day the body would be returned to its temporary shelter and you would return to other studies, the stench of the preservative stayed with you. You learned not to bring your hands to your face, you learned not to touch your lips or come anywhere near your nose. You were happy you had broken the thumb-sucking habit. You pitied the obsessive nail chewers.

There were forty-five cadavers, and we worked in small teams, each team with its own cadaver, as lecturers and instructors circulated among us, pointing out details, showing in the printed text the body part that lay under our inexperienced fingers, unknown, unrecognized, a mystery that only with difficulty began to conform to the standard set down in the anatomical illustrations that were always so clear and unambiguous. At first nothing within the cadaver seemed to conform to the illustrations. Nor did the thing on the table before us conform to our notions of what a body would be like in death. We had no notion of death at all, we were all discovering. We certainly had no notion of what a body held this way in a kind of suspended nonanimated artificially preserved state would look or feel like.

The feel was like leather, old and rough and hardened and of a color never encountered in the outside world. You cut through the tough gray exterior, hardly believing this had once been flesh, and found all was as gray inside, hard and cold and slippery to the touch. Your inexpert fingers seemed to slide off anything you touched as though you were being fended off, prevented from further exploration. Did we all think that what we were doing was a kind of invasion of privacy, something we had no right attempting? I knew I would have to lose such inhibitions if I were ever to become skilled at this necessary business.

In the first hours I was sure I would break. Not give the entire thing up but just break away temporarily from gross anatomy and duck out of the room for a breath of fresh air. I just wanted to be alone in the lavatory so that I could be violently ill, throw up everything I had ever eaten or drunk in my whole past life. Maybe that upheaval would take some of the stench with it. Maybe I had to turn myself inside out periodically to get past gross anatomy. It would be worth it. But before making the decision to absent myself from the room, something I contemplated every ten minutes or so those first days, I began to take surreptitious looks around me. I was not the only one making this quiet review. In fact, it seemed that everyone was sneaking looks to see how the experience was registering on his or her companions. But nobody broke, nobody ran from the room with hand clamped tight over mouth. We all came back day after day. We cut deeper and deeper into the cadavers before us, taking the texture and the color, if never the odor, in stride. Body parts began to resemble their pictures. You began to forgive the medical textbook illustrators for having intentionally deceived you, for having given you an absurd notion that it was all clean lines and Technicolor inside, every organ neat and precise and dressed in its own hue. We were beginning to chart a course, but each of us seemed to move at a separate pace. Some took longer than others to adjust. Verdell was one of them.

"Are you okay?" I asked Verdell as she worked alongside me.

We had been assigned to the same cadaver because our last names were close together in the alphabet, two T's. But in spite of the arbitrary fate that had introduced us, temperamentally we fit together easily and had easily become good acquaintances. We might have come close to friendship even though we knew we would not, in that driven first academic period, have much time or space in which to let any special relationship develop. At the moment it seemed that if you had a choice of whether to get to know your friend or your cadaver better, you knew what the choice had to be. I don't think either of us took offense at that.

"I'll be all right," she said in answer to my question, not lifting her head from the work she was attempting. When I continued to watch her she tried to shrug me off with a kind of smile and added, "Provided I'm struck dead by lightning in the next ten minutes or so."

"What's the matter?" I asked again, trying to show my concern but not wanting to be distracted.

"It isn't raining," she said. "There isn't any lightning."

"Okay. What's the matter?"

I didn't want to sound impatient, but I saw the instructor slowly making his way to our station. He would probably have questions before he offered any answers. "Right shoulder," she said. "Relax," I replied. "Just try to relax your arm. Your shoulder will—"

"Not my shoulder," she answered impatiently. "Its shoulder," she began, but corrected this to "his shoulder."

"What's wrong with it?"

"It's not like the left."

I stopped what I was doing and joined her in peering at

the exposed shoulder. The deltoid and trapezius muscles had already been detached from the spine of the scapula. But then what? There were the muscles, nerves, blood vessels of the shoulder. We had by then memorized the names. But what did it mean? There was more to it than naming the pieces in front of you. You also had to know where each muscle and nerve and vessel originated and where each was going. There was memory and memorization involved in that, to be sure. But there was much more than that. You had to imagine the body and all its parts alive again and functioning, everything moving together in a complex, rhythmic exchange of energy. That kind of imagination took more training than we had time to experience. At that moment and for all our concentration, neither of us could read much of anything into the barely recognizable gray shapes before us.

"Shoulder?" The young man in the long white coat had said after standing beside the table and watching us for a few moments. I couldn't immediately identify the tone in which the single word was dropped, but later Verdell tagged it to her satisfaction. Smugness. Insufferable smugness. I think I offered some feeble protest or some defense of the instructor, but she brushed both aside. She didn't ignore my words, but they acted only as fuel. She seemed to catch fire as she went on, incensed that anyone, let alone a woman, a friend of hers, would dare to come to the defense of such a creature.

Of course it was smugness, she insisted. Insufferable. And we stood there with no choice but to play the game with him. He even had the nerve to take the dramatic pause before beginning his memorized description. He even had the nerve to lean back and half close his eyes. We should have skipped out and left him discoursing with a cadaver. Let him stand there in a trance, telling the body where its part should be. We were there to be instructed but not to be patronized, not by some male memorizing machine with an ego where his soul should have been. Verdell was convinced he did it only with female students. Men know how to deal with men like that, she insisted. Men didn't put up with that kind of insult. Men didn't have to. She knew he pulled it only with women. She was going to start counting the times, gather evidence. I did not ask to what use she intended to put this evidence.

"Shoulder," he had said, giving us time to get properly oriented. The rest was delivered at a leisurely pace, with little breaths of emphasis on noun or adjective where necessary, as if he was sort of leading us in and around the things described. Speaking for myself, I would have said it was a good tutorial, if you didn't mind the attitude.

In the middle of it he hesitated for a fraction of a second and his eyes closed tight for as long. You could almost see him willing up the words onto the page etched in memory from which he had been reading all the rest to us. He concluded his delivery in a bit of a scramble: "It's separated from the joint by the supraspinatus tendon."

I felt the momentary lapse of memory had somehow mitigated the superior attitude. I might have felt all along that he was entitled to his superior attitude. Would I ever know as much?

"It's all there," he ended up, adding in what I at least thought was a sincere-enough tone, "Believe me, it's all there."

Verdell must have looked at him as though she would not believe him if he had stripped and proceeded to dissect his own right shoulder for her inspection. She might even have encouraged him to do as much, waited through the procedure and only at the end insisted he still hadn't proved the point. I think he might have suspected something like that about Verdell, but he nevertheless smiled at her with all the charm at his disposal and said, "You give me a call if you find something I missed, Miss. Or if you find something missing."

Before he left he had proved his point. It was all there, as he had said. He led us with painstaking care through each of the regions and muscles of the shoulder, losing the flirtatiousness completely in his eagerness to get us to understand the task at hand, the extraordinary piece of work under our hands. I don't know if Verdell was at all impressed.

It was an early and not then fully understood lesson for me. I, of course, knew that no woman who goes into medicine—or most any other male-dominated career, for that matter—has to be told in advance that she runs the risk of being considered a woman first and a colleague or competitor second. That's not always a comfortable position to be in. Verdell saw the risk of being, as she put it, reduced to a male definition of a woman, as not just a possibility or even a probability but rather an inevitability. If you were there in that male world, you were rated a woman in their limiting sense. To expand on the meaning of the word, you were expected to prove something men didn't have to prove. Their motives, dedication, application, diligence were all taken for granted. Yours would not be.

That was the way she saw things. I wanted to reserve judgment for as long as possible. There didn't seem much point in sharpening up my own prejudices to match those I had not yet encountered. Maybe I was not averse to a little more or less harmless flirtation. Maybe I needed the compliment, however little deserved. How long had it been since I had the pleasure of turning down a flirtatious advance? Verdell was pretty, certainly prettier than I. She was more outgoing than I, not afraid to speak her mind even before it was made up. If she was caught in a contradiction she was quick enough to pick up after herself, dust the thought off, set it right, and not be embarrassed by the need. She had a kind of natural conviction about her right to personal freedom and a kind of assertiveness I came to admire. She let you know in many ways that she was this human being named Verdell first, and then left it to you to see how she fit into the category called woman. I don't think I fully understood her. There would not be enough time to learn more about any of this from her. Perhaps it would have helped me later on if there had been.

* * *

Anatomy would have been challenge enough for one year, but
it was not the ultimate challenge, not the one that tied your
brain into knots. The text on which you found yourself sleeping in the early hours of the morning was usually neuroscience,
the structure of the human brain. At first I had taken one look
at the index and wondered, "How can all this be packed into
such a little space? How can the brain, or to be more precise,
my brain, learn all that it is said to contain?"

I woke from such troubled sleep and dashed off to hear Dr.
Norwood lecture on the subject, staring in the darkened room
at the projected slides. I sat close enough to catch the aroma of
his cologne, letting it in my imagination sweeten my introduction to the anatomy of the brain. How appropriate that the
highest human functions were being explicated on fragrant
waves of scent. I will become a brain surgeon or a neurologist.
At least I will memorize the text and pass the course.

   In time, slowly, painfully, the terms became familiar. I could
detach each from its location in the glossary of my textbook
and begin to assign it its rightful place in the awesomely complex fabric of the brain. But we were not allowed any illusions
about what we were setting out to achieve. Even if we ever
succeeded in getting it all down pat, we still would not have
the answer to the real question: How were we conscious of it
all in the first, or last, place? Where out of all these twists and
turns does our awareness of it come from?

   I listened to Dr. Norwood's large, powerful voice fill the
room like a kind of surprisingly gentle thunder rolling in from
distant hills. The voice carried clear to every corner of the room.
He was sharing with us his conviction that without belief in the
special reality, the unique essence of consciousness, its unique

origin, we were all little more than just slightly improved versions of our African ancestors, sitting around randomly flipping switches, startled and terrified by the flip that brings a flood of light but having no more understanding of the origin of the light than of the reason for the darkness from which it was suddenly drawn.

The lights went on in the hall, signaling the end of the presentation. We continued to sit, entranced. He had woven a spell around us. We knew for that moment at least why we were there.

CHAPTER 13

I came through the first half of the first year with scars that were likely to heal. You tried to forget about how some of them had been acquired. Some you were surprised to discover, like bruises you picked up as a kid on your bicycle without remembering the fall or even the pain. Gross anatomy, developmental anatomy, biochemistry, physiology of homeostasis, neuroscience—all had left their marks. Knowledge makes a bloody entrance, as someone rich and famous once said. Or was it Hippocrates? He would have known. He got us into this.

None of these subjects had lost any of their terrors. None had yielded up all its secrets. But now at least I moved more comfortably through the vocabulary. I had learned that knowing names for things helps you remember what the things are doing or are supposed to do. I had a good head for words. I must have gotten some half-acknowledged satisfaction out of casually tossing off handfuls of the more difficult terms and definitions to fellow students struggling to locate them in their overstuffed, not fully digested, only recently acquired hoard of such things. It was like tossing out a lifeline. Some liked being rescued, some didn't. Nobody, however, refused the line.

When I found myself getting a bit smug about my verbal facility, there was always Dr. Norwood's parting words to keep my learning curve in proper perspective: Just because you know the words, don't assume for a moment that you understand the concept.

Something else kept me especially humble amid all the experiences designed to keep every student humble. I knew that someday, and soon, as soon as the third year, Dr. Norwood's words would be there to haunt me. I would have to apply every word I had learned to a living patient. I longed for the experience; I wanted words, all those medical words, to become flesh. It would happen. In the third year I would finally be spending most of the day and even at times the night, on the hospital floors, not in the safety of the lecture hall. I would be with real patients, not textbook case histories. It would then be good-bye biochemistry, hello Ob/Gyn, pediatrics, internal medicine, surgery, rehabilitation, family practice. Heaven help us all. The first encounter with that reality was moving closer. There were only another thousand hours or so separating me from the real thing. It was only a question of learning as much as would be offered on infectious diseases, organ systems, pathology, pharmacology, medical genetics, epidemiology, biometrics, principles of patient care—and then being with the human beings with such organs, diseases, and needs. I stopped dreading the rigors of the lecture hall and the laboratories. I now looked upon the last year of academic courses as the last step toward home.

The hundreds and hundreds of hours of class and labs piled on us were exhausting, but they were not enough. As much as we complained about the workload the school and individual professors had set, we had all easily slipped into the same mentality. No matter how much you do, you could—should—be doing more. There were always stray hours in the week that had somehow slipped free of medicine. These could be imagined as arable plots, handkerchief-sized bits of earth, left fallow in a starving country. Not to put each under cultivation was a sin against humanity. So we formed small, informal study groups, meeting at odd hours of day or night, on weekends and rare holidays. We met wherever we could find a place—an unused conference room, a deserted nurses' lounge, a corner of the cafeteria, a storeroom with old medical records in cartons that we used as desks and pillows. It didn't matter. We weren't there for the atmosphere or to socialize. We were trying to get the material more or less down to size, our size. We whittled away at the complex concepts until they were simplified enough to be grafted onto something similar already in our brains, something on which the reformulated ideas might be grafted and begin to grow. Maybe we whittled them until they were sharp and pointed enough to stick. The idea was that if you saw how someone else was understanding a problem or, as often, misunderstanding it, you might get an insight into the problem and how it could be solved. At the very best, listening to someone thinking out loud might give you a clue to understanding your own thinking. You forgot to be embarrassed by your stupidities. To anyone keeping score, we were all equally dumb, equally bright. A kind of unavoidable democracy prevailed, and no one stayed at the head of the troop for long.

The group I wound up spending this free time with was made up mostly of male students. Not unexpectedly, since they made up more than 70 percent of the class. I had managed to convince Verdell to join me, not that she showed any special eagerness to be with those she dismissed as "med jocks." She hadn't shown much inclination to match up with the small groups of women students, either. "First-year cannon fodder," she called them. She had her own idea of why so many women had been admitted in the first place:

"Stands to reason that a lot of students will get kicked out. A lot of students have to get kicked out, if not right off, then surely by the end of the second year. By the third year you have to be doing time in the real world. In the wards, with patients. Might be a menace. Weeding out the ranks is a kind of liability insurance. Also helps to boost the morale of the ones who survive. Besides, male professors—and you haven't noticed anything other than males up there, have you?—feel better kicking out a female than kicking out one of their own. So why we're really here is to act as a buffer for the male ego. Sound familiar?"

I would not have tried to argue with her, even if I had the facts to prove her wrong. She was not looking for facts to persuade her out of the feelings that seemed to make her more and more hostile to the daily life we had to live. We all felt we were in over our heads a good deal of the time, sometimes most of the time. And we all had days of intense anxiety that quickly produced the inevitable rebound, intense depression. Most of us found an answer to either or both states by swallowing large doses of what had produced them in the first place—more work, more hours, more scrambling to keep ahead of the clock.

Verdell plugged away as we all did, but she had begun to see things differently from most of us, and certainly in a different way from how I saw them. Sure, the work, the hours, the demands were probably more than we could reasonably be expected to handle. We were, something even we forgot, young, in our mid-twenties, with very few natural-born scientific geniuses among us. Verdell had a legitimate complaint about the pressures we were under. But she was also far gone into a different kind of anger, an anger directed toward the entire system itself. It was anger directed at those who perpetrated it and at those whose lives were, for these years at least, completely under its control. She saw giving up control over her life not as a temporary necessity but as a deep personal insult, a danger she had to be on guard against. I think she also had to be on guard against those who accepted this kind of control. Verdell was one of those who could never justify any diminishing of independence, not even as a temporary expedient.

CHAPTER 14

If you had committed yourself completely, you could not say that the commitment left you with nothing for yourself. You had committed yourself completely. There shouldn't have been anything else left. You didn't want anything else. You were completely at one with your choice. You had agreed that fulfilling the promise could take as much of you as necessary, all of you if necessary.

The logic went something like that. But even as I repeated this intellectually foolproof formula to myself, I knew I was finding little emotional support in logic alone. I had committed myself to becoming a doctor. There should not have been parts of me still looking for some other kind of satisfaction. There were, however, even if for the time being I kept those voices still. Or ignored them, or let the relentless pressure of work drown them out. Still, whatever explanation I was using was enough to hold me together from month to month, course to course, lectures and labs, conferences and confrontations.

Through the first year, at least. Get me through the first year at least, I prayed, trying to strike a bargain with myself. It was as if I were offering something of myself as a ransom, a pledge of my continuing good behavior and performance. I'd redeem myself later. It was a bargain I would keep, I promised. Why couldn't I?

Verdell left at the end of the year. So much goes into getting into medical school in the first place, so much hope, so much plain hard work, so many expectations riding on you, you have to believe that giving it all up would leave bitterness and anger. Not for Verdell. No anger at all, no bitterness, no resentment. In the last weeks of the school year she gave me the impression that failure was the last thing on her mind. She was calm, casual, happy. Not just because she was getting out of the endless daily grind of it all, although we certainly envied her for that. She wasn't running away from any intellectual challenge bigger than she thought she could handle. She had simply decided that nothing was worth putting her life on hold, not for a day, certainly not for years. She didn't talk about it, but the way she looked said it all: I came close to losing who I am. And now that I finally know who that is, I'll never forget. I'll never risk losing me again. Count on it.

I think about her often. She was bright and beautiful. Probably still is. She probably is still a better person than she would ever have been a doctor, or maybe even as a doctor. Like the rest of us that year, she was trying to figure out how to be both; but unlike some of us, she was not afraid—or ashamed—to admit that sometimes you can't. Then you have to choose. Or you don't and hope nobody notices. When things go wrong, you maybe end up hoping you don't notice yourself.

Toward the end of that first year Mr. Right finally came into my life. He was a little more—how should I say it?—mature than I thought I wanted, but I did not hold that against him. He'd been around, was well broken in. This had its obvious advantages. This would also sometimes be a problem, as I soon found out. But it meant I did not have to worry too much about putting an occasional dent in his composure. He came with dents enough. He wasn't used to special treatment, and I, of course, didn't have time for that.

He wasn't American-made. He was Japanese. I called him Toy Motor, although he was really a Toyota, already several hands past second by the time he fell into my eager embrace. He came with at least 100,000 miles to his credit, but someone suggested he was cheating on his age, might even have turned back the clock. So say 150,000, give or take. I wasn't counting, I was in love. He was my very first motor vehicle. He put up with all my clumsy efforts to learn how to handle him. I was coming to this late in life for someone of my generation, when almost nobody escaped from the teens without at least one significant such experience.

Now I was finally also learning how to drive. Learning to drive was not as nerve-racking as finding your way through all the sulci of the brain, and in a way it provided the relief of a different kind of challenge. After all, you didn't actually run the risk of loss of limb if you hung a left rather than a right coming down the sulcus cingulum. But having seen traffic mostly from the safe height of a seat on a local bus, it was shocking to see how close and menacingly fast things moved down below, at the highway level. It was the thought of all the miles I had spent up there, on a seat on a bus that always made all local stops, that really spurred me on and got me past both written and driver's tests. I was pretty skilled at passing tests. And then I had the license, and it was all legal and sanctioned by the state. Now Toy Motor and I had the open roads all to ourselves.

I would not be taking the first summer off, as much as my aching brain, frayed nerves, and tired body would have appreciated the break. Having gotten up enough steam to plow through the first thousand hours, I did not want to lose any momentum. I did not worry about imposing the rhythm of unrelenting work on my own natural rhythms, physical or emotional. I suppose I had just assumed that by now I was hearing only one rhythm, the others more or less submerged under, blended into, or obliterated by that one. The descriptive phrases changed from day to day, depending on my state of exhaustion. Any part of me that was not keeping time with the rhythm imposed by medical school or was getting out of step with that rhythm would have to get the beat—quick march, double time, pick up the slack, shape up, ship out . . . something. There was probably some appropriate military expression to cover the sense of urgency that never left me. I wasn't going to run the risk of getting out of step. This is war, isn't it? I am in for the duration, am I not? Deserters get shot. Verdell was an exception, one that just proved the rule.

It was a real job, not monkey work this time. What I would learn I would use, if not at once, then someday. What I would learn would one day help me help a patient. That was how I thought of things. All that past year as I studied or listened to a lecture I would play this game, a very serious game, with myself. In my imagination I would see myself picking up each piece of information, each new fact that had to be memorized and understood, and I would imagine myself feeling it, an object in my hand, real, alive, giving off its own energy. Every object thus transformed would then respond to the energy I gave off. That energy would emanate in the attention I was focusing on the object. That step was a very practical one—I needed all the energy I could muster simply to grasp and then retain the information coming at me from all directions.

As I felt each item I would remind myself of how I had to think about it, or how not to think about it. I'd begin with: This is not just a textbook definition or a description of some body part or an explanation of a function. This is not a theory or a probability or the consensus of scientific opinion on a debatable issue. When I put this thing to be learned into my head I am putting there not fact but means. With this felt object I am empowering myself to help others. Everything is being transformed from fact to means. Everything now has a double purpose. Each thing is not the fact in itself. Each thing has become part of what I will someday be able to accomplish.

I did not describe this technique to my mentor for the summer at the government-sponsored research facility where I worked. Bill Rothman had probably devised something like it during his own progression through the many science courses that culminated in his doctorate and his long-term position as research head in this prestigious center. I tried my best not to be awed by him and finally succeeded, his easy manner making that possible after the first few hours. I learned from the other women on the project that it was perfectly all right to become completely infatuated with him. He would never do anything to encourage the infatuation or take advantage of it or give you any reason to regret that you had decided to indulge the summertime emotion. You could practice pure science and get a little taste of pure bliss at the same time. At the end of the summer you'd go back to school none the worse for the experience. You even got to appreciate how nice it was that he took off at the end of each day to go back to the wife and kids. Sometimes he'd take you along, too. That was a bonus.

We were studying the pharmacokinetics of asthma medications, how they move through body systems, are sometimes changed by rate of take-up, are distributed through the body, and how they are eventually eliminated. He thought I'd take a special interest in the work, considering the toll asthma takes on African-Americans. Maybe I'd be interested enough to come back and work on another project, try to learn if blacks had a particular predisposition to asthma, something genetic. He had assumed that pediatrics or family medicine would be the specialty I'd give most serious consideration to when the time came to make a decision. That would be a logical assumption, given that I am black and female. I would take one of the so-called female interest branches of medicine, where my feminine intuitions would come to the fore. Not necessarily branches where male interests are served. I did not know yet how general such assumptions are or how constricting they can be. I would have to challenge them first to learn the power these assumptions have, even among the most open-minded of persons.

The complexity of the chemical analyses sort of took my own breath away, but it made for an interesting day's work. But with all these metabolites and isoenzymes and so forth, I had to keep reminding myself that somewhere down the line, call it the bottom line, was a kid struggling to get his breath, his coughing and wheezing and weakness enough to drive the parents to frantic worry and a midnight rush to the emergency room. If you were the doctor on call that night the most important question would be: Is the kid taking any other medication? If so, you'd have to try to recall whether it was on the list of things that would slow the drug down or speed up its work. Try conjuring up the whole list, run your mind like an anxious finger down the alphabetical list from alcohol through estrogen and on to zileuton.

One Friday night Bill had me follow him home in Toy. It was the first invitation to join him and his family. His wife and kids were going to have a barbecue for us, and we were not supposed to do anything but relax and watch them work. I worried how I would tell them I had gone off meat since gross anatomy, but hoped there would be salad and that everyone else would have huge appetites. When we got to the simple, neat house set back against the fringe of remaining trees screening it off from the other similar new houses in the development, he led me into the driveway and then told me there was a problem. It would wait until I had met the family and had something to drink, but not wait as long as dark.

His wife was young and pretty and black. She did not show any surprise at discovering me, so I did not show any at discovering her. I wondered if I had missed something about Bill Rothman that I should have suspected. My head was so used to picking up clues that signs of some problem, something out of the ordinary, an anomaly was automatically assumed.

Why hadn't I noticed? Bill Rothman was a statistical oddity. A white man married to a black woman. In those years, the beginning of the eighties, such a union represented less than 1 percent of all existing marriages. I caught myself up short at that point. I did not want to admit that Dr. Bill Rothman being married to pretty black Selina might have struck me as a problem, something that had to leave telltale clues. At first I did not want to go into the other possible reasons for the unease I felt. But because I had been trained to examine everything, I could not turn the sleuth in me off so efficiently, even if the trail doubled back to me and something that was my problem.

Maybe I was thinking that if someone like Bill would fall in love with a black woman, what's wrong with me? Why didn't I have as good a chance as she, as any woman would, as good a chance as any to have this neat, happy, fulfilled life? Wasn't I as entitled as she? Why not with someone like Bill? Why not with anyone, anyone at all? What were the odds against me finding that anyone?

And that was it. Knowing Bill as the brilliant, dedicated scientist that he was, then seeing him here, in a loving, perfectly ordinary and normal life, made me see the difference between the path I had decided to take and this one. The odds against a marriage such as this were high, but here it was. I had to ask again: What were the odds against me finding this natural communion with a man, regardless of his color or origin or anything else? And oddly, suddenly, I began to understand Verdell in a way I had previously ignored. I had been aware only of her desire to leave a life she found she didn't want. Now I was beginning to understand that she had chosen to go forward toward a life that fulfilled her best instincts. There were messages here I obviously had not been ready to deal with.

It was twilight before Bill decided to settle the real problem I was having. Not him. Not love and marriage. Simpler. What could be called a Toy problem. Motor oil. A welcome relief from the more speculative problems in my head. He opened the garage door, found a pair of overalls for himself and another the same size for me, reassuring me the size didn't matter, I did not have to perform anything too elaborate in them. Just get on the flat, wheeled roller thing next to the one he was already stretched out on and work my way under the engine. To do this you worked your heels along over the cement-drive surface. Steering was a problem. When I found the nut that held the oil tank shut tight, the trick was to fit the adjustable wrench snugly onto it and loosen it. But not before I had the bucket ready to catch the old, very old, oil. I was performing my first auto mechanic task, the first of many. I told him I thought my teacher was overqualified for the job. And as the night finally settled in, he helped me fill the oil tank (not the one that said antifreeze, the other one) and gave me some of the best advice I had so far been gifted with.

When the oil has to be changed and you don't have time to run the car down to the shop and wait for the mechanics to notice you and find somebody to drive you back to the job and then get you back before the shop closes for the night—but usually it is closing for the weekend or long holiday weekend—at such trying times practical knowledge is worth its weight in gold. You might also want to know how to do a tune-up on your own Toy engine. Easier than brushing your own teeth and not half as painful. Then there were the brushings and spark plugs. . . .

With the help of a flashlight and Bill's infinite patience, the inside of the Toy was beginning to look less like a metal version of gross anatomy on the first day of school and more like the inside of a motor vehicle. How nice, I thought, how very nice to know a man who lives in an ivory tower and who also knows how to repair the stairs and maybe even the elevator when it gets installed. And he can take you through it all step by step without ever making you feel you aren't up to the job, will never be up to the job, should never have attempted the job in the first place, should give up the job and find something more appropriate for someone with your talents or lack thereof. How nice, how perfect, I once more concluded—and still conclude. And how rare, as rare as everything else about this neat man.

Never imagine that once having decided to become a doctor, the decision is final. "Doctor" is just the overall word for someone who does some very specific kind of doctoring. Before the second year of medical school is out, you have to have a fairly good notion of how you are going to take the abstract notion "doctor" and make it doctor of something or other. You have a wide variety of something or other to pick from: anesthesiology, dermatology, emergency medicine, family medicine, internal medicine, neurology, obstetrics and gynecology, pediatrics, psychiatry, surgery . . .

In theory, at least, you have a wide variety. Practice says otherwise. In the past, when I had time to think about what specialized kind of medicine I would spend the rest of my life practicing, I vaguely concluded that it was likely to be family medicine, or pediatrics, or obstetrics, or gynecology. However, I wasn't quite sure how these services got fixed in my head as the right kind of places to be targeting. I think I had some notion that gynecology would offer me a field in which to do some research on "women's problems." The fact that I had, from my teens, experienced some of the most miserable menstrual cramps ever recorded gave me some impetus to study this particular problem. I might just be able to come up with some of the whys and wherefores, maybe even discover a method of making life bearable every day of the month and not just a few days. Because of my sex and the problems it brought me, I think I had more incentive to examine this issue than most of the male students around me might have had.

I think I can honestly say my mind was fairly open about the choice. I would look around and then find someone to ask. I had been told that not many faculty members had time left over from their teaching and practicing duties to offer extensive guidance. As a woman I had an additional problem, however. If I thought I could confide my hopes, doubts, and dreams more in a female faculty member than in a male, I was quickly disabused of the notion. Full-time female faculty members back then were harder to come by than they are today—and today less than 10 percent of full-professor level positions in medical school are held by women. I could not go shopping around for a female role model on which to build my career when the school did not stock any models for me to peruse.

Just when I thought medical school had pretty much showed me all the surprises it had in store for me, a totally unexpected one opened like a trap. Perhaps not the best image. Say it opened like another straitjacket into which I was expected to snuggle, all meek, quiet, and compliant. I had decided, with help from all the good and kind spirits in the world, that a doctor is what I must be. I found out that choosing just what kind of doctor was not to be left to my good spirits and me.

CHAPTER 15

You can't escape your basic orientation. As a medical school student I was basically focused on research. So to get some clues as to where I might be headed in my career I naturally turned to research. I knew the findings would not serve as a crystal ball telling me absolutely where I'd be in the next thirty years or so. But I might get some clue from finding out where those others like me had finally wound up. If that didn't work, then it really would have to be a crystal ball, like the one I saw downtown in the storefront window where the exotic lady in the long flowery dress and heavy earrings tried to coax me in for an in-depth reading, satisfaction if not accuracy guaranteed.

I didn't have time to run downtown, however, and outside of research I had lost trust in the validity of any alternate way of knowing. It didn't occur to me that I could look elsewhere—say to myself—to discover the answer. I had fallen back into the habit of expecting the voices to come from outside. I was now almost two years along in my studies. Among the other things the years had meant were long hours of facing up to just how much I didn't know or understand. There were the even longer and more difficult hours of having to follow rigid and prescribed formulas for reaching the "truth" of any given situation. The hours had done their work. The more I learned the less sure I was of what I knew. I was impressionable that way. Impressed by everything else but my own convictions.

What futures had they made, the successful graduates of my esteemed college of medicine? If I could have imagined myself a part of such an all-embracing graduating class picture, then I might have felt somewhat more secure about my future. I might have experienced the security a child gets from hearing all over again the familiar memorized fairy tale, no changes allowed, no surprises, no unexpected twists of fate. Everything comes out the way it was supposed to.

Behind all this abstract, scientific pursuit of the truth and behind the research into career possibilities and career choices made was a simple fact—I was terrified. I thought I knew where I was going, but was I going to go the whole way alone? I thought I already knew the direction, but I didn't know the way was so confused, with so many unexpected crossroads and turning points that never showed up on the small-scale map I had started out with. How would I know which direction at a crossroad would keep me on the right path? How would I ever recognize when I had made a wrong turn? It was just beginning to occur to me that I had only a small-scale notion of the true dimensions of the world I had once so confidently expected to conquer. I had to get a better map if I were ever to get any idea of how vast my opportunities might be—or how daunting the obstacles.

The routes already taken by most who went before me are

well known, tabulated, documented, peer-reviewed, refereed, and printed. Research, the amassing of numbers and more numbers, is a religion whose devotees possess a faith and perseverance that easily put other believers to shame.

In one column, neatly tabulated, were the numbers who had taken the acceptable, well-trodden, well-charted routes. In the other, the less-robust column, were the meager ranks of those intrepid or just plain contrary souls who had chosen the less-familiar paths and did not return to tell about it. As intriguing as that alternate course seemed, I had a suspicion that I would not get much encouragement to add myself to that list of wayward alumni. Few had done it in the past. Why would I be an exception? As far as research went, and in a way as far as my questioning could go at that time, I had my answer. I had my future wrapped up securely in well-documented reports. Just go on and do what others have been told to do in the past. You'll have trouble enough keeping up with those demands.

I slept on it for a day or two, but in truth did not get much sleep at all. Something was bothering me. The figures I had studied, for all the air of inevitability with which they predicted my fate, did not sit well. As usual, the words to pin down and clarify the cause of the bother were taking their own sweet time getting born. Just as well, I conceded, knowing I had no choice but to bide the time. This particular matter was too important to come forth in garments more suitable to cloak another, different kind of worry. I wanted, for the moment at least, to concentrate on career decisions. The other incidental thing, the "me" in all this, could wait, would wait. I would make sure of that. I was already more than slightly embarrassed at the image of myself that rose up whenever I thought back on those few happy evenings with Bill Rothman and Selina and all the summer world I was let into briefly. Now, who is this, nose pressed close to the windowpane, staring wide-eyed with longing and hunger at all the candy jars lined up inside? Close, so close, except for the windowpane . . . and a few other obstacles in the way. Well, that's one waif going to have to swear off candy, develop a taste for raw carrots and such. Builds character, raw carrots, prevents cavities and other heartache.

I did not have to wait for a meeting with Dr. Norwood. His cologne embraced me first before he took my hand, and with a quick word of congratulation and encouragement (I did get enough of the structure of the brain packed into mine to be able to pass his course) led me to the chair drawn up, as usual, close to his desk. He sat down and waited, ready to give me whatever time I would need, knowing I would not have asked for his time unless I already had the problem formulated well enough to give him a quick notion of what had brought me there in the first place.

I thought I had, but as I began to speak the carefully worked out formulation fragmented and I heard myself beginning and hesitating, saying something and almost at once overriding the words with words unexpected, unintended, tripping over my tongue. "Why do I have to be . . . Why does everyone . . . Are they the only specialties . . . What if I want . . . ?"

I wisely fell silent after this not very promising or even coherent beginning.

"I see," he said, reassuringly.

I did not think for a moment that he was mocking me. I was frantically trying to put my scrambled thoughts together, his display of patience making that harder rather than easier. He's not going to give me all day, I thought.

He didn't.

"The one thing you'll never get to hold against me is that I made things easy for you."

He waited just for my rueful smile to start to take shape before breaking out in his rumbling laugh. "Not my fault! Just the structure of the brain itself. You're as much at fault as I am, considering you're walking around with one, same as I."

"The course was very good," I said, believing this, forgetting the pain.

He smiled in appreciation. "You lived to tell it. . . . You'll live through the rest. That's what's bothering you, isn't it? Where's the best place to put all this? That's it, isn't it?"

He waited for the expected nod of assent and then continued, more reflective now, inclining his impressive bulk toward me. I felt he was taking me by the hand and inviting me to share some truth he had been long in discovering. "The study of medicine can steal away the soul. We all look toward the practice to restore it. Practice has to be the place where we can see ourselves come whole again. You should not have a conflict with what you practice. What you do in medicine for the rest of your life has to be related to what you are."

He paused and left hanging between us the implied questions, "Have you found that out yet? Have you decided on that?" He respected my hesitation for a while longer, then leaned even closer and almost whispered to me, a confession: "You'll excuse me for playing the heavy in class. Sometimes I'm not sure I know everything I pretend to know. Sometimes the true meaning of things eludes me. That's when people become most certain. Bad habit. Professional hazard."

He raised his finger and with this gesture of caution included me in the conspiracy. "Now, all hell will break loose if talk like that gets around, won't it?"

I swore myself to secrecy without, of course, saying a word. He acknowledged it all and reverted to his serious, still slightly abstracted mood. "Sometimes we just don't know which life is best for any individual. We don't know what to advise. We can only go on past success or past failure, both of which can be equally instructive."

I finally found my voice, his frank disclosure of such uncertainty giving me the validation I needed to express my own. "Why is it just assumed that I'd do what all the other females did? Why are my choices limited?"

"Limited?" There was real surprise in his reply and some stiffening in his posture, as though he felt a challenge from an unexpected quarter. The response took me off guard. "You come back someday, maybe after you've been in practice for ten years or so, and tell me what you still haven't yet learned about, say, pediatrics, and then we can talk about 'limited' choices."

I felt that he was trying to fake me out. Although my temper might have been getting in the way of my discretion, I spoke up anyway: "I didn't say there's anything limited about pediatrics or obstetrics or gynecology. I'm sure I'll never learn enough to be really good at any of them. I'm limited. I'll accept that. But is that what my choices have to be?"

"Your choices aren't limited."

"The choices offered to me, this person, me, are. Somebody limits them. Something limits them." The tone of my voice did not anger him. His was gentle, but I could detect a kind of weariness, as if he were repeating words said so often he might now have reason to doubt their effectiveness, if not their sincerity.

"We know . . . it's generally accepted that women medical students have certain . . . difficulties . . . men don't have, or are good at hiding." When he came to an unexpected pause I heard my voice filling the silence with an edge I immediately regretted. "Such as?"

He did not take any offense at this, at least none I could detect. But he answered me with so mechanical a recital that he might have been reading the words off the pages of a journal. That was where they probably originated. I thought they might be something he had written himself. He probably had more than one occasion on which to quote them. I did not want to imagine the number of women who had listened to the words right where I was sitting. They might even have been the kind of statement some writers live to regret, hearing them echoed so frequently they become drained of their original import. I was beginning to feel sorry for him.

"For some women, integrating their identity as medical students and then as physicians with their identity as a woman proves a hazardous venture. The resulting stress is intensified when events—disrupted, aborted, or postponed personal relationships, for example—force them to believe they must choose between an identity as a woman and an identity as a professional."

Again there was silence between us. His head was drooped, and he stayed motionless for a moment until he raised his eyes to mine and said, with something of a trace of humor, "It does get to sound more pompous each time I have to repeat it. But it was well intended. Did any of the good intentions come through? I would like to believe that it still sounds at least well intended."

I meant it when I said, "Yes."

"Medicine is a hard life under the best circumstances. We just want to help you avoid the conflicts that are avoidable."

"Excuse me, Dr. Norwood, but I don't see how my being a woman is avoidable. Not at this late date." I hadn't meant to be snide or dismissive, and he did not respond as if he caught any such possibilities in my words. He actually laughed as though he thought them rather amusing, although I probably had sounded deadly serious, in the manner of medical students.

"If you want to break out of the mold, get in where you don't belong—sorry, where some people may tell you you don't belong—then you're going to be taking on more than the usual horrors of postgraduate medical specialty training."

"You mean horrors to be added to the horrors already experienced?"

"I thought I apologized for the brain."

"You did."

"Then take my word for it—no, better take the words of some of my colleagues. Talk to them, or at least try. Some may not even consider you fit material to work with. They won't hesitate to tell you so. Go shopping around. You tell me you don't like the fit of the usual thing we want to dress you in— baby doctor, lady doctor, something to bring out the woman in you, something to exploit the woman in you. Something to sort of give you a running start in dealing with patients. You don't think any of these will work for you, then you have to suit yourself. If you can forgive the pun."

"I'm sure it was . . . well intended," I said, almost too quietly for him to hear. But of course he did.

"I think I can detect traces of a sense of humor. How did that escape the last two years?" I hesitated, wondering if the question was sincere. But because he continued to wait for an answer, I said, "I think I kept it hidden."

He got up and signaled that the interview was over. I probably looked as if I felt stranded, so he took another moment to say, "Don't stifle that sense of humor. You'll need it. You're not going to get past some of what's in store for you without a sense of humor. And a thick hide. That takes longer to develop. It is also useful, but it's not as attractive. Stay with the humor. Do what is necessary to keep it alive."

I thought about those words many times in the months and years ahead. The hide seemed to thicken of its own accord; the humor tended to go into hibernation for long stretches of time. Sometimes I'd wonder if it had just given up and headed out for my congenial territory. If there had been snow I think I would have tried to follow its tracks. The new hide would be enough to keep me protected. I guess that would be considered a good enough trade-off, but I couldn't be sure if I would ever get used to it.

CHAPTER 16

The question I now had to answer could not be posed in the obvious way. I could not ask anyone, "Why would someone want to be a surgeon?" Nor could it be posed in a more general and impersonal manner: "Why does *anyone* want to be a surgeon?" The question as I heard it in my own head came with a kind of extra dimension, a question with a question inside: "Why does someone who is a woman think she might also want to become a surgeon?" And then the question had to get personal: "Why is this particular woman beginning to entertain the idea that she may want to become a surgeon? And why is there any question about it?"

I was going to have to answer all of the above, if not now then soon enough. The second academic year stretch was ending, and I still had two more years to go before graduation and the long-sought, long-desired M.D. after my name. In theory at least, decisions about what to do with the rest of my life, professional and no doubt personal as well, could be put off for a while. But perhaps only for the next year. But in the next two years I would be serving clerkships and actually working in the hospital with patients. I had to make up my mind how I could be most useful. I had to find a specialty that I could become good at—excellent at. I owed it to my as-yet-unknown patients. I also owed it to all the ones I knew who had helped me get this far.

It was lucky for me that I had the time because I did not yet have a clear notion of what I wanted to do. Surgery was beginning to seem more and more intriguing, if only because it had been presented as such a remote possibility as far as female students were concerned. But I had little concrete notion of what the training and daily life of a surgeon were like or how any of that would suit me. I had an instinctive feeling, however, that surgery was not something into which anyone jumped without first finding out how deep the water was.

I had heard stories of women who had made the reach for surgery as a specialty and had even come close to nibbling the tempting fruit. Most had failed. The results were said to be as disastrous as those that followed the first recorded temptation of Eve by the forbidden apple—sudden and complete loss of innocence, to say nothing of Eden itself. (Adams were so few and so thinly spread among the female candidates I heard about that they were, as the scientific jargon has it, statistically irrelevant.) I had the impression that just being a female guaranteed defeat.

I mulled over some of these tales as I took an early-morning run, hoping that the indignation I felt at the fate of my fellow females, gone down in that battle, would spur me on to previously unattainable feats of endurance. My once rigorous daily running schedule (at least thirty minutes) had suffered the fate of most such purely personal, selfish indulgences during the past months. On many days I had to forgo the exquisite agonies of near exhaustion, imminent muscle spasm, dehydration, dry heaves, rhabdomyolysis, and diaper rash for the simpler, more sedentary torments of pathology, general and systemic pharmacology, and medical genetics. But this morning I had stolen time off from class and labs to compete with myself. I felt I had to let my imagination roam unchecked over the fragments of supposedly guaranteed true stories exchanged in the cafeteria, bigger chunks of rumor and gossip passed only among intimate friends, more coherently presented details culled from published accounts. I thought that if I put some of these accounts to a critical review I might come up with a pattern suggesting what I could expect, and what would be expected of me, if I ventured on the same route and began to take a career in surgery seriously. It probably made as much sense as surveying the casualties on a battlefield (I had been told that 80 percent of female surgery candidates did not make it) to see if you could survive the war.

The first fact I had discovered was that females who want to be surgeons usually don't have other full-fledged female surgeons to talk it over with. You don't have one of your own to give you insight into how to live the life of a surgeon. You don't have a feminine perspective. This fragment of the picture was by no means imaginary. The point was made statistically relevant by the bewildering (to me at least) news that women then made up only about 3 percent of all practicing surgeons. I looked around: Women were even less in evidence on the teaching faculty of medical schools everywhere. Few if any full professors, few if any department heads, few administrators or deans of medical schools were women. My chances of finding myself in the same pool with one or two female mentors to buoy me up were not promising. The facts made me imagine a situation in which I might be facing a life-or-death crisis every day, but there would be nobody to talk to me, nobody to listen to me talk. I had to think about why I assumed I would be so cut off. And that led me to what everyone I had spoken with called typical male behavior in the closed-tight, uptight world of male surgeons.

Everyone agreed that male faculty members—the majority, remember—talked to students about the whys and wherefores of selecting a specialty. That was talk from an exclusively male perspective and so had limitations as far as application to females was concerned. More to my point, the male surgeons not only talked from a male perspective as well, but (many women medical students were willing to testify) also talked seriously only to other males they were certain might make good surgeons. Surgeons, the stories went, sometimes also talked to or about prospective female surgeons. A good number of the stories that circulated was calculated to make any woman's blood run cold. But should mine? What was I to believe?

I had a problem accepting stories of really demeaning encounters between aspiring female students and established male faculty members or senior residents in surgery. The stories came to me at second and even third hand. My own experience was limited to my recent interview with Dr. Norwood, who had been gentle and concerned. I had not yet tried to interest a faculty member or a resident or attending surgeon in my own still-evolving thinking about my choice of career. But I could imagine what a rebuff would feel like. I could imagine having to believe that it would be different if I were different, not female and black. I could imagine feeling that and also feeling guilty that I could entertain such thoughts. Why assume the man was discouraging or discounting me because I was a woman? Maybe he was right and I would not be good enough, would become another casualty. Who wants to waste time on a loser? On the other hand, why should I give him the benefit of the doubt and assume I would be a casualty? Labels stick only on a surface prepared to receive them.

For a moment my memory prompted me with an image of a frightened, self-conscious younger me, fearing she was over-stepping herself, waiting with dwindling but ever-renewed patience for a high school counselor to find a moment to listen to her most impractical dream of medical school. For a moment I recalled Ms. Diamond and the pained expression on her face as I described what I wanted. I heard her so reasonably, so carefully chart an alternative course, one that would not leave me open to heartbreak. I learned that the reasonableness and the concern were her way of shielding me, young, foreign, black, female, from the cruel disappointment all those liabilities made inevitable. She almost had me persuaded. It was a turning point in my life. My mother showed me in no uncertain terms that I did not have to accept the label Ms. Diamond was offering.

Were the stories I was now trying to evaluate really sketches of another such challenge, another obstacle I would have to face? I was not quite sure what to make of many of them, although each was declared to be the purest gospel truth. Maybe the tales were not so much strict liberal truth as symbolic of the fears and uncertainties—and self-doubt—women almost automatically feel as they approach such a solid male fortress as the practice of surgery. "Impregnable" was the word used to describe this particular male fortress. I soon agreed that it was a good choice. The physical impossibility and the joke implied in the word "impregnable" might have been as subtle as a poke in the eye, but the statement had validity nonetheless. This is the prejudice a woman could face in her effort to be accepted as a valid, likely candidate for a career as a surgeon. To make a long story short, the word meant, "You'll as soon see one of them pregnant as they'll see one of you a surgeon."

I had been told of interviews in which a surgeon dismissed a woman applicant with a checklist of predictions, beginning with the most predictable. "Don't waste your time and mine," he was reported to have said. "You might start off all right, but then you'll just get married, have children, give up what I spent years training you to do well. I could have been training someone who would go the course."

From this initial attack on her for wasting his time, he is reported to have gone on to show sympathy for her inevitable emotional crisis. "And if you do make it as a surgeon and you don't have time for normal things like marriage, you'll wind up blaming that on your career as a surgeon. Even if you do marry but can't find the time for children, you'll blame that on your career as a surgeon, too. Any way you look at it, you'll never be satisfied with the life you've persuaded yourself you can manage."

I had been told of surgeons who told women bluntly, "The natural characteristics of a good surgeon are not those women assume naturally. Women are just not aggressive, competitive, assertive, risk-taking. You women are not willing to give every waking hour and most of your dream time to surgery, become obsessive, even seriously obsessive, with surgery. You don't naturally take charge of a situation. You certainly don't take charge when it's a lot of aggressive, competitive men that have to be bent to your will. Most women don't even have the physical stamina required for the job. Sometimes you need plain physical stamina to get you through. These are the things you need as a surgeon."

After this recital of feminine limitations, the surgeon was reported to have traced the applicant's inevitable conflict in trying to surmount these God-given boundaries. "When a woman develops some of these characteristics, she usually hates it. At least her boyfriend hates it. She winds up blaming surgery for the loss of her natural feminine qualities. And the boyfriend. If she's smart, she gets out before that happens. My advice, and I give it to all women, is to get into a specialty where your natural instincts work for you, not against you."

There were more such stories, variations on the theme, different yet the same. They circulated freely, sort of like a flu bug. After a while you didn't think about whether they were strictly true or not. It didn't matter. The message was just there, warning you off even before you had decided to make the attempt. They made you hesitate and wonder if you ran the risk of such a put-down if you tried to talk about your interest in surgery as a career. The most disturbing aspect of the possible rebuff was that it would be delivered as if it were all in your best interest. The person warning you off, shutting the door in your face, would be using your "feminine" nature as justification. He would turn it into a case of you against you. But then, that got him free of all responsibility for a system that believed it had a right to exclude women, regardless of ability or interest.

Sometime later I sat down and read carefully the studies and the personal experiences of other women who became surgeons, or were rebuffed in their attempts, or caved in under pressure. These weren't just stories, things second-year students used to frighten themselves with. These were history. History proved the stories were pretty much on the mark. I had to call them more variations on the same theme. They helped explain the numbers I kept coming back to, the less than 3 percent of practicing surgeons who were women. Or should I have been saying, surgeons and also women? What were these women like? How did they differ from all the vast majority? What had kept them going? What gains, what losses?

I decided I would find out something about surgery. I wasn't tempting myself with forbidden fruit. Whether or not I would be unofficially but no less effectively discouraged from considering a career in surgery, I would have to learn it anyway. We were scheduled for at least sixteen weeks of surgical clerkships during the next two years. And if you liked that a lot, you had a choice of adding anywhere up to sixteen weeks more as an elective in the last academic year. But would I want to do all that work only to hang out in a vestibule when there was little chance of getting in the door? Getting in that professional door meant persuading some senior faculty surgeon that you were a good risk, really meant it when you said you were will-ing to sacrifice everything for his approval—and one of those rare openings in surgical residency.

My first impression (and this has stood the test of time) was that surgery was all-encompassing. Not just slice and su-ture and good-bye, nice to know you, but total submersion in patients, each one a unique world with its own beginning, middle, and—not end, but continuing care. I was embarrassed to discover that in my imagination surgery was more or less crisis-oriented. I held the common belief that the real essence of surgery came in those moments of high drama, with every-thing focused on the light-flooded operating table and the breathtaking procedure. And then the curtain came down at the end to resounding cheers and applause.

I had a good deal to learn—and to unlearn. I began to squeeze hours out of my necessary class work and study time to get some grasp of the dimensions of this new world. I took hours, then days, off from my prescribed schedule. I did not feel guilty or even that I was losing precious time. The hours I spent pouring over surgery texts, case studies, and patient management problems were not just teaching me something about clinical surgery. I knew I could not spend enough time to begin to understand the complexities of that. What was happening was that the descriptions of surgical patients and their care were bringing to life everything I had learned so far about medicine. Gross anatomy was not just something in which you held your nose and suffered through and memo-rized. Pathophysiology was more than the infinitely possible

malfunctions of a body system in disease. Things I had struggled for years to understand were finally coming together in a
meaningful pattern. Straight facts were becoming critical parts
of cause-and-effect relationships. Instead of paragraphs in a
textbook, I was seeing patients in need needing what those
paragraphs had taught me. I was surprised to see how useful
knowledge might be after all. It was about time.

The lecture was a kind of orientation session to general surgery, but because it was being given by the chief of surgery
himself, the room was crowded with students. None of us
knew Dr. Hall well, none of us had attended his usual lectures,
none of us undergraduates ever worked directly under him. He
was considered kindly and gentlemanly, and certainly his voice
was friendly enough as he began. Deceptively so, for it did little to prepare you for the slow transformation of what we all
thought would be a routine pitch by a department head for the
terrific wares his department had to offer. We had been exposed to such talks before.

He surprised us all. Within minutes he was not describing
surgery but was showing us the mind—and the soul—of someone who had lived it most of his adult life. He said, simply, almost casually, that he would try to let each of us see with his
eyes, feel with his hands, anticipate the next move and the
next with all the concern and anxiety he freely admitted to ex-
periencing even after all these decades. He invited us, encouraged us, to be there with him. Then, because he was a great
teacher, he said he wanted to challenge every one of us to think
with our minds, let those thoughts guide our hands, not following his but leading on their own. I felt the reality of the
scene he sketched so vividly I stiffened, withdrawing, afraid of
the trust and responsibility he had just placed in me.

Then, with the spell he had woven unbroken, he was gone
from the podium and walking among us, up and down the

aisles, calling out questions to students still too taken by surprise to answer. He meant to let us know that getting into his mind, under his skin, was no idle figure of speech. He had extended the invitation, and he wanted to hear from someone courteous enough to respond, if you please. He had a typical patient in the waiting room and wanted someone to tell him what to do about it.

I probably had blocked out his progress up the aisle toward my seat, but now there was no avoiding his outstretched hand and pointing finger. When he saw my dismay, his hand relaxed, the finger curved from its demanding position. With his whole hand he made a coaxing gesture, as though that would be more effective in drawing the answer from me. He did this once, twice, an expectant look on his face.

I should make some answer, I thought. I have to answer. But answer to what? Had I missed everything, blanked out everything that he had been asking? Why could I not pry loose from my mind the words he had just spoken, words and sentences he had in fact been repeating, with changes, elaborating descriptions, adding clues and hints, filling out the question and simplifying it and making it more accessible.

Then I gave up, relaxed, released the frantic, grasping conscious mind from its fruitless effort to remember, set it free, let it find its own way, unhampered by my anxiety. The question in all its changed parts, and the answers as well, were either there or not. They would not come if I stood in the way. I would just have to absent myself, get out of their way.

I think I spoke almost in rhythm with the gentle movement of his moving hand. I heard myself speaking, at a distance, but clearly enough. The question, really all the questions, had to do with a young man who had come to the emergency room with right lower quadrant abdominal pain.

What would I do? I knew that at the very least I would have to make a diagnosis.

Dr. Hall admitted this was a promising start. But on what basis could I do that? I said I would have to have the patient's history before the diagnosis. He looked at me and then around the room, as if to suggest that I had much to learn.

"And what would a typical patient, a typical young male patient, tell you about the vague abdominal pain that had gotten him out of bed and off to the emergency room?"

I hesitated, but even this seemed appropriate.

"Not want to tell you much," Dr. Hall said. "How do you deal with that possibility, that inevitability?"

I knew the answer to this. I would have a line of questions to ask the patient.

"Such as?" Dr. Hall shot back to see if I had read beyond that in the general surgery textbook. He smiled when everything I remembered poured out in a rush. I would ask when the pain started and where it had started and if it was still in the same place or had it moved and what was it like, this pain.

Immediately Dr. Hall stopped me, his hand up like a traffic cop. "Maybe the young man is not the descriptive type, maybe he is just typical and doesn't want to talk about it much, feeling a bit embarrassed being in the ER to begin with, and maybe worse being confronted with a woman surgeon."

I replied that I would give him a simple scale, one to ten, and ask him to rate the pain. I didn't add that it was not unreasonable for me to expect even a typical male to be able to count to ten.

"And if he rates himself at about a number eight?" Dr. Hall asked, and I wasn't too sure what to say but avoided this by saying I would ask if the pain was sharp or dull or got worse with eating.

"Is this patient likely to have an appetite?"

I had to think but remembered that that was not likely under the circumstances.

Dr. Hall gave me a moment, looking around the room to

see how his exercise was going over, encountering gratified looks from everyone who wasn't having to come up with the immediate answers.

I must have let my attention wander until his repeated "Next?" broke through.

Next? What's next? And before I had tracked the memory down, I heard myself say, "I would palpate the area."

"Just any old place in the area?" he followed up quickly, with a trace of mockery in his voice.

"I would begin at the umbilicus," I said, not totally undermined by his tone.

"Good start. Then what?"

I hesitated, then took the leap. "I would palpate the right lower quadrant."

A look of real disappointment flashed over his face. I felt at that moment that he did not want me to fail him, so I mumbled something about upper left quadrant.

He finished for me. "Because the upper left is as far away from the right lower quadrant as anatomy permits, starting to palpate the upper left is the thing to do."

He began to walk away, then turned back to me one more time and smiled, saying in something like a conspiratorial tone of voice, "That's what you meant to do, isn't it? That's what you'll remember to do, provided you remember to do the inspection first, then auscultation, then palpation. Don't mix them up."

I of course said nothing, and he walked back to the podium and made a few wrap-up comments. I tried to concentrate on these but could not. I felt uncomfortable. It was not just that I had not answered all the questions or answered them as fully as possible. I wasn't certain I should have spoken up at all. I couldn't explain what I was feeling if I had been asked. But nobody did ask. Not even those who had looked at me with only slightly disguised skepticism—or was it distrust?—while Dr. Hall was questioning me. The now-remembered looks troubled me. I didn't want anyone to think I had snatched at a chance to impress the chief of surgery. He wouldn't be impressed by a half-remembered case history. I also knew what any of my efforts to impress him would mean. Not much. I had read the evidence. I had looked it all up and knew what to expect.

The session had come to an end, but I did not notice until people began to press past me and I had to retrieve my bag from under my seat and get my things together. Dr. Hall was standing just outside the room talking with a student. He reached out and signaled for me to wait as he finished his conversation. When the other student left and we were alone for a moment he said with a slight nod of his head, perhaps as a way of apologizing, "Didn't mean to put you on the spot. But you got it right. Mostly."

"I should have remembered all of it," I replied.

"And you did. When you heard it again. In most cases that's not good enough. You have to learn to prompt yourself. In advance of the problem. But in the beginning at least someone will be around to keep you out of serious trouble."

I must have given him a look of total incomprehension because he broke out into a laugh and said, "You must know your chances of getting into serious trouble are big. Very big. Young lady surgical students like you are in trouble most of the time."

"But I'm not—" I began, but he had already begun to walk down the corridor. He did not stop but just partially turned his head, just a half look over his shoulder.

"Of course you are," he said.

CHAPTER 17

It was early in the morning. It was early in the New Year. The snow was whirling around outside the Toyota's window. Things were whirling around inside my head. I had been in a whirlwind for some time now. I couldn't tell if I was so disoriented because of the length of the storm or because of its intensity. I hadn't learned how to cope with the everyday whirlwind—orders to fill, blood to draw, lines to put in, lines to take out, new patients to interview, old patients to evaluate, reports to file—and today would bring more of the same. It was barely 6 A.M., a morning just after New Year's Day. How could I last out the year if I felt so blown about and up in the air this early?

I was a third-year medical student, halfway into the year. I would have to be ready for first teaching rounds by six-thirty.

To do this I would have to begin about six, checking up on patients, changing dressings, finding out what had happened during the night. With luck, by six-thirty I would be ready to trail from patient room to patient room, following the senior resident, the attending physician, those really in the know and about to let us know it, mainly by pointing out what we didn't know. Questions would be coming at me and at the other students as fast as the snow smacking up against the windshield, obscuring my view of the traffic light. If I couldn't see the light I could not practice my intuition. I would not be able to check the correspondence between my inner certainty that the light would or would not change just as I approached it and the light's actual behavior. I practiced my intuition on anything conveniently at hand. Sometimes I used the elevator. Which one will come first, left or right? Later I would practice on my beeper. Don't look at the number of the caller, check within first. And when the telephone rings . . . Who is calling and why?

I wasn't being swept away with experiments in the paranormal. I probably had by now pretty much gauged just how many light changes there had been before all the cars in front of me crept through the intersection. I had probably unconsciously registered when the elevator on the left made one of its infrequent visits to the floor where I happened to be waiting. I probably already knew how delayed its return would be because of the time of day and the traffic in and out of the hospital. (I sometimes wondered if the elevator cars also wandered off horizontally, but could not confirm this speculation.)

I was making educated guesses, and I was also training myself to value the unrecognized clues on which such guesses could be based. A guess could turn into a guide. I would need every possible one I could summon in managing the patients I now had under my care. I would need every guide for the unexpected course my life had suddenly taken.

*   *   *

When the six-thirty rounds got started I would have to be ready to answer any questions that came my way. I had not yet perfected my intuition to the point where I knew what would be coming. I had already learned that answering questions about a living, breathing patient, somebody, that body right there within arm's reach, was worlds apart from answering a question about a case in a textbook. For one thing, this real patient's problems, and the solutions to them, did not always match up exactly with what the patient in the text-book had. The answer to the problem in the book was usually unambiguous, based on consensus, straightforward. When pa-tient so-and-so has such and such, you did that and that, and sometimes even that. That was how it was done. It worked. Do it again.

Except not always on teaching rounds. What worked was what the man in charge, the one waiting for your answer, said worked. That was often enough some major variation on what you were at the moment frantically trying to remember from the book. Of course you could not doubt, but had to credit, the man's approach, worked out over years of experience with patients. You also had to remember the variation if you wanted to avoid a public dressing-down for your obtuseness and the stubborn determination to resist any effort to pry open the sealed mind you had just shown. You had to keep the lines open between you and the senior people, you couldn't risk be-ing tagged uncooperative. Sometimes that meant forgetting to cooperate with the way he wanted you to do things.

You had begun to learn that there was nothing like the pure and abstract practice of medicine. That was in the books; in real life there were just persons, medical persons, senior medical persons. It was best to remain on the best side of all such senior persons. The personal was the element you had to swim in or else decide to get out of the pool.

*   *   *

Rounds were over and we had missed breakfast, which ended at ten, so we had to rush off to implement orders given earlier and forget about eating until lunch. There would not be a break, and if one or the other of us worried about passing out from hunger we would resort to the usual practice, lifting one of the vitamin-fortified drinks meant for the patients. Not exactly from bedside, mind you, but from an obliging nurse.

I wasn't going to join the others in the cafeteria. Lunch or not, the break would have nothing to distinguish it from the hours that went before and the hours that were coming up. As usual, I didn't have an appetite, and the cafeteria was not the place to find one. So even if I found a telephone not located smack in the middle of the overcrowded waiting room, even if I had the patience to wait out the line of people with less-important messages than mine, people who could just as well wait for tomorrow or write a letter, even if I eventually made the call, was lucky enough to catch him before he left for classes, even if I got through and we talked as long as we could—if any or all of this happened and we exchanged a few words and then I ran back to the cafeteria for a last chance at something to eat, when I got there they would still be at it, despondently stirring empty coffee cups and nervously twisting sandwich wrappings.

And they were, chewing over the disasters that had occurred during rounds at the bedside of a patient whose gallbladder had been removed and who was running a fever. They chewed on all their delayed or wrong answers as if each was another piece of indigestible gristle they could neither swallow nor spit out. This way everyone would remember that the next time a postop patient runs a fever you do not order two Tylenol and go to sleep for the rest of the night. What you do is take off the dressing and inspect the wound and if it is red around the edge, showing signs of infection, you do a Gram's stain to identify the organisms (or bugs, or bacteria) and order antibiotics to kill or slow the growth of the organisms identified by the Gram's stain.

What was the most likely pathogen involved in this kind of infection? the attending physician had demanded. The silence was deafening, embarrassing, until he answered himself with a booming "Clostridium! Like the *Clostridium botulinum* you pick up hanging around the cafeteria all day." And then everyone remembered and nodded in agreement. The attending physician was not mollified. The interrogation was not over, for sure, and so he wanted to know what would be the next threat to the patient's life and your future as a medical student? We shuffled and shied, pretending to consider the question seriously. Someone ventured a very tentative, "Cholangitis?" The silence with which this was greeted proved it was a false move. Indeed it was: With great disgust the attending physician explained the obvious to us. Cholangitis, which in any case does not show up until seven to ten days postop, if at all, would be responsible for the fever if the bile duct had been inadvertently tied or injured.

Carried away by his own theatrics, the attending physician looked us over with mocking disbelief, a scrutiny we cringed from. A dramatic pause, and then he was off. Had he not gotten out of bed before dawn on the assumption that he would be questioning a group of advanced students? Had he mistaken us for those hardworking, dedicated, informed drudges? Had we just happened by on the way to some more demanding group activity—a game of checkers, perhaps? He would apologize for assuming that if we were up this early ("You are all up?") then we had some interest, however marginal, in patient care. Or were we brazen trespassers, molesting the sick and the infirm? Should security be summoned?

He probably had been doing a similar routine for years. He

knew when to cut it short. He did and then began to guide us to a more likely diagnosis and more reasonable approach to treatment. What you do with a postop gallbladder surgery patient with a spanking-new fever—and here he paused for a split second before delivering what he must have considered the punch line—you make the patient cough. Another split second to wait for our reaction, and then in a voice of pure reason he finished up.

"No, this is not a reversion to some simple era of naturalistic remedies. You make the patient cough to clear his lungs. The patient has not been able to cough. Bronchial secretions have accumulated. The patient has obstructive atelectasis. . . ."

He stopped short. He must have seen the ducked heads, averted glances, heard the shuffle of feet. He narrowed his eyes. We were not going to put this one over on him. He called out, "What is atelectasis? Anyone? Everyone?" He gave up. He raised his hand as if it held a baton and we were to get ready for the downbeat. He said, "All at once, after me: Atelectasis is airlessness of the lungs due to failure of expansion or reabsorption of air. When you see it in newborns you're in deep trouble. And so is the baby, if it isn't stillborn already. You also see it in postoperative patients. The patient has a fever, which can be caused by atelectasis. At least it could when I was in medical school. The patient will most likely recover from both if you get him to cough and clear his lungs. Now, isn't that simple and logical?"

I was more or less listening to the rehash of all this, maybe more interested in the sudden revival of my flagging appetite, although there was nothing novel enough on my tray to stimulate even mild activity of the salivary glands. It seems I was wedded to tuna on white for the duration. I was monogamous that way. I munched indifferently, paying more attention to the way the physician's sarcastic remarks were being repeated verbatim, not in ridicule but just as solemnly as his directives on early-warning signs of real wound infection and treatment options were being repeated.

We were all unconsciously memorizing his style as well as the content of the interrogation. I did not like to think about it, but intimidation, abuse, humiliation, even as transparently play-acted as in this encounter, are easily impressed on the mind. They can be retained, then imitated. I think you can even do it unconsciously, the way you can pick up people's speech patterns just by being around them, without really intending to.

What the doctor had shown us was an old act he had in all probability watched long ago with the same kind of fear and insecurity we had felt. He was just passing on the notion that medicine is an intimidating pursuit and we had better know what we were about before we attempted it. He was telling us we would be weeded out soon enough if we couldn't cut it. He wanted us to know we would be lucky if we made it, or if they let any of us make it. It was all in a noble cause. But I could not help wondering, What's the relationship between nobility and intimidation? Should there be one?

My appetite had come back because I had found a telephone somewhat out of the main traffic. It was in use, but then the woman ran out of change and had to hang up and it was my turn. I didn't pity her. If her call was really important she should have filled her pockets with coins. He answered and I recognized his voice, but I said his name anyway, just to hear it out loud. I heard him say yes, but it sounded uncertain, as if he was not committing himself. It may have been a poor connection. He had to have been expecting my call, so I could not really explain the hesitation and question. I felt myself beginning to blush.

Then it seemed to all come back to him and he was remembering it all. The party, people and noises and music everywhere. Interrupted conversation. Something that did not get put into words. We tried to make arrangements to meet. There were complications. He had to be there, I had to be here. Different schedules. Tight schedules. But it was all settled before my coin ran out. I could have spared some change for that poor lady who had to hang up. But I didn't feel bad. I felt marvelous. We would meet again. We might even have a first chance to be alone together. It would not be too far off, even considering his schedule and mine. It would be later in the week. This week. But still days off. I walked away from the telephone promising not to count the hours. I would just take it day by day.

We had met a week before at a Christmas party in his house in the suburbs. I was introduced but don't think he noticed. He was the host and was busy greeting people all around, sending them off this way and that, directing them to drinks and food. And I just slipped by. There were a lot of people, a lot of music. Friends of mine had insisted I go with them, even though I said I would not know a soul. And as for striking up small talk—by this time in my life I thought all I would be able to talk about was medicine and patients and procedures. Not very sophisticated conversation for a Christmas party in an elegant suburb, but every minute had to count. There was always a chance you could pick up some interesting, useful information even in casual conversation. I was terrified that if my friends went off to talk to people they already knew, then I would just hide in a corner and be silent until they took me home again.

It didn't turn out that way. They had gone off, and I was left alone looking at the huge decorated tree. But before I lost interest in this, he came up and was introducing himself. I had not been able to catch his name when we first arrived, stunned by the noise and chatter and music that came at us when he opened the front door. I hadn't planned on coming in the first place, so I paid no attention when my friends talked about the party.

"We've met," I said.

He looked uncertain. "Law?" he asked.

"Medicine," I said.

"Interesting."

I assumed he wanted to know if I found it interesting. Or perhaps he thought it interesting that I should be in medicine. I couldn't tell from his look, which didn't seem to have much relationship to the question. "Yes," I answered. "Is law?"

"Yes . . . well, sort of. My parents' idea. Yours?"

"It started out mine. But they love the idea."

"That's convenient."

"Yes, since they made it possible."

"Pay the fare?"

"No. Just cosigned the loans."

That left him with nothing to say, and I could not interpret the slightly embarrassed look he showed. Someone came up to him then and pulled him aside a bit and seemed to be asking some serious or at least complicated questions. The guy was not letting him go, so he turned to me and said, "Have to go for a minute. I'm the host." He reminded me and then he left.

The host's problems could not have been that complicated because he was back before I had exhausted the Christmas tree's possibilities. "I decorated it. Do it every year," he said with some pride.

"It's really beautiful," I admitted happily.

"I'm Nigerian. It's a British tradition. The tree. We always had one."

"You're from Nigeria. You study law here. In the States." I don't know exactly why I said that. I could have been taking down a patient's history. He didn't seem to mind the dumb echo and nodded in agreement. "Not British, I know."

"What does that mean?" I asked, finding it difficult to follow his abbreviated style. I did remember that Nigeria used to be under British control. "It means I won't make an acceptable lawyer in Nigeria, knowing only American law. It's British law that still rules there. Did you ever sing 'Rule Britannia!'?"

"I'm from Haiti originally."

"Something French, then? 'The Marseillaise'?"

"I'm an American citizen," I answered, amused by his nonsense and somewhat surprised that I was following his lead so effortlessly. There hadn't been much chance for purely nonsensical conversation in my life recently.

"There's got to be something we can sing together." He put a kind of exaggerated petulant schoolboy complaint in his statement, and I found that even more amusing.

"I think 'Silent Night' is always traditional at Christmas."

"Can we go off someplace silent then and do the traditional thing?"

"Go off? You are the host, aren't you?" I asked. He swept an arm around the room and let it drop lightly on my shoulder for a moment. "Who remembers that?" he asked.

The answer appeared immediately. She was perfectly matched to his tall and lean good looks. She matched his incredibly rich and deep color, matched the slightly feline way he moved. She claimed him at once, hardly bothering to excuse the appropriation, not giving a second's thought to the possibility that I might have any legitimate reason for detaining him. She took his arm, and he acquiesced, going and looking back at me and gesturing with his free hand. It took me some time to interpret that gesture. It seemed to offer several possible readings. I mulled over some of the more favorable. He was asking me to excuse the intrusion, don't hold it against him, wait for his return, stay, not exactly stay put there under the fir boughs all hung with tinsel, but stay somewhere.

He never did make it back to the Christmas tree, but I made small talk out of it for a while with anyone who came by.

Then I drifted around, pretending to be interested in some groups' talk, saying a few words that might or might not have been noticed. Nothing like watching a large group of friends and strangers trading life secrets to get you to reflect on how isolated and limited your world has become.

He was moving from one small knot of people to another, the young woman sometimes leading, sometimes following, him. She always stayed close. They managed to keep their distance from me. The rooms were very crowded, there were people sitting on most of the steps of the wide staircase that led to the second floor. Every once in a while a couple would wind their way up the stairs, through those sitting, excusing themselves, trying not to separate those sitting close together or knock over glasses.

It took a long time, but finally those of us who had come in the same car felt we could no longer resist the inevitable. The 6:30 A.M. rounds were moving inexorably closer, and we would have to be present, even if we would not be able to give much of an accounting for ourselves.

The last scene was straight out of one of those very old-fashioned movies I used to watch when I first came to America, watch and half understand, catching some of the words but reading the emotional undercurrent in the eyes and gestures of the hero and heroine. He had taken up the host's position by the front door, ready to open it when we had gotten ourselves together. Everyone was talking at once, but then we were face-to-face. Taking my hand to shake it in a formal good-bye, but talking to the group in general, distracting them with this maneuver, he managed to slip the paper into my hand as he opened the door for the group.

"Sorry," he said. I think that was meant for me, but he released my hand and went on, again speaking to all of us as we huddled outside, letting in the cold. "Sorry you medical drudges have to ruin my party, but give us a call. Promise?

There will still be time to sing 'Silent Night' before the tree sheds."

I could not read the note until I had been dropped off at my place. It was his phone number and his name, Chima. I imagined he had jotted down his name because he did not want me to wonder whose number this was amid all the others piled up on my desk. He might have wanted me to know what I was doing if I decided to throw it away unused.

CHAPTER 18

I tried looking the word up, but it wasn't in the medical dictionary. Everyone around the hospital, especially medical students, used the word frequently, casually, usually with some disgust, so I assumed it had to be medical. It was one of those words whose meaning you thought you knew simply because you heard it so often and had begun to use it yourself. I tried my English dictionary, so beat up and stained it looked as though someone had rummaged through it for years. Every stain, every crease and torn page looked familiar, told a little tale of its own. My own guide to America. Some pages floated loose as I searched through the S's. And there it was: scut. But the definition didn't throw any light on my situation. I read:

"Scut, the short, erect tail of an animal, as a rabbit. Or hare." (I looked up the difference, but that contributed nothing.) The entry went on to add: "Scut, slang, a contemptible fellow." This sounded rather quaint and old-fashioned to me. I've heard contemptible fellows (and girls) called many things. I didn't recall ever hearing someone shout, "You miserable scut!" Scut impressed me as very ineffectual in this context.

Scut as in "scut work" was not explained. I would have to draw my own conclusions and make whatever logical connections I could between what the dictionary defined and what we medical students complained about having to do on an hourly, daily, sometimes nightly basis.

Scut work was, in the opinion of senior medical students, all the hundreds of trivial, demeaning tasks that thousands of hours of medical education left you too overqualified to be asked to perform. Scut work, for example, was having to leap up and out when your intern or senior resident asked you to get a microdrip IV tubing and a catheter. Scut work was hurrying to Supplies, finding the right shelf, finding the right packages of tubing, the right catheter, and then puzzling over which of the several numbered sizes, what gauge catheter, would be the right ones for the procedure the intern was going to perform—and in the process demonstrate to you how to perform it when the occasion arose. The occasion for you to do the procedure, you anticipated with dread, might be the very next time the procedure had to be performed when you were on night call. With your luck it would be sooner than later that very night.

You might have begun your trip to Supplies feeling your vast hoard of medical information placed you above such menial work. Your fumbling and indecision, however, gave you the sinking feeling that you might not yet be ready even for this kind of work. Scut work: The dictionary definition sounded loud in the silent room with all its meticulously wrapped and

categorized supplies. You had better move like a rabbit, showing that little uplifted tail in haste, as rabbits in panic do, if you
were going to get through this night and all the others without
incurring the justifiable wrath of the intern who has a suffering, impatient patient on his hands.

And if you begin thinking for a moment that this work is
indeed a dictionary definition of contemptible, beneath you,
you might soon find out that the intern or resident has serious doubts that you are up to the demands of even that kind
of work.

So eventually you return, late, with something not appropriate, a cause of further delay in caring for the patient. The
look of wearied disgust on the intern's face convinces you that
even scut work is something that has to be learned before it
can be dismissed as irrelevant to a person of your intellectual
achievements. The most humbling part of all such humbling
experiences was realizing how little it took to prove you had
only begun to learn. If you were so smart, how come you
had not recognized that? It seemed that you were always a beginner and to pretend otherwise was to cling to a pride that
could and usually would be deflated by the most trivial event.
You cried a lot out of sheer frustration with your own limitations. Then you cried when you realized that you still had not
accepted the inevitability of limitations, limitations in everything we are or attempt.

I was lucky to have Ian Beaumont as my resident in those
first nights on call. He even came with what we both soon
called some fringe benefits. For one thing, he was about the
only male who was more or less at my eye level. I found this
permitted an unfamiliar view of one's fellow creatures, and he
allowed the same. In both our experiences, we found that most
male students, interns, residents, and attending physicians,
even some of the females, looked as if they had trained first on
the basketball courts, for height, and then on the football
fields, for breadth. I believed him when he said it was a relief

not to have to crane his neck to take or give an order, not to find his calves aching because he had been unconsciously standing on his toes to try to look over or sometimes around the larger bodies gathered at a patient's beside during teaching rounds.

He was also slender, still looking like a teen not fully grown into his older brother's hand-me-down white coat. He told me it was a real pleasure to have someone evenly matched with him in size and strength, especially when faced with so simple a challenge as rolling over in bed a large and unresponsive patient. The conflict he felt on such occasions in the past when he had to call one of the heavies, as he described most of the males in the place, had nothing to do with pride. He had no illusions that anybody ever mistook him for anything else but a ninety-eight-pound weakling, and he never shied from calling for help. The problem was that the big guy almost automatically, if not intentionally or literally, shoved him aside, did most of the work, not letting him contribute his fair share. His share wasn't up to Olympic weight-lifting grade, but it was a share and should have been acknowledged. Ian said he would feel the patient's weight moving just ahead of his hand but knew he was adding nothing to the body's movement. He said he used to reason with himself—he corrected this quickly to console himself—by repeating, "This is not a weight-lifting competition. It's all about knowing and caring, and turning the patient so that he doesn't develop a bedsore, given this body weight."

I knew he would not have had to say that if he had not been affected in some way by the implied rejection. Medical students competed on many different levels. Males might do it on more levels than females, although females did not lag too far behind, I came to find out. Ian knew the levels where he could not compete. He also knew it was never easy to concede the contest, not even when you knew there was nothing worth fighting for.

With me it was more cooperation than competition. That didn't reduce the strain we both felt when we took on jobs whose sheer physical demands called for a heave. Sometimes we even gave in and called for help. But more often than not, working with Ian turned the most ordinary jobs into something they often weren't but always could have been— occasions for sharing, not competing. Sharing was what Ian did better than most. He was world-class at that.

I was concentrating as best I could, but my mind kept jumping ahead to when I would be free for the evening. When would I be free? How many hours were left? And if anything delayed me, what then? Anything could delay me, everything would. Of course I trusted him to wait. Why shouldn't I? He had said he would be free. But how long would he wait? And what if he waited until just seconds before I appeared like a crazy thing, rushing out the door only to find the place where he had sat in his car and waited all that time empty now. How would I know if he had waited at all, or even come in the first place? And if he had come and waited and then gone away, why would he ever come back? He'd have missed me by seconds and would not have seen how I ran out to meet him, only to find the street empty.

Ian had noticed my momentary lapses of attention, and it caused a look of concern to come over his face as we went from patient to patient. He's wondering why I look as if I'm not taking it all in, I thought. He keeps turning to me as if he would like to answer any question or explain anything over again if I had any doubts. He's wondering why I don't have a question. I would like to ask him a question, but I can't think of anything about the last patient that I could ask him about or that he didn't explain. That must mean I was not concentrating on the patient as much as I should have been. There is always something more to find out than you can ask.

Ian had another and more obvious reason to be wary of my behavior that evening. I had been putting in an IV line. I was new at this, and I was afraid and cautious. But I had to admit that I was cautious not only because I was concerned with harming the patient. I was cautious because I was afraid I would fail what was one more of the endless tests I was now being subjected to. It wasn't the risk of causing the patient pain that made me hesitate. It was embarrassment that I would be found out not getting the needle into the vein correctly.

In those nights of first contact with patients, I was distressed to discover that protecting my ego was as important as serving the patient's need. And everything at first seemed like a direct challenge to my ego, that part of me that had mastered all the abstract concepts in all the medical textbooks. I didn't think there would be a gap between the abstract and the human being waiting for me to do something, something that was as likely to bring discomfort as relief.

Like most people I had a kind of visceral response to the idea of putting a piece of sharpened metal into living flesh. I expected that to inhibit me. But I had seen lines inserted, injections given. I had seen flesh probed. I had even gotten over wincing and feeling the tightening in my chest. I had been instructed in how to do it so that it caused the least discomfort to the patient. I was expected to be able to do it. The principle was simple: See one, do one. Then you were ready to go on and teach one. Trust yourself, get out of your own way. Do it fast, do it painlessly. What looks like coldness is really compassion.

But in spite of this I was full of tension, coiled up and defensive, protecting myself by letting my mind see the picture that traced the route of the needle into the vein. I began pushing the needle slowly, cautiously into the parchment-thin, almost translucent flesh of the elderly woman's arm. Her eyes

were shut tight. I was concentrating so that I would not hear
her sudden intakes of astonished breath filling the interminable seconds. I was doing the procedure correctly, but correctly only from my point of view. I wasn't going to make a
mistake. I was sure I hadn't.

When it was done and I was pressing the alcohol swab on
the wound, she opened her eyes and smiled at me. She said, "I
wouldn't like to have to do that." Her fragile fingers touched
my arm for a second, a touch so light I had to imagine the
pressure with which she tried to reassure me. But it was there,
if more in spirit than in flesh.

"I know you don't like it, either," she whispered, as if we
were in some kind of conspiracy and no one else should hear
this fact.

"I didn't mean to . . . I hope I didn't hurt you," I managed to
stammer. "I won't hold what you didn't mean against you," she
said in the same kind of slightly conspiratorial whisper. "Nobody will. Nobody should."

There were other patients to see. We had been moving side by
side in unaccustomed silence. Ian had not said anything about
how I had given the needle. But when he finally began I heard
the changed tone in his voice, and it alerted me instantly. He
was filling me in on the next patient, who had just been moved
to the floor from the emergency room. I was going to have to
be with Ian totally now, no matter where my head had been
earlier in our work.

"This one won't be a snap. So far it looks like acute pancreatitis, but we can't be sure until everything's checked out. Call
it acute abdomen. We know him. One of these days it's going
to be chronic. You'll get used to seeing him if you're around for
long. Like the book says, it's alcoholism in most cases. He's a
case. But he was in real pain, the pain of subacute, probably
not really full-blown acute pancreatitis, but that wouldn't have

made any difference to him. Said it felt like someone was drilling right though the middle of his belly, right through his guts and into the back wall. Classic case. Abdominal pain you could die from, sweating, rapid pulse, panic, can't breathe, fever, nausea, vomiting. And pain. No way he could twist or turn or sit or stand to escape it. No warning, he said. . . . He forgot the last time."

Ian's voice dropped, and he reached out to stop me. We were outside the room now, at the half-opened door. He pulled me away so that nothing of this could be heard beyond the tight pair we made. He was speaking now as if what he was saying was not for the patient's record but for my own benefit, enlightenment, some important part of the learning experience that I would need on some personal level but would not be tested on.

"They already took the history, so don't waste time on that. Don't ask him questions. He's likely to be embarrassed talking about it, think you're too young for his history. He thinks his life is likely to shock you. Don't be surprised. He thinks you should be spared the details even if you're running around in a white coat. He even tried to spare me at first. He's young himself, not even forty. You'll see. He's messing himself up thoroughly, been doing a thorough job of it, but he can still think about how you'll take it. You should remember that when you talk to patients like this. They worry that you'll think as little of them as they themselves do. Maybe you can let him know that's a mistake."

Ian stopped for a moment and looked at me to see if I was getting the whole picture. "Remember what it said about pancreatitis?" I flipped wildly through my mental card catalog, racing down the alphabet to the letter "P." He watched me, figuring out that I would sooner or later call up most of what I had found in the textbooks. It wasn't an uncommon disease. It was especially common in alcoholic men. If I knew anything at all about the inner-city population this hospital was serving, I should have gathered by now that men with alcoholic disease were no rarity. Ian wanted to know if I had a realistic idea of the population I would be dealing with. He thought that was as important as knowing about pancreatitis. He was telling me again that I was at one of those crossroads where facts and people intersected.

I began in some disjointed fashion, first echoing what the book said about clinical signs, going on about diagnosis, tests that should be done to support a suspicion of pancreatitis but won't be diagnostic of the disease, films to detect abnormalities of the abdomen, treatment options . . . I ran out of steam. His still unsatisfied look was clearly saying we know all that, so then what? His eyes challenged me to answer.

"He should have a nasogastric tube, central venous pressure line, and a catheter to monitor cardiac function . . . and . . . fluid replacement. . . ."

I faltered again, and now Ian picked up the recitation. "Up to eight liters a day. Vital signs monitored hourly. More often. Arterial blood gases. Urine output. Electrolyte assessment. Then there's the risk of infection, respiratory distress, renal failure, cardiac failure, stress ulcer . . ."

Now it was his turn to falter and let his voice fade away. I wanted to hug him right then and there. Instead I said, "All that. And the patient is too embarrassed to even talk to an idealistic, immature, uninformed young person like me."

He hung his head in mock despondency for a second and then shrugged his shoulders. He held his hands out and turned his palms over, showing me he had nothing left to add. But he did sneak in, "All that, and terrible diarrhea, too. Really bad. I mean, this is steatorrhea plus."

"Thanks," I said.

"I told you it was a classic case."

"Am I ever going to see this patient?" I asked. "To see him is to serve him," he answered, giving me the true dimension of the case and what the near future held for us both.

"Every hour, on the hour?"

He hesitated, then, very straight and serious, capped that with the only applicable word: "More."

But before he pushed the door open he looked carefully at his watch, as he had seen me do over the last several hours, and said quietly, "If you want to take a break first . . . something like some personal time . . . ?" I couldn't tell him that by then I was certain the street was empty, his shiny car long since gone. And if I missed it by mere seconds, I would never know if it had been there for me at all. I followed Ian into the room.

CHAPTER 19

I saw a movie once, not a feature but a short documentary about the marvels of American industry and manufacturing, something I probably saw when I was in Miami, where I sat glued to the television learning English, learning about my new country. I had never seen anything like the process that unfolded in this film. Inside a great building, an industrial plant, thousands upon thousands of yards of carpeting were being created before our very eyes, carpeting in multicolor patterns, massive rolls of carpets in brilliant flowering patterns.

Complicated devices shuttled back and forth faster than any human hands could, shooting out what seemed like infinite strands of colored yarns that were caught and woven into place on the mesh that would be the foundation of the finished carpet. How amazing that each separate strand of wool was directed to its proper place and no other. Each color found the right place, so that its individual tone could be added to those already bound into the background weave of the carpeting. Each strand added its own tone, a different meaning almost, to those already in place. And there before your eyes, the rose that was the center of each pattern emerged and grew into fullness out of the separate, limited strands that were thrust at the underlying web by the device moving faster than a human hand could, faster than a human mind could control. It was foreordained that the rose would emerge in the carpet's pattern. Each length of yarn had its predestined place and made its necessary contribution to what finally emerged. Nothing was wasted, nothing forgotten, nothing lost. Watching the documentary on how a rose-patterned carpet was made showed how carefully everything could be contrived to contribute to perfection of the whole.

As I approached my final year in medical school, I found myself recalling this image over and over again. I did not have to let my imagination dwell long on it before I saw how I had become the web that began vacant and unworked at first and then was made to receive from all sides strand after strand of individual colors, forcing them together into some meaningful pattern. And I knew I was imagining the daily variations in the rhythms of my life. Each strand was another learning experience, another night on call, another emergency room crisis, another medical problem or challenge that had been thrust upon me to solve.

What I had to learn from each of these new experiences would have to be integrated into what I had already learned and woven into place. With luck, everything would form into a pattern that would adjust and satisfy the needs of yet another patient, another emergency. The only place where the image broke down and did not apply was in regard to predictability. The rose in the carpet was guaranteed to emerge a fully formed rose, barring mechanical mishaps. No such guarantee was likely to emerge for the well-trained physician I thought I was destined to become.

First I had to learn the rituals surrounding each major event in a hospital. Then I had to remember where my place was as each complicated movement unfolded. Code Yellow in the emergency room brought me running, but only as far as the exact spot I had been taught to occupy. A precise choreography had been worked out to save an emergency victim's life. This did not permit any improvisation on the part of a minor player like me, and it would remain this way until I had worked up the intern and residency ladders. I was there to do the medical equivalent of fetching and carrying and was also expected to learn from the pitiful examples, the scarred and broken human bodies stretched out before us all.

Somehow you get things in the right priority, at least as far as your emotions are concerned. If it was my task to insert the large-bore nasogastric tube into the patient, I had to cancel out thoughts of the pain this would cause. I threaded the tube as carefully as possible, but I did not let my hand be stayed or falter because of the shudder the procedure evoked from the patient. I eventually learned how to sidestep the sudden burst of vomit that some patients could not control. I learned how to position myself to save my shoes. I don't think I was becoming calloused. There had not been time enough for me to develop that kind of emotional self-protective armor. Training was teaching me to look ahead, to look past this immediate convulsion. I was beginning to connect the procedure I had to do with something much larger: the success or failure of other procedures still to be done. I was in the process of integrating my work with the work of everyone who would collectively labor to save the patient's life.

The nasogastric tube would contribute to that work. The patient would have to be moved to the OR for exploratory abdominal surgery. That would require anesthesia. Given the hour of the evening when the automobile accident took place, we could assume the victim had eaten. Anesthesia would almost guarantee vomiting and aspiration of food and fluid into the airways. He'd simply choke to death, something I had to help prevent by threading this tube carefully down into his stomach and decompressing it by drawing off fluid and air. It's routine work, something a student standing as precisely as possible in the place allotted her would learn to do extremely well. Every step forward depended for its success on the care with which the previous steps had been executed.

No one guarded the rituals surrounding entry to her domain more fiercely than the operating room scrub nurse. A floundering student got no mercy. Even the student who learned every detail of the ritual was shown scant appreciation. Without discrimination, all were made to feel unwelcome intruders on the territory Mrs. Peacher had guarded and ruled over since, it was rumored, ether was discovered. If you thought being a woman would give you some special claim to Mrs. Peacher's attention, you discovered your mistake soon enough. She was living proof that the instinct to protect territory sprung from stronger roots than the instinct for female bonding. If you made the even graver mistake of assuming you automatically had some claim on Mrs. Peacher because you were both women and black, you would get even less consideration. Mrs. Peacher, from her exalted position, could not imagine a black woman needing special consideration.

I thought that my turn to scrub would come, had to come.

Eventually. Then the minutes ticked by and I began to doubt that initial assumption. Perhaps I would never live to see the surgeon, then the first assistant, then the second, then the senior resident finish each of the prescribed ten-minute scrubbings, scourings. I spent the time craning my neck for a glimpse of how the brushes were being worked over every nail, every digit, every fiber and hair follicle of hand and forearm. Those days of heroic scrub work are largely gone now, replaced by heavy-duty germicides, but no one who has ever seen those old-fashioned marathons is likely to forget the experience.

Mrs. Peacher ministered to each of the scrubbed men in turn, a high priestess in the magic circle of those she considered her equals. When they were all gowned and gloved and masked, I stepped forward, presenting myself to her. One look told me I had already failed. My arms had not been lifted in the prescribed manner, my hands were not properly crossed. I had displayed a dangerous tendency to lean toward, if not actually on, things. I risked contamination of person and place. I might have to be banished back to the sinks. I would have to scrub again. I read it all there in Mrs. Peacher's glowering look.

It was no wonder then that I willingly agreed to banishment to a place distant from the operating table itself. It took only a slight shift of Mrs. Peacher's chin to put me there, not quite out of sight, perhaps not even out of harm's way, but too far to grasp any of the procedure itself. I had reviewed the operation the night before I knew I would be allowed to be present. I would try to follow it step by step in my mind, making up in my imagination what I could not see in reality.

"What do you expect to learn back there?" the voice boomed over the suppressed murmurs of machinery and the tight grouping of men hovering over the anesthetized patient on the table. The head surgeon had not straightened up, nor had he lifted his eyes from the operating field. "You are here to learn something about this procedure, aren't you?"

Avoiding Mrs. Peacher's look, ducking my head in her direction as politely, as apologetically as I could, I hurried to the table. Without any more direct acknowledgment of my presence, the others shifted positions a bit, some more, some less. There is little personal space at the scene of an operation. All the conscious bodies are concentrated on one small area, concentrating on the one unconscious body, but not the entire body, only the small portion of it that has been opened for their inspection.

I was unprepared for what I saw, although I had heard it described so many times and seen illustrations that were said to be faithful renderings. The assistant held back with clamps the layers of flesh and muscle, creating a window into the glistening world within. It was not just the intense overhead lighting in which everything was bathed that gave the organs this glow. It was life itself. No matter how carefully the patient's consciousness had been suspended by anesthesia, the independent life of this inner world of vital organs continued. It would continue even if consciousness was lost. It would continue as long as blood and oxygen flowed.

Rapt in wonderment was not a state encouraged in the operating room, certainly not from a student who had shown so little incentive that the back row sufficed as a vantage point. But rapt I must have been not to have heard the beginning of the question. I knew it was a question because the surgeon's scalpel hovered over the vessel, making little insistent probing motions in the air as if to rivet my attention.

"What is it?" he asked, perhaps even for the third time. I hesitated. I could not recognize this unfamiliar branching of vessels. He moved the scalpel to an adjacent area. "What's this, then? Look like something you found in a book?"

I leaned closer, obstructing his line of vision. One of the senior residents corrected me with a quick nudge of his shoulder. I pulled back, but I could follow the head surgeon easily now that I had been able to orient myself to the tangle of branching vessels. He was exploring the celiac axis from which the hepatic artery fed into the liver, the left gastric artery into the stomach, and the splenic artery into the spleen.

"Celiac axis," I said.

"And moving up?"

"Hepatic artery." He nodded quickly. "You ladies are getting smarter. I have noticed that about all the ladies around this place. So if this is the hepatic artery, this big pink thing over here must be . . . ?" I had to force some small degree of normalcy into my voice, but I did manage to get out the word, quietly, controlled:

"The liver."

But I couldn't let it go at that. Leaning again over the opened body, risking the attendant's shoulder, but pulling away in time, I think I actually ducked my head in agreement and smiled at him. "Yes, that is the liver. I believe it is."

He was not fazed by this but continued his exploration of the patient. He spoke as his fingers moved quickly, with practiced skill through the layers of tissue. There was no sarcasm in his voice, but each word was like a slow needle pushing layer by layer through my thin skin. "Very good. Now, for next time, perhaps you could ready a little presentation on aberrant hepatic arteries and where they arise and where they wander. This patient has aberrant arteries, as I attempted to bring to your attention. It wouldn't do for you to come here unprepared for them, not after cutting this far inside. Now would it? This patient is not going to be too comfortable lying here opened up this way while you rush back to anatomy class for a quick review. He's doing his best to oblige, but he can't wait on you forever. No matter how young and pretty. Won't take that for an excuse."

I moved back and let the others close in tight again. I looked at their broad shoulders and the wall they made working in such close quarters. As far as they were concerned, the wall was a natural barrier. They were not going to let me cross it easily. They probably imagined they had nature on their side when they reached that conclusion. I was an aberrant.

I felt another suddenly renewed flare of indignation when I tried to describe the experience to Ian. It was a slack moment toward midnight when I was again on night call with him. We were tying knots, surgical knots. Medical students are always tying knots in their spare time. It takes a great deal of practice to tie a good knot. A good knot is one that is not going to break when a patient turns or even moves in her or his sleep. A broken knot can lead to all sorts of problems for the patient and for the student who tied the knot in the first place. As a student your surgical experience is often confined to working with an assistant, closing up after surgery, tying knots after hernia operations, after appendectomies.

Ian is left-handed, so I was learning his way, meaning that I would wind up being able to tie with my left hand quicker than with my right. His knots are as good as anyone's. As he reminded me, with something of the defensiveness of the discriminated-against lefty, "Who can tell the difference between a proficient right-handed pianist and an equally proficient left-handed one, except maybe her mother?"

As we both tied he would sneak a glance at what I was doing and then silently correct me, making sure I was controlling the short strand of thread with my thumb as the index finger of my left hand passed over the right strand of the thread, then passed under, picking up the tail end of the thread and bringing it through the loop. It was important to let the left index finger follow the resulting knot all the way down so that it would lie flat, next to the previous one.

Under the best of circumstances, tying together could be a soothing experience, something like you imagined would happen in a country quilting bee or sewing party. Sometimes, if you got the rhythm right and were making neat rows of perfectly matched knots, not a granny among them, you sort of let your mind loose and said what you had been trying to keep to yourself all day.

That's what I had been doing as Ian watched my knots build up, quietly correcting the fumbling that came and went as my annoyance built and receded. I think I was somewhere in the middle of describing my reaction to being in the operating room the day before. I didn't waste too much time on Mrs. Peacher. She treated everyone the same way, male or female, young or old, black, white, in between, handsome, pretty, beyond the pale. She never assumed you'd use any of those accidents (liabilities without distinction, in her honest opinion) to get you anything. You'd at least have learned that much before entering her chambers.

As for the surgeon, what right did he have to assume that I would use being young and female—forget the "pretty" nonsense—as an excuse for not knowing my work? So maybe he was right in saying that I should have been aware of the possibility of aberrant vessels. What did that have to do—

At that point Ian broke in, saying, "Yes, they aren't unheard of." And when I shot him a glance that might have held more anger in it than I intended, he continued, as quietly, "They aren't unheard of. But how often they might be heard from in a procedure you had studied up on . . ."

"You mean I should have known it was to be expected in some percentage of patients? You mean he had a legitimate reason for complaining about me on that score?"

Ian corrected another carelessly begun knot and stopped my hand for a moment, not taking it in his but just making it come to rest with his touch. "He would have found something else. Having you in the OR is supposed to help you learn. But some teachers think you learn better if you remember the pain it costs as well as the lesson that is being taught."

"I doubt if he would have suggested to a young male student that he was relying on being young and male and attractive and big and strong and all that to bail him out of a stupid mistake."

Ian moved off, leaving the knotted strands of thread dangling from the arm of the chair (we tied on everything, chairs, lamps, beds, table legs, anything). He was getting his things together, signaling that the break was over and we had to check up on patients again. He probably assumed I was behind him. I did not follow at once but called after him: "Would he have?"

He stopped and faced me, answering me with more friendly casualness than I perhaps deserved at the moment: "You left out rich and famous. Young, attractive, rich, and so on."

I wasn't amused. "Answer my question," I said with not very pleasant insistence.

"Maybe he's been around long enough to suspect that young men sometimes rely on that."

"Well, I don't."

"Good" was all he answered.

"I don't have to," I insisted.

"Then you'll be able to recognize when someone is trying the maneuver." He walked out of the room, not stopping to see if I was following.

CHAPTER 20

I imagined that everyone knew, and what they didn't know they were making up. I imagined weary students and hassled interns getting their second wind by sitting around trading surmises and conjectures about me and the rich romance they were making up for me. I have to admit that at first I was embarrassed by what they might have been imagining. Were they thinking that true to form, female form, I was running out on my medical career and opting for the more natural life of love and marriage? Did they think that I was taking the easy way out, sparing myself the rough work? Did they conclude that I just didn't have what it took, was not up to the competition and the daily grind?

I decided that if they chose to weave exotic details into the

fleeting, speeding-off-into-the-night glimpses of Chima and me, they were benefiting from the exercise. Making up stories did better at keeping them all awake for the duration of yet another interminable night on call than more cups of rancid coffee. Far better then caging another, the absolute last and final, cigarette and sucking in the nicotine boost.

Whatever they thought, I knew that I was using the relationship with Chima to restore my sense of myself as a woman and to help keep that alive. As I advanced in medicine I saw that this would become more and more a necessity. Strange that I did not recognize the task at first. Strange that it took me so long to wake up to the pressures that were slowly forcing me to shed the inconvenient realities that go with being female. Strange it took me so long to see how untrue to myself I was becoming.

One such blind spot gave a clue to seeing all the others, clues only a willingly blind person could ignore. No matter how well you get yourself to perform, you always labor under the impression that you should have done it better. What you were blind to was that you had swallowed the prejudice without a challenge. You had gone along with the unspoken assumption that you had to prove yourself more just because you are a woman. Since you don't have any rules of your own, you have to play by the established ones. You did the extra work, you stayed the extra hours, you crammed the extra facts because you unconsciously agreed that you had to, just because you were you.

The attitude kept you from ever becoming lazy or slipshod. It kept you from ever assuming you knew something without making sure you had it down word for word, airtight and double-checked. That was good. But the attitude also kept you from the simple joy of knowing you had gotten it right. You always found yourself thinking I got it right, even though some of those men are still wondering how I could have done it, what with being a woman and all that. And if you told them you had worked to get it right, they had an answer to that as

well. You had to do the extra work. None of this came naturally and easily to you. It wasn't supposed to with women. You
found yourself wishing they would forget you were a woman
at all. Sometimes you found yourself wishing you could forget.

When you found yourself thinking that way, you knew you
were ready for an interlude, the more impossibly romantic the
better. Let them all try to imagine what it will really be like,
you found yourself saying. They won't be able to do it as well
as I can. I just need some cooperation from Prince Charming.
But I'll trust him. And then fate cooperated, as it sometimes
does, if only for a brief time. I didn't mind that possibility. This
romance would not have to break any long-run records to
serve its purpose. It was real, then and there. It was enough. I
was in love. Would it last? Who knew? But I did find out that
his name, Chima, meant "God knows, God knows it all."

It was close to 3:30 A.M., and I was going to try again. I had
gone to Mr. Pullman's room twice before. The first time, at
2:30, I had stepped into the quiet room and to his bedside with
confidence. It was 2:30 A.M., and I was there to draw blood. I
should not have been drawing blood from one of Dr. Brown's
kidney transplant patients. That was the responsibility of an
intern, not a student who wasn't even a member of the transplant team. But in an emergency, when everyone is running to
his or her station, you go where you are sent. Even if it was to
one of Dr. Brown's patients, whose blood had to be drawn at
the prescribed time, or else. I already knew, as did everyone
else, that all surgeons used the hospital's own lab technicians
to draw blood. But Dr. Brown wanted blood on his schedule,
not the lab technician's, which was why I was there, more or
less pitching in.

I touched Mr. Pullman's arm carefully and whispered his
name. I assumed he did not hear me because the only response
I got was a swift jerking away that broke off the contact. Sleep

had a right to protect him from such intrusions. I gave sleep a few more seconds. Dr. Brown would understand . . . or would he?

"Mr. Pullman," I began again, calling up my most reassuring but still no-more-nonsense voice.

"No," he said before I got much further.

"Mr. Pullman, I have to draw blood."

"You got blood."

I heard myself slip into reasoning that might apply in ordinary life situations, a mistake I still made. I said, sweetly but no less firmly, "That was on the earlier shift."

He pulled himself up in bed now and peered over at me. He was not in the mood for any sweet talk. "I don't give a damn which shift and which one of you done it. It was my blood, and that's it!" The encounter was ended as far as he was concerned. He turned away and lifted his shoulder into an unnatural position. I thought he might be trying to see if it would cover his ear, a flesh-and-bone barrier to further communication. Maybe he was too polite to stick his fingers in his ears. Maybe that would come next.

I could not wait. It was some minutes past two-thirty already. I addressed the shoulder. I began, "Mr. Pullman, perhaps if I explain you'll see how important this is. The blood I draw will be used to do the kidney transplant battery—"

It was an unfortunate choice of words. Why had I not just muttered something about the need to test the function of the kidneys, to make sure there was no rejection and so on about dialysis. Maybe he'd relent if I told him we were totally dependent on his cooperation to discover such mysteries. He didn't give me a chance. He turned and lifted his chin to me. I must have stepped back instinctively because then he leaned awkwardly, dangerously out of the bed. He had the advantage now, and no little lady with a sharp needle was going to take it away from him.

"Battery!" he cried. And in case I hadn't gotten the point,

he rammed it home with the next cry. "Assault and battery! That's what it's been. What'd you do with all the blood I gave you—sell it?"

Mr. Pullman wasn't one of those patients who insisted on learning just about all one could on the intricacies of preop and postop transplantation. So there was no point in my telling him that with just one stick (hopefully a successful one) I would draw enough blood to fill three tubes. One would be specifically for kidney function testing; one to test the level of cyclosporine, the antirejection drug. If that level was too low, it would mean that he was rejecting the kidney; too high a level would mean toxicity. The final tube would give twelve different results, including liver function and such things as calcium, magnesium, phosphorus, and uric acid levels.

"Mr. Pullman," I began once more, all reasonableness and faked calm, "we must test your kidney function. We must know in advance if you have problems with your transplant."

"The kidney's working fine. I don't need dialysis. I don't need anything. Period. I need to be left alone. Is that too hard to understand?"

It wasn't said in anger. I had to realize that more than anger it was self-disgust, contempt at himself for what was happening to him. He didn't have any enthusiasm for what we could do for him. He didn't want to be reduced to being a patient. Everything happening to him now was reducing him even further in his own estimate. He was slipping into the despair that was waiting to take over when a patient drops his guard and questions every reason he has for being here, in our hands. In those dark moments everything gets questioned and all the once accepted answers fail. I hate to wake patients in the middle of the night, when they're most vulnerable. I left him, hoping he would sleep again, hoping that another half-hour delay in collecting the blood wouldn't make much difference. I hoped no one would notice.

When I came back at three, he seemed to be lying in the

same position as he had been when I left him earlier. He could have been sleeping. He did not respond to my approach, but I did not call him by name. He needed the sleep, if sleep it was, more than I needed his blood.

At three-thirty I looked in again, but only from the half-opened door. He had changed his position and was lying on his side, his back to me. His body was curled slightly, his knees partially drawn up. I think his arms must have been drawn around his knees and he was trying to make a small, protective circle of himself. I would not invade that private space. Perhaps if on waking he thought of how he had banished me, he might feel he had gained some small degree of control over his life again. As a kidney transplant patient he had already been told enough about what was good for him and what was not. He would understand that refusing a blood test was not a good thing. I had not returned to insist on taking blood. As a result he might even worry that I might turn out to be the weak link in the chain of professionals who were going to haul him to safety. If I couldn't stand up to a cantankerous patient in the middle of the night . . . ? But then, he might be able to think all this and still be grateful for the small chance to reclaim his independence. He did not have to know what I felt about it to enjoy that rare experience.

I was giving Ian an abbreviated account of my futile efforts to draw blood from Mr. Pullman. His head was bent down in concentration, and he nodded from time to time. We were waiting outside Mr. Pullman's room for Dr. Brown, who would want a complete account of the patient's condition and the results of all workup orders to date. If they weren't ready, he would send you after them. He would assume that you would run there and back.

Dr. Brown kept very tight control over every one of his patients. Following his workup orders exactly as issued gave him the means to exercise this control. He once said that not carrying out an order was like a deliberate act of sabotage during war. You knew he meant that the practice of medicine had much in common with war, that we have much in common with the ordinary foot soldiers in war, that he had much more in common with the commander in chief. He did not bother to say that traitors to the cause not only deserved to be shot but that they would be, and were. You had a feeling he turned such admonitory events as shooting a traitor into state occasions. Attendance was probably mandatory. Such stories were in circulation. Some were believed to be true. They apparently served a purpose. They inspired dread of Dr. Brown. Incidentally, they inspired awe at his dedication to his patient. They convinced you that you, too, owed those patients every ounce of your strength, if only because he was giving every ounce of his. If it was true that he taught and led by fear, it was also true that at some point you forgot the fear in your determination to live up to his demands and then up to his expectations. You were thrilled to find he actually had expectations—and was determined that you lived up to them.

"So you gave up?" Ian asked, not raising his head until my silence confirmed his suspicions. "We are in for it," he added with what I thought undue calm.

"But it's only one—" He cut me short, using both hands to wipe what I had said out of the air quickly lest it be detected and used against me.

"As far as Brown is concerned, every one is the only one." Then he looked up and moved closer to my side as if to serve as a buffer. I saw Dr. Brown approaching. To be more precise, I became aware of a parting of the ways, a gathering to either side of the corridor of the men and women, nurses, orderlies, housekeepers, patients, wheelchairs, all the usual early-morning hospital traffic that had been moving back and forth in casual flow. All moved aside as the figure of Dr. Brown appeared. And it was really as though the figure of Dr. Brown had announced itself first and then the person himself materialized out of this. We were witnessing a living demonstration of the saying "His reputation preceded him."

He had been handed Mr. Pullman's chart and was totally concentrated on the pages where Ian had gathered and summarized all the results of workups over the past few days in a brief note. I did not expect much time would elapse before he came upon the blank where an entry should have given the results of the blood tests that never were.

Ian was the senior resident, so he caught the chart as Dr. Brown relinquished it, not so much dropping it or tossing it but simply letting it go out of his hand as if it were something beneath his interest in its present state. Something not ready for his inspection.

"Well?" Dr. Brown said.

"Yes," Ian began, but he was cut short before he could elaborate, if indeed he had any such notion in mind.

"Yes, you forgot? Or yes, you didn't get the results?"

"Yes, there aren't any results."

Dr. Brown responded to this with a slight grimace of annoyance at the insidious spread of incompetence and indifference that was undermining all his efforts to save Mr. Pullman's life.

"Get them now. Wake them up in the lab. Don't hesitate. Barge right in. Tell them they don't need more than twelve hours of sleep a night. You didn't get twelve hours last night, did you?" Ian smiled weakly. He probably hadn't had twelve hours of consecutive sleep in the last month. And wouldn't soon.

Dr. Brown looked as if he remembered how much sleep a senior resident on call was likely to have had the last several nights. With a slight lightening of his voice, perhaps a shade of contrition, he said, "Stay with me. Send someone." He glanced over the small group, and then his gaze came to a halt at me. "That young lady. She'll be able to, say, cajole them into releasing the results. Lucky for the future of medicine at this institution, we can always find some activity where the essential feminine instincts can be given free rein. Cajoling is an essential feminine instinct. Feel free." And then he took the chart back from Ian and began to study it again.

Not a single word had been overemphasized, not a single suggestive pause used to highlight any of the phrases. It was all delivered as if the statement was a cool and dispassionate entry in a dictionary. This is the way things are. I felt the blood rush to my head. I thought, how can this be? Where is this extra shot of blood coming from? Is this an attack of hypervolemia? At my age? But hadn't most of the freely circulating blood gone pounding into my head when Dr. Brown first appeared and I knew the moment of reckoning about the absent blood test results was upon me?

In that same split second I knew why I felt my head ready to blow. It wasn't fear or even embarrassment at having to confess in public that I had failed to follow up written orders. Especially when the orders were not merely written. Having come from Dr. Brown they were orders more or less engraved in stone. I had been indoctrinated into all of that, but now I didn't care. What I felt was pure and simple indignation. How dare he talk to me, about me, that way? How dare he use such language? How dare he dress up his gross prejudice in such cheap, obvious pseudointellectual terms? As if citing "instinct" was going to give his bias a coating of respectability.

"It was my responsibility to draw Mr. Pullman's blood."

Dr. Brown made a pretense of scrutinizing the chart, then he waved it at me, saying, "You are responsible for this, then?"

"Yes," I answered. "I saw Mr. Pullman."

"And was it a nice visit?"

I hesitated. He was saying nothing, there was nothing in the tone of his voice that was designed to release the pounding in my head. I had a feeling he was well aware of that.

"He was not . . . not cooperative," I managed to get out.

"How inconvenient for you. But what about the blood? Did you manage to get around to that?"

"He did not want . . . I could not persuade him to let me draw it."

Dr. Brown pretended to have difficulty hearing or understanding this. He peered at me in an exaggerated manner, as though the meaning of my words was beyond him. He said, " 'Want'? 'Persuade'? I do not understand you. You had read the orders before you entered Mr. Pullman's room? That was the reason you were in Mr. Pullman's room in the first place?"

"He said he did not want me to take blood. He said he was tired. I left him. When I returned he was asleep. I returned again, but I did not think I should disturb him."

"But you knew the orders I had written?" The question was not meant to be answered, so I remained silent.

"And instead you let the patient sleep."

I wanted to say, "He needed the sleep more than you needed the blood workup." I did not say anything.

"You let the patient countermand my order. You countermanded my order. You have an interesting relationship with this patient. Unfortunately, it is not one in his best interest."

Then I said it: "I decided he needed to rest undisturbed and sleep if he could sleep. I thought that would be of greater benefit. He appeared under considerable stress. Sometimes a patient feels the treatment is the cause of the stress he feels. That's why he resisted . . ."

I trailed off before he spoke. "Very nice," he said, without the vehemence I was prepared for. I wondered if I could risk going on. But he was speaking again with his voice under the same control. "Why did you not ask for assistance?"

"The decision not to disturb Mr. Pullman was entirely my own."

He did not bother to bring Ian into the argument directly, and I was relieved at that. He said, "The senior resident is always available. There are standing orders that I can be contacted at any time. Are you aware of such orders?"

Everyone was aware of such orders. Dr. Brown's orders were notorious. He was to be contacted anytime one of his patients was in difficulty, and the word was to have the broadest possible interpretation. When patients most likely to be in difficulty—his preop and postop transplant patients—were on the floor, Dr. Brown was usually within range of any call. That was because he would usually spend days and nights at the hospital, four or five at a stretch, appearing anytime he was needed.

"I did not want to disturb you," I said, the anger I had felt now giving way to a renewed sense of the doctor's immense dedication to his patients.

"I don't give you the right to make that decision!" he literally thundered at me. "You don't tell me if I should sleep."

He turned away and began to consult with Ian. I heaved a sigh. In spite of all my justifiable anger and outrage at his putdown of me and women in general, I was glad that this particular moment was over. I was convinced that Mr. Pullman's sleep (if he had been sleeping and not trying to get rid of me) did him more good than the absence of one blood test did him harm. But I knew I should have been more persuasive—or did that mean I thought I should have exercised more control over the patient and not let him dictate how his care was to be delivered?

Dr. Brown was not finished with me, however. Before I had resolved any of these tormenting questions, he flung the final insult my way. He said, "You're not going to practice good medicine until you learn if those celebrated feminine instincts have any real use. They may just be excess baggage. You don't need any of that on this trip."

He might have gotten carried away by his own eloquence at this point because he came right up to me, almost face-to-face. I looked at him closely for the first time. I could have called him. He had not slept, he was waiting for anything to happen. I could have called. I could not now blame him for making it so difficult for any of us to break through the wall of fear he had built around himself. But he was there, waiting. Next time I would find the courage to do what he so earnestly wanted us all to do—trust him to be at our side when we needed his guidance.

He didn't speak at once, and I thought he was somehow understanding what I felt. He shook his head as if to cast off something he had intended to say. He seemed to find his way slowly. He said, "You want to make it a great mission, soaring through the muck and up into the ethereal regions. But every steady climber knows that most of it is mountain and there are only a few moments on the peaks. You have to make sure of every step along the way. That's where the spirit is."

Not insult. Challenge.

CHAPTER 21

It's 6:30 A.M. on Saturday and I'm waiting, but not waiting to draw blood. I am waiting, however. And drawing blood gets to seem like a distinct possibility. I have been waiting for at least thirty minutes, minutes I could have devoted to sleep. It is Saturday. A dog in a nearby building noticed me when I got out of the car and rang Erich's ("with an 'h,' " as he was condemned to say all his life) apartment. It barked in a sort of indifferent, this-is-what-dogs-are-supposed-to-do manner and then gave up. I gave up on the bell after a while. Erich wasn't ready to answer or wasn't there to answer. I went back to the car and got in and waited. Eventually, Erich was driven up in a taxi. It was past seven. It must have been a late party, judging from the way he looked, the party-used-up look. It must have been a party not in the vicinity, judging from the long consultation and increasingly animated conversation between Erich and the driver. I got out of the car and went to Erich's assistance. He gave me a curt nod, meant to do duty as greeting, apology, and, possibly, thanks for the cash. He paid the driver and hurried into his building, and I got back into my car to wait. Would he deduct the cash I had just given him from what I would owe by the time he was finished with me? Would he even remember I had bailed him out with the taxi driver? Would I remind him? I tried to put the annoying questions out of my mind. I knew the answers. I wanted to drive off. I wouldn't. Erich needed the ride. I needed Erich.

It all began when a friend suggested I try a different hairdresser. I assumed she meant to be helpful. After all, she hadn't said, "Try a hairdresser, any hairdresser." But if hairdressing had ever made my list of priorities in the past year and a half, the notion had to compete for attention with more pressing concerns.

Erich naturally thought differently. He thought I was a mess, even if he didn't say it in so many words. But it was all there in the way he lifted my hair with his comb, pulling the shock from side to side, giving that one up and sectioning out another hank, looking at each first in puzzlement, then in dismay. He gave me the impression that the best approach would be just to shave it all off and make an appointment for later in the year.

From a practical point of view, I did not have the time to hang out in his elegant waiting room (the ones I was used to were usually filled with children screaming, mothers frantic, addicts nodding, alcoholics sleeping, old men moaning, young women fighting back tears and boyfriends, and so on and so on). So we struck a bargain. He would see me on Saturday, his busiest day, which also tended to coincide with my rare day off, if I would pick him up and drive him to his salon. And then in all peace and quiet he would continue the miraculous work of transforming me into the woman I had left behind years ago. Over the months the job was getting done, and my friend began to notice. My hair, which to the best of my recollection had more often than not usually been hastily tied up in a bandanna, was now intricately braided, row on row, each strand of hair coaxed into place and made to stay. And woven into the braids were bright beads, and the end of each braid was caught and held by beads of even more intricate workmanship. It seemed that my hair was being sculpted into some traditional ceremonial work and I would be bearing this reminder of my origins for all to see.

After his work was done Erich turned me over to another magician who transformed my face—yes, those familiar, uniform planes and peaks, that once evenly colored skin that covered all the serious work going on within also changed. A sweep of an incredibly soft brush I hardly felt brought a touch of subtle color here, a different tone there, and I felt as if another version of me was emerging from the basic previously unadorned template. I was a woman of color from the beginning, but I had never imagined I would be a woman of such diverse, blended color. One could call it magic, but did I need any such magic in my life? Was it magic or just a reminder of something I had forgotten? No one ever forgets she's a woman. There are—what shall we say?—built-in reminders of that. But what I was now being able to face, looking into the mirror at a startlingly new face, was how little in my present world made much of my being a woman. My womanliness had more or less taken a backseat while I learned another role, the role of receiver and more recently dispenser of medical information, technique, accepted practices. Oddly, I don't remember hearing any of the men in my group complaining that their manhood had been put on hold.

Such thoughts came uninvited as I gazed at the unfamiliar figure looking back at me in the mirror. I knew I would have to

remember each detail, because it would be up to me to re-
create the face in the days between these sessions. When it
was all over Erich would usually appear, make some adjust-
ments that appeared necessary to him, and give the signal that
released me from the spell.

Sometimes he would say something like "He shouldn't
have anything to complain about now." As if "his" complaint
had brought me there in the beginning, I protested to myself,
knowing I wouldn't be there otherwise. But I had never discussed Chima with him. I don't know if my friend had filled
Erich in on this point, although there was enough gossip float-
ing around the hospital to make this a possibility. I don't think
I was upset by the thought that she might have betrayed a confidence. I had never confided in anyone about him, even
though we had been seeing one another for months by now. I
took a last look. Erich was right. I looked like more than a
woman used up by her job. I looked like a woman. His parting
flourish, meant to get me out of the chair and on my way, confirmed what I had been thinking: "You're on your own now,
young lady, I've done all that art and my arcane science can do
for you."

I came to know the nice house in the elegant suburban development well. I even had my own private place, a small room
where I could hole up with my books and be more or less
undisturbed for long hours on end. I did this often, in spite of
the continual comings and goings of Chima's friends, relatives,
fellow law students, and others who did not appear to fit into
any of these categories but seemed to me as welcome as the
others. It was all conducted like a traditional village extended
family where everyone knew the role that had to be played
and no one transgressed on the prerogatives of the other.
Everyone recognized Chima's preeminent position. I tried not
to give much thought to where or how I fit in, but I did know
that the order as I was seeing it had existed before my sudden
advent. For all I knew, they were just observing a familiar

routine by acknowledging my place in the general run of things. It might have been a piece of luck that I had to spend a good deal of time at the house studying and preparing for the inevitable return to the hospital after a day or so of freedom. I was glad that most of the free time I had I could spend alone with him.

There were times when I would be away for several weeks at a stretch. This was when I had to do a clinical rotation at another hospital. I was usually so overwhelmed with working in a different environment that I had little time to think about a nice retreat in the suburbs and an assigned place at the table—and in everyone's expectations. Every medical student thought about these rotations as the experiences that would make or break you. As a fourth-year student with so much new clinical experience to be digested, you had doubts enough about whether you really did fit into that white coat, short as it was (only the graduated M.D. got the knee-length coat). On a rotation at an unfamiliar hospital you felt somehow alien even to what you thought you had learned. In a way you were right.

Medicine isn't monolithic, practice isn't identical from institution to institution, procedures and preferences change from physician to physician. You, a bit player, a fourth-year student still, didn't dare make any statement about which approach to the patient struck you as the better one. You just hoped you remembered the difference between what you were used to seeing done "back home" and what the preferred method in your temporary place of business was.

I usually came off one of these rotations with my head doing its own rotating. Just a few days before the end of the rotation, for instance, I had to deal with a diabetic in a crisis. What was wrong with what I thought would be the best way to manage the diabetic when his glucose level was ripping through the ceiling? How much time did we have before the man would be in hyperglycemic shock, with cerebral impairment and coma likely to be not far behind? I thought everyone knew you had to put in the IVs. Get the high-dose insulin going through the vein to bring down the glucose level, get the fluids in to rehydrate. Keep it all going until there was evidence of recovery. Well, not everyone agreed. In fact, nobody did. At that particular institution what I considered therapy was regarded as the certain route to a malpractice suit, to say nothing of a patient fading away in a diabetic coma.

I was asked if I wanted to drop the man's blood sugar so fast that he'd wind up as bad if not worse than when he was admitted. Yes, I did know that diabetics in crisis run the risk of getting too much insulin too quickly, but that's what bedside monitoring is all about. Except at this institution. No one was taking a chance on too much IV insulin resulting in too low a blood sugar level. Low-dose insulin injected under the skin was what you gave, or you had to answer for it. So you swallowed your reservations and hoped for the best. And as you watched the patient rally without a hitch, you began to question if what you had accepted as the best therapy might have to be reconsidered. Maybe the low-dose approach was as good . . . maybe better . . . and would you risk saying as much when you went home?

But this was my life. You think you have everything down pat, and then you learn that there are other options and choices. You try to keep your mind open, even when it is spinning like a top. You had to try to see things from as many different angles as possible, not just your own. Spinning could help you do that. In many instances, there was more than one way to see things. You had to keep your options open. You couldn't grow otherwise.

I decided I would drive directly to Chima's house, not even detour to my own place to rest or pick up some fresh clothing. It would be a long drive, but if I left first thing, I would be there before the end of morning. I had the next few days free. I'd

spend them in completely mindless, domesticated contentment. I'd do my laundry, his laundry. I'd clean the house, wash
windows. Maybe I'd cook. We would go shopping and select
everything we had told each other was special, all our favorite
foods. I would make romantic dinners for two. There had to be
candles, if only the red ones from the last holiday. They would
serve for a festive touch. Maybe he'd remember we first met
during a holiday. He would open a bottle of wine. I might take
a taste. I would not open a book. I would not think about medicine or surgery or rounds or patient care or controversial
approaches to the management of chronic diseases.

I had spoken to him several times during the past weeks,
hurried conversations that left everything unsaid but were all I
had time for. He was not always there when I called. I never
knew exactly when I could get to a phone, and it would have
been too complicated to have him try to reach me. But whenever I called the house someone always answered, recognized
who I was, offered no explanation for his absence. I never
asked for one. He wasn't going to wait around for my call. I
never expected that.

I saw the rest area and the telephones, and because no one
was using them I pulled off the highway. It was still early, and
the traffic was very light. My abrupt maneuver caused only
a small but rather shrill ripple in the scant line of cars that
passed me, a few angry blasts of horns. I should have taken
more time to signal, but I had come upon the area unexpectedly and I guess I had made up my mind without thinking. The
phone stands were not being used, and I didn't know how far
off the next rest area would be. I thought I still had about another hour or so before I could get off the highway and onto
the more familiar county roads that would take me to the
house. I didn't remember seeing rest areas with telephones
anywhere along those roads. I'd feel more comfortable if I
could reach him.

He sounded still mostly asleep, so I repeated everything I

had said until he answered, "Yes, yes." He seemed confused about the day I was getting finished with the rotation, but I told him I had served my time, every last hour of it, and was free. Time off for good behavior, you know. It was still too early for jokes, even old ones that didn't need much explaining. I repeated that it would be at least an hour, perhaps more, but I would not disturb him when I arrived if he was not up. I would have a lot to do on my own. I think I told him I had brought my laundry. I could do his.

The road that branched off from the main one and led up the hill to the small group of houses where Chima lived was wide enough to let two cars pass. But I almost always pulled to the far side and slowed down or even stopped to let someone else pass. Perhaps the change from flat road to incline played tricks with my perception and I could not believe there was ample room for two. So I had slowed down and was moving to the side as the other vehicle approached, concentrating on hugging the edge and not taking any of the encroaching tree limbs and shrubbery with me. As it was, I could hear the faint brush and drag of branches and leaves against the car fender and door. I could have been deep into the weeds.

I was looking directly at him without registering who it was, not even thinking to myself, But I should know who this is. I should. The effort to identify the man was probably being short-circuited by the nervous energy focused on my efforts to recall the woman beside him. Forget what was actually before me. Forget the tousled hair, the stripped, chastely unmade up face, the evidently borrowed sweatshirt sagging about her shoulders. Forget all the evidence before my eyes. I dressed her instead in the sleek party dress that moved like a second skin. My imagination took those limp strands of hair and in a flash had them piled high on her head again. I did it up grand. I hadn't spent all those hours and bills on Erich in vain. When I was done, Erich would have been proud to own the job himself. I threw in the earrings and painted nails, the high heels, the seamless hose. I even threw the Christmas tree at her. And all the traditional, terribly British, been-in-the-family-forever decorations. I gave her season's greetings.

It was enough, but I would have found more, except that now it seemed that something was pressing on me from all sides. It wasn't a thing, however, it was a sound, sounds. The whole car was being flooded with party sounds and music, music, music. The sound was building, going up, straight up like rockets on the Fourth of July. The sound was coming from all over—no, it was coming right out of my head, which was now going off like a rocket on the Fourth.

I must have smiled and waved as I let Chima and his passenger inch past me. It was a slow process because I had moved somewhat closer to the middle of the road from the shoulder I had hugged at first. It might have been that he had to inch past my run-down car carefully to make sure that his own more impressive vehicle was not bruised in any way. I let him pass, and then I had the open road ahead of me and the house as my goal. If there was a speed limit in the area, I did not have it in mind. I had other things on my mind in addition to the rockets.

I slammed to a stop at the house, grabbed my bag, used my key, and ran to the kitchen. I knew where the knives were kept. And then up the stairs to the bedroom, which bore the signs of hasty tidying up, more indicative of true guilt than the incriminating rubble I would have encountered had not the unused telephone beckoned to me from the empty rest stop.

I pulled back the bedcovers. I wanted a clean field. Of course it was a water bed. He was just the type to have a water bed. He talked a lot about its advantages. You did get used to sleeping in one, even if at first it felt as though you were, well, sleeping on water. I had to concentrate at times in order not to feel the nausea creeping up on me. It would not do to give in to nausea, not after having had all the advantages described to you. I used to pretend it was just like sailing. But most of the time it was like sailing and getting seasick with no solid land in sight.

I must have assumed the water was under pressure and would gratify me with a great plumy geyser, straight up to the ceiling. Sure, I washed the windows!

It was not so. My application of the knife had been skillful. I had decided on an incision that I imagined running from the suprasternal notch to the pubis, a most generous cut. But instead of a plume all I got was a lot of water sloshing to and fro, as if hesitant to try out the offered freedom. Until I continued with the cut and ran my blade down the sides. That was more gratifying. Much more.

I didn't hear him come in. I didn't connect the faint squishing sound with someone walking softly over a water-soaked carpet. There wasn't any dry place to put me, and the bed had deflated sadly, so he picked me up and carried me into the small room that was considered mine. It had a daybed on which I sometimes dropped when I needed a few minutes' break from studying. He had managed somehow to snatch up a towel and was drying the tears that had spilled down my face and that I hadn't noticed enough to wipe away myself.

I said as clearly as I could, "My feet."

He did not understand but did not seem to want to pursue the issue and question me.

"My feet," I repeated, pointing down to my wet socks.

"Oh," he said, understanding. "Mine, too." From his kneeling position he attempted to lift one foot to show me. He pulled off my socks and began to dry my feet.

"Your shoes?" I asked him.

"I kicked them off. First . . . when I saw . . ."

"You're so clever," I said.

"They're good shoes."

"London?"

"Yes. But I had them resoled here."

He had finished with my feet and settled down on the floor, from where he was pulling off his socks. "Let me," I said, taking an end of the towel. He did not let go but used it to pull himself closer to me.

"I think there's been an accident," he whispered. I tried to hide my face from him, but he turned me around so that I had to look at him. He waited until I could bring myself to speak.

"Can it be fixed?" I finally said.

He looked at me closely in silence.

"Do you want it to be?" he asked.

He was asking for a yes or a no. And I had neither answer ready. Yes, I wanted for us to go on and for me to let him make me continue to feel complete again, not riven by conflicts over what I was and whether I had lost some essential part of me in all the long years of making myself conform to what my profession demanded of me and would continue to demand. Yes, I wanted to go on believing that with him I was a woman and that was enough to be, that it could be considered a very valid full-time occupation. I wanted to believe as he did that becoming a doctor really added nothing to all that was basically me. I wanted to go on telling myself that we were enough just being here the way we usually were. It was all right here for us. You didn't look for anything more because there was no need. No need to look any further.

I wanted to answer no. Enough of this, as fine as it has been. He was there beside me now, and all I could remember about us was that we had been here this way before, many times before. And could go on, but wouldn't get any further. Once, a long time ago, I had thought I was looking for something, some meaning that gave meaning to other things and events, lent them significance. Something that didn't end where it had begun. I wanted to say no because I hadn't really learned anything I could not have found out for myself. If I had the courage. I would not have needed him to convince me I was still a woman, if I had listened to the voice within that could not possibly, ever, have told me otherwise. For a time he gave me a quiet place where I could hear his voice assuring me. I loved him for those moments. I loved him. I knew there were others; I was naive but not that naive. I could write them all off because they were temporary, but I remained the one he came back to. And if I stayed away too long, he called out for me. It was as simple as that. We called out to one another, and we heard what we said. I wish we could have gone on listening to what we always had to say to one another.

CHAPTER 22

I didn't give up the comfortable private place he had made for me and I had accepted. I needed a place to get away from the increasing pressures that went with being in my final year of medical school. He asked only that I keep my place on the terms I had already accepted—and not change the terms in any significant way. You could call it compromise. I did. But then, I must have known the terms from the beginning. I tried not to let it bother me too much, and I didn't make an issue of conscience out of it. I did not think I was deceiving him. Our relationship went along more or less as before. When I was with him, I was there. He didn't have to know more than that, or that I was only there more or less. More or less as before. I had to get over the notion that he would want anything more

from me.

When I had to be away for those longer or shorter periods on rotation at a nearby or faraway hospital, I tried to block out most thoughts of him. I trained myself not to imagine what he did from moment to moment. Maybe this, too, was compromising, giving up any real claim I might have had to him. But then, more realistically, maybe most of his life was just none of my business, given that I knew the whole continuing relationship was compromising. I needed his companionship and affection. He gave those things. Like many women who have been in my position, I would no longer risk asking for more than he was willing to give, or at least had shown his willingness to give. And to be perfectly honest, I knew I had stopped asking myself to give much more. I wouldn't make that mistake again. In this sense, we were evenly matched. That's why we got along so well.

I can't say I plunged into work to escape some of the disappointment involved in seeing the limits of my romance. You didn't make it this far in medical training unless you had already plunged way in, up to your neck in the element and kicking your feet, methodically, steadily to stay afloat. If the need to escape from some purely personal conflict motivated you to spend an additional hour or two when your allotted time on call was over, no one had to know your reasons. If you volunteered to take over for a colleague who had some personal crisis to attend to, you just earned some personal points and no one had any reason to doubt your altruism. And if you always seemed available to serve as the least significant assistant during the least glamorous piece of surgery, your eagerness was attributed to the competitive spirit you seemed to be acquiring, in spite of all your other noncompetitive, very typically female characteristics.

That was a sure way to get to see a lot of routine appendectomies and hernia operations, a lot of repair work for dog bites and gunshot wounds and the various and sundry insults motor vehicles and heavy-duty equipment can visit on the fragile human frame. You usually assisted at these procedures from the end of the table, craning your neck for a better view, memorizing every cut and maneuver the surgeon made, feeling envious at every contribution the senior resident was allowed.

But gradually your presence seemed to arouse some slight recognition and maybe even interest. You did get to hold the clamps that spread the body open. You forced yourself to hold them wide and steady, resisting the body's natural pull in the opposite direction. You braced yourself, trying to get traction from the very floor beneath your feet, literally digging in. You trained yourself to release the tension in the muscles of your arms in split-second intervals, imagining the eased fibers reviving, lengthening, breathing, and then happily resuming their work. You tried to do this without betraying your fatigue by an uncontrollable tremor and a shameful quivering of your hands. You even learned how to relax your jaw so there would be few if any remaining external signs of how acutely you were feeling the sheer physical stress of surgery. You reminded yourself that getting physical about yourself, getting your body to function at its peak, keeping it there—none of this was vanity or self-indulgence. It was a matter of life or death. And not just yours but also the human beings who would depend on that strength.

That part of it came as a not-so-welcome revelation. You knew you'd never concede that surgery was strictly a male domain. You'd go one-on-one with any man when it came to discussing the finer points of, say, percutaneous femoral vein cannulation or the most accurate method of accessing an abdominal aortic aneurysm. But when you had to compare your hands with one of theirs, measure your shoulders against theirs, your back, their backs, structure, body weight, muscle mass . . . yes, being male usually came with built-in, obvious advantages. You could not minimize these essentially male attributes as just so much brute force. Force, with luck and gentleness, with the best luck lovingly applied, has its place in surgery.

I almost always got to close at the end, getting better and faster at it with each procedure. If I was lucky enough to have Ian as the first assistant, he stayed with me and we ran a kind of minimarathon of one-handed, left-handed tying. His knots fell neatly into place, mine came a beat or two behind, not too far off from his own meticulous standard. In this as in other things, Ian remained my mentor and steadfast friend.

I did not have to keep him informed in so many words of the course of my relationship with Chima. He knew that against the odds Chima and I had agreed, as it were, not to disagree further, to continue for the time being if not as two together then at least as two companionable people side by side. We could not live with one another, not together, but we did manage to live side by side.

Ian gathered all this not so much from the few comments I made along the way, the few casual and brief explanations for my comings and goings over the last months. I did not feel I had anything to hide from him. I knew he would not ask for anything more than I felt free to give. He didn't have to. He was better at penetrating disguises than I was at devising them. No matter how well I made up my face to reflect a pretended ease and contentment, he read beyond the facial expression. He saw in my eyes the exact state of the spirit within. I read back from his the understanding I needed. I felt in my bleakest moments that my unresolved emotions were a painful, nagging misery and, worse, a mystery. His look told me that whether the feelings were mystery or misery to me was beside the point. They were what I felt, I felt them as they were.

But they were more, Ian was telling me. They were a part of me that had to be recognized and accepted. I could not disavow or disown them because they did not conform to my idea of what deep, true emotions should be like. Never putting it in so many words, he was saying I had no right to pretend to more than I was. I couldn't make an orphan out of my own flesh and blood. At the moment, for the moment, I was those feelings—confused, mysterious, miserable. I should at least be honest about it. He never said it in so many words, but he told me you could never be free within yourself without first being honest with yourself.

There were more practical, day-to-day problems for me to try to work out with Ian. Dr. Brown was a major one. I had gotten somewhat used to the aura of terror that surrounded him, largely because I had learned some insight into the man, who, I decided, rather enjoyed projecting terror. Certainly his thunderbolts fell indiscriminately, striking everyone from senior attending physicians to hospital administrators to janitors to those even lower in the pecking order, namely, medical students barely learning how to crawl. So there was apparently no individual malice intended in any of these outbursts. I decided they were just slightly exaggerated expressions of justifiable indignation at jobs poorly executed, lessons half learned, care ineptly delivered. The sin, not the sinner, was the target. Nevertheless, the humiliated and chewed-out sinner wasn't usually interested in the fine distinctions. A public acknowledgment of error was invariably in store for the offender, although the confession always struck the rest of us as totally superfluous. Dr. Brown's judgments of wrongdoing were never questioned because they couldn't be. He did not waste a chastising bolt on an error that might have some partially valid excuse for existing. He never took aim at a dragon that was not a menace. Would I willingly stand in that line of fire? There was much to learn from Dr. Brown, not just surgical technique, even though that in itself was surgery of the most demanding nature, the intricate maneuvers of transplantation. Working with Dr. Brown meant learning all the other steps necessary to bring the patient in the best possible condition to the operating room. After transplantation there would be the demands involved in monitoring recovery hour by hour, as many hours of your time and life as that required.

As Ian reminded me, in the few years that had passed since Dr. Brown's kidney transplant unit had begun to function, not a single senior medical student had chosen that service as an elective. Ian did not have to amend this statement to include "And never a woman." This was one instance where men and women were equal, equally cowardly. No one could legitimately point a finger at me and call me a coward for not venturing where no one else had dared. But I was beginning to feel some peculiar stirring. Everything else in my pursuit of a medical career had appeared first as an impossible challenge, an improbability, a hurdle too high for my legs, a remote possibility needing a miracle to bring it into reality. Seen in the perspective of my life and career so far, Dr. Brown was beginning to exhibit some recognizable characteristics.

"He isn't always kindly disposed toward women. At least women in the profession," Ian offered, somewhat tentatively in my opinion. "Kindly disposed"? I rejected that notion at once. Everyone knew Dr. Brown was a totally unregenerate, solidly entrenched, unreconstructed male chauvinist and would probably remain so if 90 percent of the medical school were female. I knew Ian was reminding himself of that even if he didn't say so out loud.

"He isn't disposed. Period. Not kindly, not ever," I corrected.

"You noticed," he replied, rather sheepishly, I thought.

I reminded him of just one of my earlier encounters with unredeemed male chauvinism. Dr. Brown was lecturing on the surgical strategies needed in the construction of a vascular access for patients with kidney failure who had to go on hemodialysis. He said he wanted to impress on us the importance of learning well what might seem like dull, pedestrian, routine surgical technique, opening veins or arteries and threading tubings and wires so that the kidneys could be flushed and the patient kept alive. He stressed the hard discipline and even drudgery involved in learning and doing the various procedures. He regretted he could not offer more in the way of glamour and heroics. He implied that these were qualities that he imagined had originally attracted women to consider medicine or even surgery. He recommended television for glamour and heroics.

Unfortunately, he went on, in the real world of patients with end-stage renal disease and kidney failure, there was little chance for the heroics of transplantation. There were patients on dialysis, about 200,000 of them, the numbers increasing from 10 to 20 percent a year. In contrast were the eight thousand to nine thousand luckier others, those freed of dialysis by a kidney transplant. So all of us, especially the more naturally romantically inclined ladies, would have to lower our sights and accept that the success of dialysis depended on doing the venous access correctly. Could we stand the jolt of reality? More to the point, would we learn access surgery well enough not to do harm to our trusting patients? Would we learn well enough so as not to disgrace the school, our teachers, and, incidentally, ourselves?

Ian listened without interrupting me and did not even attempt to calm me down as I went back and forth over some of the more incendiary moments. When I was finished, he shrugged his shoulders, held out his hands, and said, "That's why there are no takers for his transplant service rotation. One place where males do not feel the urge to compete. With medical students there's an instinct stronger than the competitive. It's the survival instinct. The ones who don't have it . . . well, they make themselves known by their absence."

"I'm still here," I said with some annoyance.

"You've got the instinct."

I gave him just a second and then said, "I signed up for the service."

"The service?"

"Yes. I went home and practically memorized the book on vascular access for hemodialysis. I concentrated on memorizing the illustrations. There are a lot of them. I felt he couldn't turn me down if I had everything memorized. Not that I knew what it all meant. But I got most of it right when he asked me. I could have drawn pictures of what I missed and gotten it all right."

Ian said, "He wants you to learn. You don't have to be brilliant when you get to him, but you do have to work. Hard, conscientiously, past what you would expect of yourself. That's how you have to leave his hands. In a way you have to make up for all those who don't or won't or can't make it. So if someone like you tries to give up, you get the wrath. But if you try to keep up, you get the pleasure of his laughter. So both the wrath and the laughter mean something. He's got it all calculated. Both tell us that nothing us smart, privileged, coddled intellectual black folk ever do is done just for ourselves. We carry the burden of all those who don't do, won't do, can't do. If you come this far, through all kinds of nasty stuff, and you don't make yourself go more, you feel the wrath. He wants you to feel how hard the judgment must be. He's also sort of willing to give you a little taste of how good the satisfaction of getting close can be. He wants you to compete, even with him if necessary. He wants you to compete against history and life itself, the life most of our own people have had to live. He wants you to help rewrite history, and the pain. He's familiar with pain. So are you, and you'll get more acquainted with it; it will come to have a familiar look and feel. You'll help change it, get rid of some of it, have some success that way. You won't do much for his pain, however. His pain comes from looking behind him and seeing how thin the ranks of followers are, how few to come and replace him and the few strong men of his generation still left. He wants his work to pass into other strong male hands, and he looks back and sees how thin the ranks, how limited the possibilities. He's in pain because he fears that the instinct for survival is being ground down and out of the men of this generation. He'll accept you for the hardworking, conscientious, careful student you are. But when he sees you, he also sees all that is absent. He'll help you make it, but he'll make you work for all the rest as well as for your own goals. Your miracle has to sustain you and all the rest who with any luck or guts can hurry up behind you."

Everyone came to my graduation. Everyone else also fell into the arms and took the warm embraces and grateful kisses of all of their own who had come from near and far to celebrate that most improbable day. My own came from New York and Miami, Boston and California, and Haiti, in numbers I found difficult to believe. Brothers, sisters, uncles, aunts, husbands, wives, girlfriends, boyfriends, children, babes in arms. Nobody had waited on my doings to get on with their own lives, their courtships and weddings and babies and children. I felt I had dropped out of at least a whole generation of family growth and would never catch up. But nobody hinted I had lost out on something. I had won the prize, and they could not stop hugging and touching me for having done it. And for that time anyway they had all convinced themselves that it was the prize most worth the running, most worth the separation from the rest of life that they themselves had known.

And in what I will always remember as the most solemn procession, my ancestors from Haiti came forward to share the time with me. My grandmother, now as frail as a leaf, leaning on the arm of her son, my uncle, who had also sustained me for so many seasons of my schooling. And there were my other near relatives, all with the marks of age and care engraved on their carefully composed faces. Each of them seemed to me at first to compose themselves as they approached, for I was now the titled one in the family. And then each face dissolved

in joy and tears, and I could have been no more than a child in
a white dress ending another grade school year with good
grades and the nuns' approval.

My mother and father stood together at the ceremony,
companionably, as if they usually passed the time through such
long formal events by turning often toward one another, dip-
ping their heads to avoid being heard, whispering whatever
stray observation the speaker, or more likely some unusual
sight in the surrounding trees or garden, occasioned. From my
place a distance from them, on the stand where we all were
marshaled together, I watched them, kept them steadily in my
eye, accepted from time to time their gaze, once or twice the
hand uplifted in greeting, encouragement, advising patience,
promising that even famous speakers eventually run out of
words. I gathered them all to my heart. I knew I had needed
all the strength they had given and would continue to give in
the coming years. I knew I would never have cause to question
the miracle of such love coming that one day from so near and
so far.

CHAPTER 23

I always wanted to return to the Eden of my childhood, but there is no Eden on earth and what you return to is not Eden and never what you remembered. But I went back to Haiti after my graduation from medical school, brought back by my uncle who had worked so hard to sustain me through all my schooling. I imagined he thought it would be some recompense for having had to exile myself from so many things, for having to spend so much time in my closed-in world of medicine. He knew how hard it had been, but he must also have felt it had taken me away from the real world. Perhaps he and the rest of my family wondered how I would be able to enter the lives of suffering men and women and children and understand that suffering when I had spent so many years with books and study, answering only the demands of that limited life.

Every day and everywhere we went they told me about this one and that, a distant relative, a friend or neighbor, some people who lived nearby for a time and then were not heard of for years. Some names I could just barely remember, and their sounds teased me like fragments of forgotten songs. Their names sounded so musical in my old language. Faces were like the names. Some were called up at once, but others, most others, came back to me only hours or days after their stories were told. And then, with so many newly told stories to remember, with so few memories to fasten them to, forgetting them so quickly, the names and faces seemed to wander about loose in my head, looking for a home again, until I realized I had come home again.

I went up to my grandmother's farm and saw that the land had gotten poorer, acres not even planted but abandoned as not worth the effort. I could not remember from my childhood a single handful of earth she would have discarded without effort to coax something from it. But the worn-out soil stretched away from us. The barren acres seemed to encompass much more than I thought were her former cultivated fields, until it came to me that the forests had also moved away, the great green veil of them that once hung between us and the sea now only a thin change of color seen at a distance. The trees and undergrowth had over the years been cut away, piece by piece, then acre by acre, hillside and valley. The woods had became the only source of fuel many could afford, and so they were consumed. Now the soil they once shielded was exposed, unprotected, unnourished. The sun was more brilliant than I had been used to for many years. It seemed I had not been living under the sun at all since I left my home. But once back I could easily imagine everything exhausted under such an intense glare. I knew the sun would bake the earth and exhaust it.

I watched my grandmother from the veranda of the old house. She stared across the fields as someone in a painting stares out at the sea. She stared at the lands she had worked and that had been the source of all that sustained her and those she protected. It was unimaginable that the land should be exhausted, as unthinkable as the sea drying up. Whatever she thought, she did not speak of it.

My uncle's house, where I was staying, was in a pleasant and secure part of town. He was not a man of any significant wealth, but he had prospered, and his two-story house was large and surrounded by well-kept yards. He thanked God for his good fortune by His generosity. From the balcony on the second floor where I had my room I could look down and across the wide yards and to the very border of the property, where people had put together tiny shelters, little huts of discarded wood and tin and paper, things that had no better use. In these tiny covered places people came to spend the night when there was no other place for them. By day these huts would be deserted, as their temporary inhabitants went off early, before dawn in most cases, to seek work. I knew that they would first go quietly to the house and stand by the kitchen door before they left, looking away from the door as if their presence were nothing but a coincidence and not meant to alert anyone inside. My uncle had someone there with orders to give these unfortunates something to help tide them over the hours until they had whatever pay they could get for their labor that day. He told me people came and stayed a while and then moved on. There was an endless stream of such people moving about the land, and one man's generosity could do only so much without endangering his capacity to do anything further. This was sensed by the others as well, and so the human makeup of the place was always changing, although the face of anonymous misery represented there was always familiar, always the same black face of want.

In the days at my uncle's place I was always up early enough to see the woman leave her shelter. She would go to the kitchen door and return with something that she gave to the little boy, crouching down next to him and guiding every mouthful. She would leave him then, turning back several times with her finger to her lips until his voice no longer tried to detain her. The child would be quiet and alone. All the others had gone off. The shelters were acknowledged to be only temporary respites, so no families would come if there were possibilities elsewhere. But certainly families had to have been forced into separation on occasion, leaving one here, one another place for a night's rest.

It seemed to me this child was too young to have to learn such a hard lesson. I thought someone would come in time, and even if the night had been cruel, soon enough he would have companionship until his mother returned.

My few remaining days were full. I left the house, was called to the last of the many visits that had been arranged to accommodate all the friends and relatives who wanted a last sight of me, to have a long talk about what I had done and what I would do next. I came back and had some moments to prepare for the next hasty venture off into another nearby town and more gossip and tales. Each time I returned the boy was there, like a solitary survivor of an unrecorded natural disaster. He was alone in the settlement of makeshift shelters, having ventured not much farther from his own doorway at my latest sighting than he seemed to have done at the first. He might already have investigated to his heart's content each dark doorway and the unlit, mean spaces within. If so, he had returned with nothing to occupy his hands. He still sat by the opening to the shelter. He waited, as though waiting was the only thing anyone had found time enough to teach him. As if waiting was the only skill he would need. How could he bear the minutes and hours? He was a frail black boy in a far corner of a kind man's backyard on an empty afternoon. He had no idea of soon, or later, or before nightfall. Everything in his world was only now, now, why not now? And nothing answered, and nothing came to fill the emptiness. It seemed to me that there could never be enough later in his life to fill such a vacancy. It seemed he would always be in dire need of anything life had to offer to get over such absence. Where in his world of deprivation would anything at all come equal to that task?

I would not lessen in any way the immense private human tragedy of this child by calling him a sign of something else. He had painful meaning enough in himself. And if by chance he were indeed solitary, unique, the only example that could be cited, even that would be too painful to accept. But he was both. He was tragic enough in his own solitude. He was tragic in that his condition signified the isolation and abandonment of so many others.

Over and over during the next years my work would bring me close to men and women and children cast as far adrift as this child had been. Many had learned only one lesson from life, the same one he had been taught. Yes, there might be love, there might be the possibility of comfort. But for many of these there was only the reality of the long, long wait.

When I went back to the States to start the long years of surgical residency that lay before me, I brought back the image of this child with me. At first I thought I remembered simply because the image was too painful to forget. But then I understood what was keeping the image fresh: my accumulating experiences as a doctor. The abandoned, waiting, yearning child was what I learned to seek and find in every isolated, lonely, angry, self-destructive, and wounded human being who came to me for help. I finally began to learn that they had all been waiting, long, longer than anyone should have to wait. When the need is as great as in those I served, there is no soon, no later, no before night or dawn, there is only now. I would try with all I had learned and all the skills I would continue to perfect to bring the waiting time to an end, to make love and comfort and healing happen now.

CHAPTER 24

I was at last a doctor. Once I had returned from my vacation in Haiti and had let those impressions become permanent, I had a chance to let the reality of my new position in life sink in. After all the stops and starts, the impossible challenges and the slow inching up one rocky slope after the other, I was at the top. Except, as in the past, the top turned out to be the bottom. In spite of the letters after my name, I was in reality just a first-year resident in surgery, still liable to scut work of all kinds, still the one with the least authority. This was the first of five years during which I would have to learn how to become a skilled surgeon or get out.

I like to think back on those five years as the time when I was "perfecting my skills as a surgeon." Nice phrase, even though there is a slightly disembodied, abstract sound to it. It might look good on a résumé and add a certain tone to the routine list of more modest accomplishments, but what the phrase really means is that I had spent many hours standing by in the operating room and watching the really skilled senior resident or attending surgeon perform the procedure. Watching and waiting for the inevitable questions and hoping I could answer most of them on cue, without fumbling or evasions, speaking up loud enough to be heard, risking the exposure if I had it all or even partially wrong. Exposure was a little too mild to describe the kind of disdain and disgust you risked.

As I discovered, it was back at the bottom again, with the additional realization that as a woman in surgery the bottom, the end of the line, was assumed to be your rightful place. The end of the line is working the OR as little more than observer or, with luck, second assistant, more or less where you had been as a third- and fourth-year medical student doing your surgery electives. You held a clamp, got to close the incision and do the final suturing, and so on. After a few months of this the conviction dawned that if I wanted to get ahead, I had to muscle in, and they all had more muscle than I. The alternative approach was to watch, wait, and catch the opportunity when brain would count more than any quantity of brawn. You struggled to avoid fantasies of stepping in, the lucky understudy, for the stricken star, saving the day modestly but brilliantly. Chief surgeons are stars who do not fade or step aside for understudies.

I was becoming more and more convinced that surgery had a side not thoroughly described in the books. For sure, surgery was life-restoring techniques meticulously applied, split-second decision making, risk taking—all that and more. But on the beginner's level, surgery was often simply competition. The first hurdle I faced was the need to convince the head surgeon that I was good enough to work alongside him. Before I would have a chance to impress him in the operating room, I would first have to get his attention by standing up and being heard. I had to take courage in hand and decide where I would shine out among my fellows.

Would it be during morning rounds, patient management rounds, attending rounds, major conferences, or grand rounds? Every occasion was a potential test of how well I understood the patient and the problems presented. And at every occasion questions were flying through the air like shrapnel. Except no one could duck for cover. Duckers were dead. I had to know in advance what questions would likely appear to trip me up into exposing all I didn't know in spite of the hours I had spent going back and forth over the books, hounding everyone who might have had experience with such a case in the past. It was a slow process of being noticed. There was no place for that feminine reluctance to compete. Wallflowers were known to wither in the harsh winds that whipped through a surgeon's world.

Nobody wanted to compete for the opportunity of treating Palmer, not even with the certainty that there would be no difficulty coming up with the most likely prognosis. He was no stranger to the clinic and to the nurses and residents who staffed it, although that was something you would not have gathered from their absent or at best perfunctory greetings. As I soon discovered, they were not at all subtle in the way they avoided him. When he hobbled in, they were suddenly distracted by more pressing emergencies that took them out of sight. Nurses who could not find a legitimate excuse for leaving the room banded together in intense consultation that defied anyone to interrupt. I had first noticed him, bent over and forlorn, waiting for some recognition. I had something else to do and passed quickly by.

I don't recall exactly how Palmer was first shunted off on me, but after that he was considered mine, my patient. Whether he had been given specific instruction to claim me I never knew,

but in a very brief time Palmer himself considered me his doctor and waved aside any other intervention until I was available. No one contested his exclusive claim.

The reasons were too obvious. Palmer was considered one
of those hopeless cases, a repeater, a chronic waster of professional time and medical resources, a manipulator, a self-
destructive leech. Palmer represented, all rolled up in one wasted
human being, everything guaranteed to provoke negative feelings. He was the patient nobody wanted to acknowledge, the
one who made you hate. No one wanted to treat him again,
and not just because he had been in and out of the clinic for
treatment more times than anyone bothered to count. No one
wanted him because everyone knew he sought treatment only
to get back enough strength to continue his self-destructive
course.

When I first brought him into the room for examination, I
did not know enough about his history to feel so intensely
about him. I just knew that I had to get a strong hold on myself
to avoid throwing up. I did not know if that would have embarrassed him or not. He might simply have attributed it to my
youth, for he had raised his eyes slightly when I began to examine him and gave me the familiar look of one who believes
he has reason to doubt my credentials. He was fairly well ravaged by his drug habit, but he was young, perhaps not much
older than I. He might have thought that reason enough
to doubt my competence. Why should he give the benefit of
the doubt to a black woman like me? Who gave black women
any right to act better than black men? It was an attitude I
recognized.

I would have been humiliated by losing control, and I
struggled to regain it. I kept telling myself I had seen worse,
smelled worse, had to deal with worse. That was not true, or if
it was I had cut the experiences out of my memory. They were
not the kind of thing designed to keep you slogging away at
becoming a doctor.

I could not cut out Palmer. I could not ignore the running sores on his arms that oozed pus and sent up what seemed like waves of decay, a stomach-turning cloud of decay that enveloped him and reached out to pull me into its ghastly aura. It was too late to put on a mask, I thought. He would know why I was seeking even that little protection. He had probably seen this happen before. Later I wondered at myself. Why should I worry about my behavior embarrassing him when he showed no embarrassment at all himself? He never had the slightest hesitancy in talking about himself—no, not himself, rather, as he put it, his case. A case was what he seemed to consider himself. Some of the medical experience had rubbed off on him. Given time, it will do that, even in the most unlikely instances. It took me a while to understand that seeing himself as a case was how he had managed to retain some pride. No female doctor was going to take that away from him. He was going to make sure that I saw him as an interesting case. What I or anyone else thought of him as a man or a human being had probably long since stopped interesting him.

Palmer was a heroin addict. He was also a self-taught expert on human anatomy. He had squirreled away information gained from repeated visits to the clinics that he supplemented with data from various illustrated medical manuals. He used it all to help himself discover the most useful veins into which to inject the drug. He had, he told me as I examined him that first time, gained a certain local reputation for possession of this invaluable knowledge. He had also learned the approximate tracks of all the major veins. He had learned how to palpate the artery to find the vein lying next to it, a vein that was not so obvious to the touch. He would then plunge in blindly with the needle, after the desired vein that would send the drug to his heart and head.

Of course I saw his point. For persistent intravenous drug users, a supply of healthy vessels made life a little easier. Given all the hassle a user had to put up with—the daily cost of the habit, the need to juggle job and family concerns, coping with cops and other legalities, and so on—owning a body that could be made to cooperate conveyed a considerable advantage.

Palmer told me he had been giving his arms a rest recently. He held out the inadequately healed wounds on one arm for my inspection. Every time he moved I felt myself drawing away involuntarily. The stench seemed as equally solid an extension of himself as the arm. He did not notice my reaction as he pushed up the sleeve on the other arm and offered that next for my inspection. He asked if he had done well to lay off the arms until the scars formed. Was that the right thing, in my professional opinion? I think he wanted some praise for the prudence he had been showing. He leaned closer with his arm held between us, an interesting specimen to be contemplated by two experts. I felt he was treating me as an equal in this investigation and would next inquire as to my opinion on the need for therapy.

"But I don't know, Doc," he said. "Still not sure the veins can be trusted. What do you think?"

Would he have spoken so openly to anyone other than a young and inexperienced woman? I wondered. But I did not want to be drawn into bantering diagnoses with him, so I told him that his arms, both arms, were severely infected and he would have to be admitted for blood tests and most probably IV antibiotic therapy to catch the infection before it became systemic, invaded his entire body. Given his overall condition, there was a risk of sepsis. He understood it all, including systemic and sepsis. He nodded appreciatively as I spoke and then considered it all for a moment until asking, "How long?"

"Until you're better."

He just shook his head and gave me a kind of pitying look at the simplicity of such a thought. "I mean for the IV," he said.

"Five days," I replied without really thinking, just to end the discussion. I hoped five days would be enough.

"Longer than last time," he said, again with the same expression, now meant to pardon my inexperience.

"I'll write the orders. You'll have to be admitted. You understand that, don't you?"

"As I say, it's longer than last time."

"I didn't treat you last time."

He stood up now and came after me until we were walking more or less side by side. Ahead of us at the desk the nurses were watching our approach with wary expressions. Palmer touched my arm to stay me and leaned closer, almost whispering into my ear, "Tell them it's for three days." I felt he was about to add, "Believe me, it's better."

I did not wait for that or for any other dialogue with him. I motioned for him to take a seat and wait while I went to the nurses' station to write the orders. When I handed them to the nurse, she made a show of studying the paper carefully, then looked from Palmer to the paper and then to me.

"It's longer than the last time," she said after all the carefully studied delay.

"Is it?" I began, pretending surprise at some other physician's habits. "I was not giving the orders the last time."

"He's back regularly," she replied, as if that took care of any reason I might still retain for giving her such orders.

Even low rank can be pulled, so I pulled it. Palmer was admitted, and the course of IV antibiotic treatment begun. He was my patient now, and I would have his care to add to the others assigned to me. There would also be the need to follow up on whoever was admitted during the nights I was on call. And when there was a jam-up in emergency I would have to be on call for that as well. I had to be ready for morning rounds and conferences and work in the OR when that became possible. There were tests to be ordered and X rays to be studied, nasogastric tubes and catheters to be placed, physical examinations and patient histories to be taken and recorded, and patients to be moved and brought back again and made comfortable and reassured. There were telephone calls and beepers to be answered and a thousand explanations to be given and received. There was more to be done than hours to be doing it all, but that was not always taken into consideration. It was all in the practice of medicine, but somehow much of it seemed like run-around work someone else should be doing. And when you looked around there wasn't anyone else but you and the likes of you to do it.

As it was, Palmer turned out to be not the least of my concerns. That was because in the staff's opinion he had already exhausted any claim to be a serious concern of theirs. They followed the orders, but the minute I appeared they were elsewhere, as much as to say, "You think he should be here all this time, then you can have him."

I changed the dressing on his sores when it had not been done or when I felt I could not count on it being done soon enough. I saw that his vital signs were checked regularly. I had to change the IV when I saw a risk of another infection developing at the site. His nutritional status was as poor as you would expect considering the life he had led, so I had to see that his daily intake was carefully monitored. I made a note to speak with the dietitian about supplementation. I could not be sure that any such order I wrote would not get shoved to the bottom of the pile. A special diet for a regular like Palmer? I had been made to understand that he had long since sacrificed the title of real patient. I was his nurse and nurse's aide and orderly and social worker. I was having to struggle to remember that I was also, if only incidentally, the doctor on the case.

I thought I owed him another kind of care, so I tried. He listened with what seemed unfeigned attention as I spoke about wasted opportunities and new chances, new hope. I felt embarrassed at offering advice based on my own limited experience. I think that once or twice he even helped me out with the right phrases when I came to some kind of dead end. After all, I had little experience in counseling and what I was saying must have sounded like predictable platitudes. He even offered encouragement for me to go on, remarking how unusual it was for a young lady in my position to dial into the, well, concerns of a man in his. It gave him a new insight into women like me, he suggested. He would have to do some new kind of thinking about some of his previous attitudes.

He agreed to look into some of the outside agencies that were available for further counseling, drug rehabilitation, job training. I had the social worker pull together the most recent information, and he accepted the printed pages with the names and numbers of individuals and groups. He seemed to give the sheets a quick, summary glance, nodding as if he had already heard of some of these workers, pausing when a name or agency rang no bell. When he was discharged after five days, the nurse on the floor returned the material to me the next time she saw me. She said she supposed Palmer had gone off in a hurry and forgotten to take them with him. She couldn't forward them because he never stayed in one place too long.

There would be more of Palmer a year later, but I can tell that story now because in a sense it doesn't matter when or where the rest happened. In spite of my attempts to deny it, his life had in fact turned in its predictable course and he was back again. I gathered from his account that he had spent the ensuing time studying the veins in his legs. Their use would in his opinion save his arms from any risk of reinfection. He asked my opinion on that, but I was no longer interested in taking a case history approach to his problem. As usual he pressed his luck further than he had any reason to believe it would go. When he had exhausted the peripheral vessels in his legs, he probed even deeper and found the femoral vein, the main conduit. It gave ready access for his needle and drug and then exacted the price. He limped into the hospital with a

raging fever and leg abscesses that needed immediate attention. He did not have to remember my name or request to see
me. The staff saw that I was called as quickly as possible.

Palmer insisted that he had used only one leg and that had
served him well for some time now, meaning that the veins in
the other leg had not been invaded and so were clear of infection. He brushed aside my efforts to do a more thorough examination. He joked that he would not sue me for what I didn't
treat. As long as I took care of the problem that got him to me
in the first place, everything else would be forgiven. He wasn't
out to have me cure all his troubles, much as I had shown my
willingness to try. He said he really appreciated all the interest
I had shown in his problems in the past. He'd remember that.

It was a fairly uncomplicated operating room procedure,
and he seemed to follow my description of how he would have
to be anesthetized to allow me to drain the abscesses that were
causing the fever. He signed the consent papers. The procedure was to be confined to the one obviously infected leg because he had no problems with the other.

A different story unfolded on the operating table. I opened
and drained the abscesses in the right leg, more thankful for
the necessary masks and all the rapid removal of putrid material than a surgeon perhaps should be. I was glad so much decay could be cut and removed and carried off so quickly. I
made sure the femoral vein was not in any way compromised
by the procedure, trying not to think of the abuse to which it
had been put and would no doubt have to endure again. I had
already gotten to think about each inner part of the human
body as an entity with its own life, facing its own risks and
challenges. I could conceive of Palmer's vein as if it had a destiny separate from his. I could wish it had.

He had lied to me. Under the probing light in the operating room I could see that the other leg was also infected and
that his needles had already begun their destructive work.
Abscesses had already formed, infection was present in spite

of what he said. If I ended and closed the left incision, it would
be only a matter of time, very little time, before he would
be forced back for a repeat of what I had just done. The
thought crossed my mind that some of the staff might even
begin to view me as an accessory, setting Palmer up for yet
another return.

He needed a similar procedure on his left leg. He was there on
the table, here and now, not off somewhere carrying an infection like a ticking bomb, daring the fuse to burn more slowly
while he tried for one more high. Strictly speaking, in order to
give him the kind of treatment that would be most beneficial I
needed his informed consent or that of some close relative. But
I could not wake him and then have him put under again.
Since he had lied about his leg to begin with, I could not trust
that he would agree to the procedure that would unmask the
lie. He did not mind lying, I had already discovered, but the
lies had to be on his terms. He didn't like to be found out so
bluntly. And as far as family was concerned, Palmer always presented himself as a solitary and there was no record that anyone had ever come forward to claim him after any of his
innumerable stays before this.

I decided that I had just cause for operating on his other
leg. There was sufficient evidence that the abscesses, if left un-
treated, would be as dangerous a risk as those for whose treatment he had already consented. I was convinced that it was a
legitimate decision, and I went ahead with it.

We were back in the recovery room. I had hurried to his
bedside as quickly as I could, wanting to be there as he came
out of the anesthesia. Maybe it was taking an unfair advantage.
I had a feeling, however, that I would not have as good an opportunity as the present moment afforded. Palmer was still not
totally out of anesthesia, but he did respond to my voice, and I
continued to talk to him, getting him to repeat his name and

then mine after me, making sure he moved steadily into full consciousness. He didn't react any differently to my next words, and indeed I tried to make them as bland as the questions about his name and mine.

I said, "You used both legs. You had abscesses in both legs."

He mumbled something that sounded like the endings of my sentences. So I repeated the words, and he did, too, even picking up the "Yes, both legs" that I used as a variation the last time I spoke.

Palmer was silent then, but from his breathing I knew he had come over and was past having to be coaxed into a simple thing like remembering his name. I was pretty sure he was lying there with his eyes consciously closed, trying to pull out of his memory what had just transpired between us. He was not going to make his move until he was clear on that point, not if he could help it.

He opened his eyes and caught mine. I had the distinct feeling he had not fully taken in the fact that both legs were bandaged. Or perhaps he caught things faster than I recognized and was aware of everything that had happened. His survival skills were well honed, and it would be no problem for him to keep their use well hidden from a simple observer such as I.

So I accepted that he caught it all when he said, "What happened to my leg?"

I repeated as calmly and as innocently as I could the tag "both legs." He did not like it. He said, "What happened to my legs?"

"Both legs were infected. They're both treated now. You have an even chance. No limping."

He didn't like the feeble attempt at a joke, either. He said, "You were only supposed to operate on one."

"No extra charge," I said.

"I didn't say operate on both."

"You didn't say you had used both and got both infected."

"You didn't have permission to—"

I cut him short. "If you lie to me I can't treat you. Your body didn't lie, so I treated it. Remember when you first told me Palmer's body was like a case history we could both examine? Palmer's body gave me the go-ahead. Palmer is lucky to have a body that keeps up with him."

He drew back and was silent. It was a complication he had not anticipated. He would have to consider how to deal with it. He did.

CHAPTER 25

I picked up my messages and scanned through them. I didn't bother to read the one from Palmer. I didn't have to. The messages did not vary much, the only changes being a slight modulation in hostility from time to time. I attributed this to the curve he happened to be on at the moment he decided to try to get through to me. Yes, Palmer was enjoying a good high that day—the threat was veiled. No, it had been a bad trip and he was not in the mood to disguise his anger. He had not appeared in person since I treated his legs. But he continued to hold me personally responsible (for his cure, I could only assume) and was determined to sue me for a large sum of money. I sometimes worried about how he might extract this sum should these quasi-legal means fail. Short of hiring my own personal bodyguard, I didn't know what to do about him.

I had explained the episode to the hospital administrator and was reassured that I had acted responsibly under the circumstances. I would have endangered his life if I had not treated him as I did. That explanation carried no weight at all with Palmer. He had let me know that in more than one message. Now I just crumpled up the message slips and tried to put him out of my mind.

I had enough to occupy me. Someone once wrote that doctors fresh out of four years of medical school and working through residency years (and mine would stretch to five because I had chosen surgery) had to wear at least six separate hats. Residents were still students and still learning and being tested daily. Residents were also teaching those just a few paces behind them, undergraduate medical students such as they had recently been. Residents were required to function as part of a complex health team. They had to be involved in ongoing clinical research projects. They were responsible for the many patients in their care. Then, on a very practical business level, residents were just plain hired help and had to answer to the hospital administration that employed them. Not that the pay would ever spoil your future enjoyment of a living wage. Still in all, you were careful not to endanger it, not just for fear of getting evicted from your humble flat but because fired residents were not considered very desirable employees by other hospitals.

I found it a scramble to remember which hat I was wearing at any particular time. Then I found out that it didn't matter. The roles overlapped, and I was responsible for all of them simultaneously. The end result was that they had you coming and going, but you tried not to think about it that way. You also tried not to think that in addition to the six hats you also had to find room in your head and heart for the rest of life, the normal round of living. You still had to find time to be with the one you preferred and not feel guilty about it. You still had to find time to think about your family and when next, if ever, you could be with them. You had to find time just to think. It was no wonder that being pestered by messages from an irate but usually spaced out former patient was the least of my problems.

One of the real persisting problems was finding my own voice, knowing when to speak up in spite of the pressures that said, "Stay down, in your place, don't ask for trouble." I never realized how little power those newly inscribed and probably still wet letters after my name actually conveyed before that night in the emergency room when every voice in my head was saying, "Trust yourself. Don't you trust yourself? Why don't you trust yourself?" And I did not respond until it was too late.

I was on call that night, and because it was the weekend I expected there would be enough emergency room activity to interrupt any sleep I might catch. But somehow you always try to grab any slack moments. The slack tightened up just about the time my eyes closed and I was up and on my way to the emergency room without knowing what I was doing. I was jolted awake soon enough. The emergency medical team had radioed in that they had a knife-wound victim and we had better have an attending surgeon ready for him.

When they wheeled in the patient we were all in our prescribed positions and began the usual routine at once. I could feel the sudden hesitation that came over us all at the same time as we removed the covering and saw that boyish body, that gawky teenage frame still nowhere near full growth, nowhere near a man yet, but certainly never destined to flesh out into one of the heavyweights. We looked quickly back and forth at one another with the question unanswered and unanswerable in the air around us. "What is this kid doing out on the streets? Was anyone with him? Where are his parents? Does he have anyone caring for him?"

We were almost asking, "What is he doing here?" It was as if we did not want to find out what danger threatened him, so inadequate did he seem to the challenge of those we were so used to seeing here in this place.

A nurse cut away his shirt, and again we hesitated. The boy's flat black chest moved up and down in short, jerky breaths, but that might have been his anxious response to the strangers gathered around him and to the rapid movement of others he could have caught out of the corner of his eye. What had given us that split-second pause was the perfect wholeness of his flesh, as though nothing had as yet been written on it.

But it was there, the violence that had stalked and found him. It was a tiny opening, little more than a quarter of an inch. Little blood or fluid escaped from it. It seemed that little could come from so superficial an opening. X rays were taken and the IV line put in and blood drawn. It was not necessary to intubate him, so I asked him what had happened and did he have any idea of how he had been hurt? I almost wanted to ask him if he yet knew he had been hurt.

How did he have the time or the presence of mind to concoct such a story? I wondered as he told me his unlikely account of the event. He had been walking along with his girlfriend down a neighborhood street. There weren't many kids around, nobody looking for trouble, not on that street. He wouldn't have been walking with his girl on a street where you could find trouble or have it put on you. And he never saw the guy who did it to him. Never turned around and had a look at him because there was nobody else but him and his girl in the street when he got a chance to sit up and look around. He told his girl to run for help, and then the medical team's ambulance came and picked him up.

I didn't ask how a guy coming at him from behind had

managed to get an arm around him and cut into his chest so close to his heart. I was listening to his shortened breathing and to the muffled sounds from his left lung now.

The X-ray films had not come back yet, but even without them I felt certain there was internal bleeding in spite of the dryness and apparent superficiality of the knife wound.

Something told me that I should deal with the bleeding now, not wait for confirmation from the films. I told the boy I would have to put a tube into his chest, but he would not feel it because first I would numb his chest. He stiffened, and his breath came in quicker, more shallow bursts as he felt the needle and the burning of the anesthetizing drug. I threaded the tube carefully between his ribs, concentrating on that and not on his rigid body and labored breathing. The suction yielded little at first, but within the next thirty minutes fifty milliliters of blood had been collected in the chest tube. In the next hour another fifty milliliters. We took him to the ICU. He appeared stable, but within the following two hours another two hundred milliliters drained and there was a drop in blood pressure. More large catheters were inserted, and I ordered the nurse to start blood transfusions and increase the saline infusion. I could do all this, but I could not make the most significant decision—whether to take him at once to the operating room and open him and find the source of the flow of blood and then stop it. I would have to wait on that decision until the chief resident and the trauma surgeon came up to the ICU, had time to read the X rays, and then evaluate the patient on their own.

As the minutes went by fast, I watched the boy's vital signs become more and more unstable, his breath more erratic. The chief resident and the trauma surgeon arrived and began to discuss the case between themselves, including me in the discussion at times but not often. They put in a call for the heart surgeon. By now the boy had received four units of blood and many liters of saline solution. His blood pressure had finally stabilized, but I instinctively knew that the improvement was temporary. His blood pressure would bottom out again. And as for the flow of blood: I thought of a cup with a fine, almost invisible crack in it. You could fill the cup to the brim, but within minutes the water would sink, slipping out and away, leaving the cup empty if you did not replace the water again.

I would have moved him to the operating room if I had had the authority. But it was more than authority I needed. I knew that. I needed the conviction that I was right, that I was right in believing the danger was great and thus had the right to act on this belief. I should have taken the boy to the operating room and found how damaged he had been by the knife wound. I should have done this when I saw the increasing amounts of blood flowing through the tube I had placed in his chest.

The chief resident and the trauma surgeon continued their long discussion but still did not often include me as they considered the moves they could take. They had called the heart surgeon and now, in anticipation of his arrival, had the boy at last moved to the OR.

As soon as the surgeon opened the boy's chest, his blood pressure began to drop. I could see that the opened chest revealed a field filled with blood, yet there seemed to be no immediate source for this leakage within the chest wall. The clamps I held to keep the chest open required no special energy on my part. I could concentrate on the operation itself, watching the surgeon's hands as they moved toward the heart. With great care we began to evaluate the pericardium, the membrane encasing the heart, in its entirety. The tiny tear in the membrane was so small it took minutes to find. We suctioned away the fifty milliliters or so of blood in the pericardial sac, and then we saw the corresponding small tear in the heart itself, a mirror image of the outer tear.

The small knife had been plunged with such vehemence into the boy that it had pierced straight into his heart. I saw the heart muscle contract and release, and with each move-ment blood pulsed from the wound. The pericardial sac had contained the blood at first, preventing it from gushing out and warning us. And then the volume was too great and the blood had seeped through and into the chest cavity from which I had tried to drain it.

The tiny wound in the boy's left ventricle would need no more than two or three stitches to bring the heart's muscle to-gether. But already the loss of blood was more than he could withstand, no matter how we tried to replace the loss.

In the end, none of our desperate measures were strong enough to call him back, and his vital signs went down quickly and he was gone almost before we realized it. I wanted to cry out after him, tell him to wait, we would make up the time lost, it had not been that long. But the time had been lost. I had let time and that life slip away because I had not learned how to listen. I did not lack medical knowledge, but I was still defi-cient in knowledge of self, especially deficient in the first step toward that knowledge. The first step turned out to be sur-prisingly simple and obvious. All that was involved was learn-ing when you could trust yourself. If you learned that, you would never have to worry about lost opportunities again. You would always be on time if you knew when was the right time to believe in yourself. But if I couldn't do that, it really wouldn't matter how much knowledge of self or of anything else I piled up. None of it would be accessible to me if I couldn't learn when it was safe, when it was best, when it was most beneficial for all for me to believe in myself.

For that year's holiday Chima's parents came from Nigeria to stay at the house. They helped him unpack the Christmas tree decorations, marveling at each in turn and the memories of some almost forgotten family event each evoked. They told me that decorating the tree was an old family custom and how it had always been done as part of a family ritual. Many people could not understand why it was so important, but such a ritual helped remind them all of the importance of close family ties.

His father handed each decoration carefully to me as I reached for the higher branches. A poorly secured decoration fell from a branch, and broke, but they made light of this, insisting that I must not risk a fall myself by trying to reach farther than I could with safety. They suggested I help them unpack the decorations and Chima, with his height, finish placing them. Branches that could not be reached would have to remain bare.

They were both very polite and very formal and did not ask for any details of my relationship with their son. I assumed they had been given some information about me; at any rate they did inquire about my progress in my surgical training. They seemed especially interested in the career choices that would be open to me. I had the feeling they were as interested in all those that would not be. Chima's father was a physician. He did not offer any information on career choices available to women in medicine. I did not pursue the topic of career opportunities for women physicians lest they assume I was interested in a career close to them.

I gathered soon enough that they were both very protective of their son and were especially eager for me to understand the problems he would face on returning to Nigeria and establishing himself as an important member of the legal profession. It was not to be questioned that he would in time be an important member of the profession. The question rather was how to minimize the problems he would encounter with his American law school training and other American ways and manners. They asked my opinion on just how like the other Americans I knew their son had become. They stopped short of asking what I thought could be done to reverse the process, although I think they would have appreciated my opinion on that as well. They stressed that law as taught and practiced in England was more appropriate for him. They asked if he had indicated any resistance to the idea of continuing his education in London. I think they wanted me to sound him out on this point. They extolled the virtues of London, how many of the old traditions were still alive there, how much a young man would benefit from its liberating influences. They spoke enthusiastically and gazed at me as if to have me visualize what they had delighted in on so many occasions. When they said that English ambience was very persuasive, I believed they hoped that Chima would be persuaded to try it, live it, be more English than the English—in England. I believed they expected me to be the vehicle for that persuasion. They'd write the airfare ticket, but they wanted me to coax him into using it.

As I was being led in and out of these conversational ways and byways, I had the feeling they were bringing me into their confidence, treating me as a friend of the family, one they could trust to give them an unbiased, objective opinion of their son. Maybe they thought my training as a doctor had already equipped me with tools precise enough to give an honest diagnosis and prognosis where he was concerned. They never gave the slightest hint that they feared some purely personal response on my part might cloud my judgment where Chima was concerned. I could have been an elderly relative, an old friend, a faithful family retainer, confidant. I had become like someone who had fondly watched the lad grow and still had his best interests at heart.

I went back and forth to Chima's house as often as my schedule permitted. The holiday season is always a busy time of year at a hospital for every surgery resident because we have to cover the emergency room for trauma cases every three to four days. Trauma coverage is especially hectic, and we could expect at least two or three major incidences in a single night, sometimes with multiple patient involvement. The same would be true all over the city. There was another consequence of the holiday surge one did not like to dwell on but one that was nonetheless a reality we had to be prepared for. The season of giving was also the season for organ donation as accident victims tragically supplied the desperate needs of Dr. Brown's kidney transplant unit at my hospital. If I was not needed in trauma, I would try to let the chief resident know I was fresh enough and ready enough to go through the long hours of a kidney transplant.

There was no chance I would have time enough to visit any part of my scattered family for the holiday. I had also agreed to work some shifts for residents who were married and already had small children. Chima explained to his parents the reasons for my several absences. They did not ask me to expand on what I had been doing on my own. They seemed delighted to serve as host and hostess to his friends and compare at firsthand his Americanization with that of his friends and fellow expatriates.

On the days immediately before they left they were more eager than ever to bring me into their confidence. They took me aside and with anxious glances around to make sure that Chima was preoccupied, again stressed how important London was for the full maturing of his talents and the success of his future. We could have been senior attending physicians in consultation over the future course of the patient waiting for discharge. Our final prescriptions would make sure the patient would not have to be seen again. It would be a farewell, of course, but a separation in the recovered individual's best interest. I was a physician, I thought they were now happy to acknowledge. I would have to appreciate and even applaud the decision we had reached by mutual consent.

I did not talk with Chima about some of the impressions his parents left me with. I wasn't very good at putting impressions into so many words, and if he had asked for the words themselves I would have been at a loss. They were all so pleasant and polite. But I knew what they meant. It all added up to a final judgment. Whatever existed between their son and this woman was not to be taken seriously. It would carry no weight when his career choices had to be balanced out. I carried no weight. Our relationship had no weight. Once I thought I was walking on air, off on a cloud, light as a bubble and carefree as air. That was correct. I felt all those things. I just had the reason all wrong. My relationship with him made me feel as though I were walking on air, being all those unreal, insubstantial things because there was nothing in it solid enough to ground it in reality. I have to give his parents credit for helping me see that. I quickly got over the feeling that they had slighted and dismissed me. From their perspective the relationship with Chima was to be dismissed. They should have dismissed it and did so. But they had the reasons for doing so all wrong. Our relationship wasn't a threat. It just wasn't. It ended more or less at the same time that Chima decided to answer the call to find his true destiny in an English ambience. It was time I began to remember the call I had once heard.

Dr. Brown's kidney transplant unit had been busy, and Dr. Brown had not been away from the hospital for days. As proof of that all you had to do was listen. His voice, identifiable at all times, was now both unmistakable and unavoidable. Even if you did not have any of his preop or postop patients in your charge, you cringed when you heard the voice thunder. Your heart went out in pangs of sympathy for anyone who had failed the ultimate challenge. Once, a long time ago, you thought that transplantation itself was that. More recently you discovered that the real challenge was working for Dr. Brown. Every surgery intern and resident was, however, required to rotate to kidney transplant. No choice. Of the eighteen general surgery residents who started out, only six staggered to the finish line at the end of the year's training.

On the morning of the most commotion I had ever encountered, Dr. Brown had sent out a call for an early assembly of the entire transplant team. He arrived before anyone else, even before the chief resident, who should have known better than to let that happen. The resident finally rushed up, gray and red-eyed from his all-night duties. We hung back and let him open the door. Dr. Brown's voice seemed to reach out and drag him in by his white coat lapels. We followed like lambs, trying not to flinch from the verbal brickbats that flew in all directions.

When I say loud and thunderous I don't mean vague and indistinct. Each brickbat came precisely etched with the crime that justified its use. In this case the resident was being pelted with everything from the more or less acceptable and run-of-the-mill "incompetent" and "inept" through "useless," a "threat," and off into "practically murderous."

Our entrance distracted Dr. Brown, and he turned with a furious look and challenged us all with his question.

"What do you do when you suspect murder?" Our naturally dumbstruck looks did little to soften him. "What do you do when it's murder, practically premeditated murder?" he again demanded, now pointing at one hapless resident, who either looked particularly vulnerable or had the bad luck to be in Dr. Brown's line of vision.

"Ah . . . Ah . . . ," the poor man began, and then took a running leap into fantasy and let the words come tumbling out. "If there's a murder, I think we should call the police."

The idea struck Dr. Brown as eminently sensible. "Exactly!" he shouted. "Call the police!"

The man looked appalled at what he had begun. He gathered up all his remaining courage and ventured in a tentative voice, "If it is murder . . ."

"If?" countered the doctor, then narrowed his eyes with suspicion and asked, "Do you think I am a fool? Is that what you think?"

The man literally jumped back, as if that blasphemous idea was something alive and present and he had to disassociate himself from it at all costs.

"I'll show you if I'm a fool or not," he began, and motioned for the chief resident to move to the front of the room. He gave him just enough time to face us before hurling the first bolt at him.

"Why did the patient call you?"

The resident began bravely enough with "He said he had a fever."

" 'Said'? You had reason not to believe him?"

A pause of a minisecond, and then the resident accepted the correction: "He had a fever of 101.5."

"And you said, 'Take two Tylenol.' " We made the fatal mistake of interrupting him with some slight titters, having assumed that this was meant as a joke. Dr. Brown would have reared up on hind legs if he had such. But in our imaginations he did the equivalent, letting his voice peal out in indignation. "He told the patient to take two Tylenol and call him later!"

We pondered this for a silent moment but were allowed no more respite.

The doctor again spoke directly to the resident. "You knew the patient. You knew the patient's needs and the dangers he faced."

The resident nodded.

"Tell us."

We ached for the man standing there in such dejection. We wanted him to feel that we understood a mistake had been made and that he would have to publicly admit it, make this public confession. It would teach him humility. It would teach him never to take a moment of patient care for granted, never to forget a single step. We knew the lessons had to be learned. At that moment we almost agreed that this was as valid a way of teaching them as any.

The resident struggled to regain his composure and began, "The patient had undergone a kidney transplant three weeks previously. He did not mention any clinical signs other than fever. I told him to take his temperature again in two hours and call."

"If he died in the interval, who was responsible?"

We saw the resident stiffen but not back down. He said quietly, "I should have had him admitted at once. I should have found out for myself if he had other signs of possible rejection. I would have proceeded at once with the established antirejection protocol. I did not. At the very least I should have persisted in asking. No matter how carefully they are instructed, patients don't think about warning signs . . . they don't want to."

The mood in the room had changed during this quiet account. Dr. Brown had his arms crossed over his broad chest, and his head was bowed, listening with great concentration to the resident.

The resident went on after his brief pause, speaking calmly, delivering a report that he and his superior would ponder over and then work toward some conclusion.

"He did have the good sense to get to the hospital, even though it was by then almost dawn. I examined him at once. The graft was tender and enlarged. He told me then about the gain in weight, the swelling in his legs and ankles. He said he did not think either of these was important enough to mention. He had been told they were possible warning signs, but he probably did not want to think about them that way."

Dr. Brown interrupted him here, speaking calmly, with a slight shrug of resignation. "He only wanted something for his fever and headache." There was not a trace of sarcasm or irony in any word of it. He recognized that the resident had understood the patient.

I felt we had all moved closer together. The air seemed to have cleared, defused. The real threats had been identified. We would begin again to work toward solving them. Dr. Brown moved to one side, leaving the open space for the chief resident. He unclasped his arms and with one broad gesture told the man that now the presentation was his, rightfully earned. I had discovered again that none if it was ever going to be easy. No step could be skipped. Every step had to be taken in turn. You would never dare a shortcut.

CHAPTER 26

The first few times he tricked me, and I called the unfamiliar numbers that showed up on my beeper. Then I tried screening any unfamiliar numbers against a list I made up of those I normally would have to respond to. But Palmer's essentially nomadic existence gave him a variety of places to call from, and he used every available number to continue his campaign of casual intimidation and petty blackmail. The price he asked to absolve me of the sin of practically saving his life fluctuated from week to week. I pointed out the inconsistency to him, but that only led him to conclude that I was willing to bargain. I did not bargain. Sometimes these totally irrational and even paranoid conversational breaks provided a little surrealistic diversion from the usually grim realities of nights and days as a surgical resident.

I had no idea how he got hold of my beeper number or the number I had switched to after his first call. The most obvious answer was that he had some inside accomplice. Not an unreasonable supposition, given the frequency with which he had availed himself of hospital services. And Palmer could be very charming and persuasive if he thought it would be worth his while. I think he was one of those men who went through life securing accomplices rather than friends or loved ones.

I did not want to think about it, but the chances were he had actually persuaded someone in the hospital that he had been wronged by me. Even though I was only a woman I had the advantage of being part of the system. Over the course of our conversations Palmer had said as much, and more.

One day I had just automatically called the unfamiliar number on my beeper and given my name to the tired old man who had answered. Not Palmer, I sighed in relief. The man apologized, began to explain that he had not called, then checked himself and repeated my name, remembering something, putting things together. It was Palmer, all right, but not the one I knew. This was Palmer Senior, and he had gathered enough about me and my encounter with his son to want to apologize. He did so, beginning in slow, halting words, as if he had the greatest reluctance to say anything at all about his son. Then he seemed to gather his strength for the unwelcome task of answering for his son yet another time.

He understood everything from his son's stray talk, heard during the few times they had been together recently, the few times, he corrected, that he had allowed the boy (he corrected that as well) back into the house. One of those times was unfortunately earlier that day, but it had been enough for more damage. He understood his son had been making contact with me. He knew a little of the reason why but would learn the rest. He apologized for the call made without his authority from his home. He assured me he would see to the matter and, again apologizing, hung up.

I put all that aside in the following days. I was doing a rotation in intensive care and would be on call every other night for three months. The unit had only twelve beds, and not every bed was always occupied. But every patient in the unit had to be followed round the clock, so that meant you always had someone needing care at any moment. I tried not to let it all become a blur of vital signs and blood tests and IV drips and tubes and high-tech equipment humming and signaling in the background. I had to remind myself that all these potentially life-sustaining things were doing what I was trying to do, sustain the patient. I didn't want to think that in some cases the machinery was doing a better job than I could, was doing things that were simply beyond my capacity—not just mine but that of any human being. Giving technology the least gracious compliment you could think of, you had to admit that most of the machinery did certain things faster than you could and did them without getting distracted or tired or confused. Machinery could also provoke other thoughts, the kind of thoughts that almost made you envious. Machines never questioned whether they were really doing the patient any good. Machines did not wonder if they should turn themselves off when they became intrusive. A machine always was certain that what it did was in the patient's best interest.

I had to replace the IV line in one of my patients that night. I would have to find a usable vein, tighten the tourniquet on his thin arm until some possible vein came into sight. What chance of that, when he was so wasted that the veins seemed flat and collapsed. They seemed barely capable of their primary function of returning to his weakened heart the blood that sustained him. I would have to intrude on that primary function. No patient could die without an IV. That seemed a kind of unwritten but strictly observed law.

He had already had several operations for the stomach cancer that had long since spread insidiously through his body and would certainly kill him, soon, later, with or without the benefit of the machines. His wife and grown son had been there all day, every day. They had come up to me on every occasion and asked again what could they expect, what were the chances, when would I be able to tell them something? They could not or would not see the answers to those questions in the futility of everything that had been done so far. Now they were pondering a decision about further surgery. I had tried to lead them close to accepting that nothing would add significantly to the days left him and any further pain would give even that little time less meaning. I could only lead them so far, and if they did not yet want to cross over to the truth of the man's situation, I had to respect that, the only decision they could make at the moment.

He had not opened his eyes when I entered and began to speak to him. I asked if he wanted me to put the line in his right or left hand, if he thought that one would be easier than the other. He did not answer, and I knew that it would not matter. Either one would be painful. I examined both arms and hands and found little to choose between them. I continued to talk, telling him what I was doing, step by step. He kept his eyes closed as I went on with this almost meaningless description, telling him that I was opening the IV kit and removing the bag containing the nutrients and fluids, was connecting the bag to the tubing, hanging the bag, opening the clamp on the tube so that the fluid could run down, removing any air from the tube. . . .

I could feel how tired he was, tired and afraid of what was happening to him. I could not go ahead and tell him that I understood what he was feeling and that I had read fear in his silence and that he could admit the fear because it was real enough. I went on with my simple description, telling him how I would proceed once everything was readied. The words seemed to form a bridge between us. I could sense that he was listening and concentrating on them, almost using them to pull himself back into a world that contained something more than his despair and pain. Even words that amounted to little more than package instructions were managing to do that for him. He knew that I was taking time to reach him.

I tightened the tourniquet and held his hand in mine. I asked him to make a fist and guided his hand as he did so, moving my hand slowly to his slow rhythm. I stuck the needle as quickly as I had ever done, but still I stiffened, expecting the gasp of pain I had always dreaded. But there was no gasp, and after a few moments he opened his eyes for the first time.

"I don't want any more of that," he said.

"I'm sorry it hurt."

"No," he said. "It was . . . gentle . . . more than most."

"The IV will help . . ." I began without much conviction.

He sensed this. There was not a trace of anger in his voice when he said, "Them. Not me. Helps them." I took his hand again and felt the slight returned pressure as his eyes almost dared me to deny this. I just nodded, and he went on, "They see the line and think something's being done. Lifeline. Stupid, isn't it?"

"No," I said. "It helps."

"Them. Right? Them." When I agreed he seemed to settle back against the pillow, satisfied. I did not want to break this kind of pause. I waited until he said with the lightest tone I had yet heard, "You wouldn't think a man in my condition would be able to do anything for anybody."

I felt encouraged enough to make one of those statements that are better read than spoken. I said, "You can help them let go. Show them how."

"Sure, sure," he said, dismissing this. Then he took my hand in his again for a second and leaned his head a bit toward me, getting confidential. "Listen," he began, and then gave the IV line a tug, "since this thing is only window dressing, do it without the needle next time. Promise?"

I gave my promise, but it was one I did not have to keep. He was so tired. He finally let go the next day. He would have given them more time to catch up with him, but he was so tired he had to let them find in their own time the peace he knew he would have.

Palmer was waiting for me one afternoon as I was leaving the hospital. Perhaps one of his inside agents had tipped him off as to when I would be leaving. I had had no beeper contact with him for several days and accepted the calm without undue speculation about the cause. So what if he had gotten himself arrested? It certainly would not have been the first or only time. Or the last. Whether he had desisted from pestering me further because of parental pressure or even respect for his father I doubted strongly. Palmer Senior, for all his evident goodwill toward me, seemed too downtrodden by his son's behavior to exercise much control or influence.

Palmer looked in fairly good shape as he walked across the street toward me. I waited on the hospital side and let him come near, feeling a bit more secure on my own territory. I found myself checking his gait as he approached but quickly shook off the idea that I was looking to see if he had even the trace of a limp. Cleaning out his abscesses would not have resulted in a noticeable limp even if the procedure had been done by the most inept, ham-fisted, amateurish, beginning surgeon. Someone with those limitations would not have survived Dr. Brown's wrath for a minute, regardless of the, shall we say, moral character of the patient.

As usual the area in front of the hospital was crowded with visitors entering and leaving, staff going on or off duty, patients with family members carrying belongings, vases of flowers, semiwilted but still capable of giving pleasure, balloons limp but still partially aloft. As Palmer came close I noticed he had gotten a fresh shirt and jacket since I'd last seen him. He seemed surprisingly together. I couldn't quite make out what he was saying over the noise of the crowd, so he raised his voice and repeated the words:

"I said, 'I decided against pressing charges.'"

Same old Palmer. However, I did not say anything at all like that. I didn't want to remind him that we had any kind of previous acquaintance on which I could base such a comparison. I just shrugged my shoulders, telegraphing, "I give up. No contest."

He seemed to accept this, but with ill grace. Actually, he was plain sour when he said, "Okay. So now it's over. Nobody's holding any grudges." He turned and even spun on his heel, a maneuver I watched again with a keen and thoroughly reassured professional eye. He did it right smart, but the effect was spoiled by the abrupt appearance of a wiry little man wearing a straw hat that came no higher than Palmer's nose. But it was high enough to stop him, which then gave the little man a chance to pull the younger by the arm and turn him around to face me again.

Mr. Palmer Senior took off the hat, nodded solemnly, and made the unnecessary introduction. I wished at once that he was not there, did not have the need to be there, had never had to do it before or ever would again. Mr. Palmer said, "That's not what he meant to say."

"You couldn't hear what I said," the younger man answered, again with surprising ill grace for one who had little else to trade on but grace.

"There wasn't enough time for you to say what has to be said. I could see that without hearing. I believe more in what I see." He didn't have to finish the thought. He had long ago given up believing his son's words. To his lasting sorrow, he knew his actions.

For a moment it seemed there would be a standoff between the rigidly determined father and the evasive and angry son. I tried to catch the old man's eye, to let him know that I would

consider the matter ended, that I had already accepted whatever it was the young man had offered as sufficient apology,
recompense, act of contrition, purpose of amendment, all of it.

Palmer relented and began. The phrases were not his, but
he had memorized them well enough to give them some sem-
blance of sincerity. The father had used the language of his
own era to forge such an apology, and I heard it as though he
himself were speaking. How often in the past he must have
had to do such a thing for his son, and how painful for him
to have learned what little use his intervention ever was. It
was one generation apologizing for the sins of another, sins
whose cause or meaning or justification they could not begin
to fathom.

Palmer never got to the end, although he was well into admitting that he had abused me and denied my good intentions
toward him and had maligned my character and had been
guilty of slander and had no right in law to testify against me.
Maybe having to say the words that officially put an end to his
efforts to make me pay up proved the last straw. He'd gladly
admit to anything, but not to the collapse of his dream, always
the same dream, the dream of an easy source for a quick fix, a
deep source, good for many a fix. At the stage Palmer had arrived, things were that simple.

He spun on his heels too quickly for the old man to intervene and was off and across the street at what I thought a
pretty fast clip for a man with his leg problems.

The old man had suffered worse defeats and worse humiliations. He accepted my brief thanks and offered his hand
in farewell. He held my hand for a minute, and his eyes
searched my face before he spoke. "He thinks your getting
ahead holds him back."

I might have looked as if I were going to protest, even
though I was not. He held up his hand to stop me nevertheless
and continued. "You don't think about that. Everything held

him back in his opinion. But himself. Only thing in life free of any responsibility is himself. You understand?"

I did not have an answer, and he did not really want one. He finally let go of my hand and adjusted his straw hat. "Where's he going?" he said, searching my face again. I was silent.

"I'll be burying him," he began suddenly. "Everything else failed, and all I'll be good for is burying. Yes. I told him that. Know what I told him?"

And now I knew he wanted me to find the answer for myself.

"You know, don't you?"

I nodded, and he said the words carefully. "I told him it would just be returning the favor because he done the same to me."

CHAPTER 27

The operating room was cool, but his brow was glistening and furrowed with concentration. I always imagined I could physically feel the concentrated will with which Dr. Brown moved through each second of the transplant procedure. I did not have to look over and see the strip of gleaming black skin between mask and head covering to know the toll the work took. I felt the concentration like something forcing me into his field of control and bending my will to his. With the rational part of my head I knew that some maneuvers were more complex, involved more risk, demanded more meticulous technique than others. In spite of this I came away from the six or so hours believing that every second had been the most critical. He kept everyone to that level of intensity, the intensity with which he himself was fired.

I was serving as a minor assistant during a kidney transplant, holding the retractor that pulled back the lower muscles of the abdomen, exposing the femoral vein and artery that would supply blood to the transplanted kidney. Dr. Brown was dissecting along the superficial femoral vessels, working quickly but carefully to avoid any damage to the vital structures. The donated kidney would be carefully sutured to the patient's own vessels, and then the blood flow would begin and the organ would start to function. By that final miracle of joining vessel to vessel, a miracle added to the scores of others accomplished so far into the operation, the new kidney would become firm and pink and alive within minutes. But until the anastomoses was completed, until Dr. Brown and Ian, the second assistant, had placed every stitch, the patient's femoral vein and artery had to be clamped off to stop the flow of blood and to keep the operating field clear for the suturing.

I had not noticed who had been responsible for the clamps, but it was probably something that Dr. Brown would let his chief resident, George, do. George was one of the rising stars of the transplant service. His position as Dr. Brown's protégé had been confirmed, for in a few months he would be sent off for a two-year stint at the country's foremost liver and kidney transplant center. On his return he was destined to be put in charge of starting up our hospital's own liver transplant unit.

Four clamps were already in place above and below the sites of the joining. My attention was focused on the donor kidney as Dr. Brown began to join the vein remnants in the donor kidney to the patient's own. But a slight movement just above his hand caught my eye. One of the arterial clamps seemed to be slipping, not accidentally brushed by the surgeon, but slipping, coming loose. I knew that if a clamp slipped and did not hold, there would be an instantaneous, massive outpouring of blood. A patient who sustained such a loss could die in minutes.

My hand shot out, and I knew I had obscured the surgeon's line of vision. That was not acceptable, I knew, but I managed to catch the clamp and hold it. Ian saw in an instant what had happened and took the clamp from me, letting me get back into the position to which I had been assigned. Dr. Brown looked across at George, at Ian, and then at me. At first I assumed he had not noticed my movement and reach. He glanced furtively at George and the clamp. And then I saw that Dr. Brown understood what had just happened. He had barely stopped his work except for the second he had focused on George. A surgeon's eyes never left the operating field. Dr. Brown did not look at me as he returned to the work of joining the patient's artery to the donor artery. But I knew that the slight bending of his head as he picked up the next suture was an acknowledgment of what I had done. And of George as well. He had said all that was necessary. All I would need. All anyone concentrating on the job at hand would want or expect. It was enough.

Word of the near accident, or of my interruption of something that might have caused an accident, got around. Some joker congratulated me on my careful staging of the event, just the thing to get the chief's attention and win some points. I even got credit for daring to take such a high risk for a little career advancement, even if the risk was more the patient's than mine. There were not that many opportunities for humor, even simple-minded humor, in surgery, and I didn't mind at all.

After that experience and after I had several other occasions to watch the kidney transplant team in action, I felt that I was getting ready to make another important decision. I felt that I was being led in a direction I would not have considered earlier. But then, I was only just beginning to feel confident that I could manage to stick it out through the remainder of the residency program. I would become a surgeon. But after that? Perhaps there might still be another challenge I would have to consider. From the beginning, medicine had meant one challenge after another. I had gotten into the habit of peering over the present obstacle to get some idea of how steep the next one was. I wanted to judge what kind of running leap it might take to make it over.

I talked with Ian and finally got up enough courage one day to ask him outright what he thought of my chances of getting into organ transplantation. "You mean Dr. Brown's service?" he asked, as though I had just stumbled through the hospital doors and hadn't gotten to know who was who among the powers that be.

"Ian, please don't make fun of me."

"I won't make fun if you promise not to make mincemeat—of yourself."

"I've worked with him. He's not as bad as that."

"Of course he's not."

"Don't say he's worse!"

"He's a great surgeon. Great doctor. Would give his life for his patient. Comes too close on too many occasions, in my opinion." I nodded at each word. It was all true. Ian did not need me to say I agreed with him. He knew I did. I gave him a minute and then I asked, "Then what's my problem?"

The answer came instantly. "Proving you're good enough." Then he hesitated and added, "Somebody worth the investment he would have to make in you to get you good enough."

"Is anybody?"

"Beside the point when you're the body in question. You know what happens to such bodies?" I nodded. Mincemeat. We sat in silence. I stole a glance or two at him, but he was too preoccupied to return my look. Then he had it. He began, "Don't ask him."

"But if I don't, how . . . how will he know?"

"Don't ask him right off, like 'Hey, take me on! Teach me transplantation.' "

"I would never—"

"Even if you whispered it would sound like that. Don't get

too close. He won't take to that. Take an indirect route. Let him know you want to do some research. Say all you want to do is gather data for a paper. Ask him for help. Just say you want to work under his supervision. Not the OR. No, certainly not. Not you. Not doing transplants. Just some research. Say you'll tabulate his patient data. Computer scut work. You won't be too much of an investment on his part that way. You won't be raising expectations or anything."

I could readily agree to this, but there was something about the way Ian was putting it that disturbed me. "I won't ask for him to invest anything."

"Good girl."

"Doctor," I said pointedly.

"Right. Catching the clamp might have reminded him of that."

"It was a lucky save. A one-shot. An accident."

"Accidents don't happen in his operating room. He assumed you caught it because you were trained to catch such things. In any case, you scored points with him. Use them wisely."

I felt he wanted the discussion to end, but I could not suppress the feeling of unease that came over me every time I recalled the operating room scene. I just let the first words that came into my head spill out. I asked, "If accidents don't happen, how come that one did?"

Ian dismissed this quickly. "You made up for it. That's enough."

There wasn't anything like free time off for the leisurely pursuit of a research project. If you wanted to do research, it had to be shoehorned into the ordinary day-and-night schedule, right along with rounds and patients and even the rotations that took you off in all directions to other hospitals for weeks at a time.

Dr. Brown did guide me toward a project. It seemed daunting, just from a statistical point of view—examining the outcomes of kidney transplantation in his service over its entire ten-year history. What was the rate of success, what the rate of failure? If a patient's body began to reject the new kidney, what had been done to reverse the rejection and save the kidney? Did some of these desperate interventions work better than others? How long had it taken before the best means of preventing rejection were proven?

Gathering all this information and sorting it out and keeping track of the changes in incidences of rejection and variations in success with different kinds of antirejection therapy would require more than my effort alone. The research team I eventually worked with would take many long hours scrutinizing every record and patient history before a clear picture emerged and all the clues to the best means of saving our most vulnerable patients were discovered and defined.

As we read through the statistics, another picture bled through and we were faced with the reality of individuals and not just numbers. And with it for me came a new appreciation of Dr. Brown and what this reality had meant for him over the years we scanned. I could not look at the records of his patients without seeing the man himself, for they and their world defined him and his.

He had all these years been reaching out to save the most endangered members of the most endangered community. His patients were those least likely to survive in spite of his intensive efforts to give them a new chance at life. Understanding the odds against any one of his patients surviving gave an insight into the almost fanatical dedication he brought to his work. The tyranny he exercised over all who worked for him was nothing willed by a tyrannical personality. It was merely a reflection of his understanding of the odds against any success whatsoever.

The patients over the years had been almost exclusively

black, largely male, invariably poor, often poorly educated. Poor meant poor: Almost 70 percent of patients had no income at all; 30 percent had poverty-level incomes. These patients had developed end-stage renal disease as a consequence of hypertension, a condition to which blacks seem to be more prone than whites. Intravenous drug abuse and diabetes were also significant causes of kidney failure. Many were still in the prime of life, most still not fifty years of age.

These were the odds. These were the factors that mitigated against any effort to bring as complex, costly, and risky a procedure as organ transplantation to such a population. These were the odds that made each successful transplantation a miracle in itself. The miracle was not that by the end of more than a decade, 92 percent of transplanted patients were surviving. The miracle was that the effort to win these men and women back to life was being made at all. The victory finally documented by the study would not have been so sweet if it had not been so difficult to achieve.

We fitted together the pieces, small pieces representing hour-by-hour daily care of the transplant patient. We documented all the ifs—if the white blood cell count is less than five thousand, if severe acute tubular necrosis is present, if dialysis is necessary. We documented each change in drugs and drug combinations from day one through the prescribed lifelong regimen. From year to year we watched for the drugs and the regimens that were associated with fewer incidences of kidney graft rejections, those associated, however statistically insignificant, with a higher incidence of rejection. As the research project entered its final stages, I realized that I had been living each of these cases, following the numbers as though they were patients I could easily visualize. I could now easily imagine myself being called to the patient with severe acute tubular necrosis or threatened rejection of the newly transplanted kidney. I would be ordering dialysis and add antilymphocyte globulin and a change in immunosuppression drug dosage until dialysis was no longer needed. As each patient's record was examined, I found myself anticipating the appropriate regimen. I had met the next challenge. I could begin to judge the height of the next hurdle.

What I could not judge as well were the intentions of the driver coming up on my left, and fast. I was moving along at a slightly, admittedly only slightly, slower pace, but it was early Saturday and the highway was not heavily traveled. I might have braked faster had I anticipated that a driver in the left lane on an early Saturday morning would be unfamiliar with his exit and accelerate and cut across me. My logic was logical: If it was a crowded Friday night he would be a commuter and know when his exit was coming up.

Logic ran through my head as the absurdity of an accident swept me away, out of control, into the dividing concrete and then out and into it several times for good measure before I came to a grating halt. It was early and the countryside had been quiet, so I concluded that the racket of jabbering birds must be coming from within my head. I sat there dazed and befuddled until I was aroused by a knock on the window and a close-up of a face with an anxious look.

In time the police came, then the ambulance. There was a hospital nearby, but I felt I should go home to my own kind, as it were, and the ambulance crew was finally persuaded after the obligatory showing of rank. I think they assumed that as a resident in surgery I wanted to be on home base so that I could run my own case.

They could not have gotten it more wrong. I was met with Code Yellow in its most formal garb. I lifted my head from the gurney and recognized all the old faces. They were coming at me with scissors and had sliced through everything I had on before I could protest. I resolved that would be the first practice I would try to abolish should I ever win any clout in emergency. The scissors told me that I was to get the entire treatment I had visited on so many over the years. The tunnel effect of the CT scan, the roll this way, roll that way of the X ray, the blood and the IV—especially the IV. I realized no one had yet come up with a totally painless insertion of the IV needle.

Only after all this was done and I was wheeled up to a room for an overnight stay did I begin to register the bruises and aches. And the fatigue. It must have been this unique chance to see a hospital room from a hospital bed that let me imagine myself a patient for a moment, which I now was. I was unexpectedly happy to have the ordinary routine of life suspended. In the corridors the sounds of the hospital rose and fell. It had become so much background noise for me over the years that I hardly took it in. Now I began to pick apart the seamless fabric and marveled at how many different noises, signaling so many different intentions had been woven in.

As the afternoon wore on, I rose and sank into sleep or half sleep, thanks to the sedative I had been given. At times I woke and felt submerged in dense silence, which had its own pulse and feel. I imagined pressing my body against the silence and feeling rather than hearing it. It was a very reassuring, comforting feeling. In one long sequence, whether long in terms of actual time I could not tell, but in one ongoing sequence I felt I had gone inside the silence so totally that I had brought it inside me and we were breathing the same air, quietly there inside. I understood that I had not stopped in ages to listen to the silence or breathe with it so intimately. I had been racing and catching my breath in order to race on faster. But this was the first time I had stopped to listen to the breath of life within me. I drifted off again, wondering if I would ever stop long enough to listen to myself and was that something I could learn how to do? Did someone know how to teach me, and what would I ask to be taught?

* * *

Sounds changed, became more clearly separated. I was coming out of sleep again and now could distinctly hear short intakes of breath. I opened my eyes and could not see anyone in the room, which was now softly lit by concealed lights behind the bed. I had been given one of the rooms reserved for special patients, and soft lighting was part of the extra-charge atmosphere. I heard the sounds, one short intake, a pause, another. Nothing mysterious. Someone had the sniffles, and I hoped it wasn't contagious with me in my precarious condition.

"Need a tissue?" I asked the silence. A long arm reached up and pulled one out.

"Take two," I mumbled, and then Reggie, one of the transplant attendings, rose up beside the bed.

"Just came by to check the vital signs. Heard you got smashed up."

"Car did. Totaled. I got a rest. But they said they would have to tow it away. I wanted to wait to see."

Reggie sniffled again and didn't bother with a tissue. He muttered something that sounded like a good-bye, and at the door I saw him almost collide with Ian. Reggie's greeting was indistinct, and Ian came to the bed with a slightly puzzled expression.

"Not staying for dinner?"

"He has a cold."

"I hear they serve only lobster in this suite. Too bad you're on the IV."

I said, "What's the matter with Reggie's nose?"

"Postnasal drip."

"It's drugs, isn't it?"

Ian responded in a mocking academic voice, "Alcohol and drug abuse are common among physicians in general." Then he went on in his normal voice, "And there are any number of reports from Boston to L.A. that will give you the figures on tranquilizers, opiates, marijuana . . . and cocaine. Let's say they got the figures and we got the problem."

"Reggie has."

"Brown has."

I didn't say anything for a moment as all the pieces fell into place. Then I almost whispered I was so touched, "That's sad."

Ian gave me a gentle shove on the shoulder. "No, sweetheart. That ain't sad. That's tragic. The stuff of true tragedy. Native-grown variety. Nothing about it especially rare or exotic. Our own natural produce."

And there it was. Dr. Brown had pinned his hopes on this bright, energetic, really competent, achieving, out-of-the-ordinary young black man and pulled every string imaginable to get him a fellowship to study at the country's, the world's, foremost transplant center. And Reggie put it all up his nose and blew it. All the usual explanations come to mind. The pressures of medical school and surgical training are too great. I can attest to that. The spotlight is always on you, not so the audience can applaud every great move but so that every slip can be duly noted and criticized. I can attest to that as well. Maybe Reggie just got tired of always being reminded of how unusual he really was. Not exactly a compliment. Tends to give you something like what's been called the survivor's syndrome: Why should I have been spared when all the others went down? Why should the burden of living and attesting be placed on me?

As a young black man trained as a skilled surgeon Reggie was the survivor supreme. Somewhere along the line someone must have shown him the figures. Say there were about half a million young black men of college age in the United States (which is not to suggest that many of them get there). Surveys showed that only one half of one percent were prepared to study science. That figures out to less than 3,000 black men even

remotely ready to march alongside Reggie. Only a minute percentage of that number climbed as far as he had. He might just
have gotten lonely. Or too depressed at the thought that on
his only-too-human shoulders the weight of so much expectation and hope deferred had to press.

Dr. Brown was like a father with a gifted son, one who
needed in his opinion only discipline and application to succeed. He might not have wanted to take into consideration the
emotional factors that derailed the young man. For a while he
took to ignoring or excusing Reggie's slipups, as long as they
were minor—a patient's preop test forgotten and not scheduled, a patient's history not scrutinized carefully enough, a no-
show for a teaching conference. But he knew Reggie wasn't
making it. Like the father with the gifted son, he went on hoping and taking still another chance. All along he was waiting
for the final thing that has to be excused but cannot be. He
waits for the time he will have to cut his losses and with it all
his hopes.

Time was getting late for Dr. Brown and he had thought
he was preparing for that by grooming Reggie to succeed
him. Reggie did acquire the skills of a competent surgeon, but
the kind of successor Dr. Brown demanded could not share his
time with a destructive habit he wasn't willing or able to break.
Finally he fired him.

Going to conferences is as much a part of the life of a surgeon
as tying a knot. I got early training. Because I had already been
working on a project detailing our transplant service's struggle
to improve kidney patient survival rates, I was asked to deliver
a speech on the entire ten years of transplant experience at the
hospital. Daylong professional meetings in big hotels in big
cities probably all get to seem the same after a while, but to me
it was all new enough to be awe-inspiring and somewhat terri-
fying. I was going to be standing on my first lecture podium,

delivering my first paper, being scrutinized by my peers and by the major figures in the field.

The conference was in New York, and so was my sister, who was attending a meeting of a spiritual lodge to which she belonged. I would not join her, but I would take from her the calm reassurance she always brought. "Lean on me," she said when I first embraced her. "Lean on me. You look like you need all the support you can get."

I tried to attribute my nervousness to the talk I would be giving, but she brushed aside such an easy excuse, and put her finger on what my hectic schedule was costing.

"You're not spending any time with yourself, getting to be a stranger." I had not told her about the accident and my night in the hospital and the sense of calm and silence I had experienced. I said vaguely, "I don't have much time."

She did not take this limp excuse, so I added as a kind of explanation, "You know . . . there's always work."

"Time for work but not time for yourself? The work's that important?"

I treated it like a joke. "Of course you know it's important."

As usual she had the trump card. "You shouldn't let someone you don't know do it."

I knew exactly what she meant. I just didn't know how to do it, how to get hold of myself again.

As if reading my mind and seeing my question, she took my arm and brought me closer to the large groups of men and women clustered about in the hotel corridor. They were, she told me, come together from all over the world and from all nations. Such divisions didn't matter, she said. They all understood one another because they were thinking the same thought. Slightly moving her hand to include them all, she continued, "They practice. They seek guidance from above, from one another, from within. But they practice listening most of all."

I recalled the moments of silence in the hospital room again, and I said, "I think I understand."

My sister said, "Yes, you understand about listening. You have been a good listener all your life. How you keep it all in your head I don't know, but you must have there everything you ever listened to. Now listen to something you don't take time enough to listen to."

We were together as much as we could be during those few days. She introduced me to friends who were attending her meeting. She told me there was a place near me where I could go and meet such people. It would give me a way to break free. I said yes, more to humor her than out of any certainty I would ever take up the suggestion. If she had intuited that, she never let on, considering her suggestion accepted. Later I realized she was right as usual.

I delivered the paper, more relaxed about it than I expected to be. I heard the sound of my voice as if it were coming from elsewhere, and that gave me a chance to change the tone and pitch as I went, as if I were playing on an instrument that responded to any change at once. The applause was reward enough, but I did not want to accept it. Instead I pointed to Dr. Brown in the audience. He had been watching me closely during the entire presentation and had been applauding more vigorously than anyone so that he at first did not respond to the people around him turning now and redirecting the praise to him. It took several tugs on his coat to get him to his feet, and then we all gave what reward we could for the work I had only chronicled but he had performed. When the committees awarded a prize to my talk, we all knew that it was meant for him as well. I knew it was for the goals reached and also for those that, for all his labor and care, could not be.

Soon after there followed a period when one day pushed away the previous with what seemed a relentless burden of patients

to be cared for, families to be counseled or consoled, conferences to attend or address. In the midst of this I received a call
that brought it all to an abrupt halt. My grandmother was dying, and all who were scattered were trying to assemble at the
old farm for her last moments and blessing. I felt the incredible
tug to go back, to break away for as much time as it would be
and be there with them and for that unthinkable end of that
life. But I said no, no one to wait for me, no one to make any
plans, there was no possibility I could leave all that remained
unfinished . . . and when that was finished another thing would
be ready to be faced and dealt with.

I made up my mind and gave my excuses and regrets and
gave my messages of condolences and thanks and wishes for
safety. And the next day, when all the family had gone ahead I
changed my mind, suddenly, without a thought. How absurd
of me to think I would not be there for my grandmother's last
moments of life. I had no time to do anything but arrange a
flight, find enough willing residents to cover for me, and pack
a small bag. The airport in Haiti was actually closer to the
farm than to the city, where most taxis wanted to return.
When I finally convinced a driver, the one with the least desirable cab, to take me up into the mountains, I also had to
convince him I knew the way. I did, in a vague, that-looks-
like-the-kind-of-place-you-turn-at way. There was nothing
like an official address, but the few farmers we encountered
acted like relay points, giving us just enough direction to get
us to the next miraculously appearing farmer, who then did
the same.

The place was hushed when we drove up in a cloud, I having urged the driver on the last few remembered miles with
desperation and fear that I would be too late. Far from the
house, up a slight incline that was one of her last cultivated
strips of land, the small tent kept the sun from the mourners. I
ran up the slope, and everyone turned to me, looks of amazement on their drawn faces. As I came near they let me through

without any attempt at greeting, and I saw the coffin moving slowly on straps the four men held and were letting slip through their hands. They looked questioningly at me, but I motioned them to continue. I came with nothing that should stop them. If I had come in her last days or hours, I would also have been with nothing to stop her going. And I looked around at the land, looking back over the growing field I had come through, looking then at every face that kept gazing at mine as though I had come out of nowhere, could not be accounted for by any normal explanation. I went from one to another then, taking hands, kissing and being kissed, staying for an embrace and tears with some. And while this was being done the coffin was already lying deep in the earth, waiting for the living to remember it for the final ceremony. She was back home now, at rest and free, becoming all spirit now and always ours to keep.

It was the end of my fourth year in general surgery and time for me to make a final decision about a subspecialty. I would need a senior faculty member to sponsor me. And because I had made up my mind that I wanted to become a transplant surgeon, I would need to ask Dr. Brown if he would sponsor me. I believe the last person to have asked this, several years earlier, was Reggie. I did not know if that would count in my favor or automatically against me. If Reggie, a gifted male resident, could so disappoint all the hopes placed in him, what chance did I, a woman, have?

These and similar reasons to turn around, leave before I approached Dr. Brown's office door, all rushed through my head. I knocked on the door and waited. I waited a long time before trying again lest I appear impatient or uncivil or too convinced of my purpose there to tolerate any further delay. I waited even longer for a response. I took the silence for the answer I feared would be inevitable in any case. No one is answering because the answer is no. I went away. I waited for the elevator. I automatically began to imagine which would arrive on the floor first.

I do not remember if I had intuited the right elevator, but when the doors opened Dr. Brown stepped out and at once took my arm and brought me back down the corridor with him. I cannot remember if he asked me why I was there on that floor or where I was going. I think I caught up with him somewhere in the middle of a sentence or a second paragraph. Perhaps I had been following unconsciously, having known in my head and heart what he had to be saying, having known them since Ian spoke about Reggie and what had never materialized.

I was walking with him with my head bent, but I would nod from time to time. Yes, he was not getting younger, might even be said to be getting older. Yes, it was wise to—no, stupid not to—have someone trained to carry on the work. Yes, the certificate of need to begin the liver transplant service will be granted, and they will have a go-ahead to begin this desperately needed service, which would begin to reclaim the lives of so many men and women in the city who had never had the chance that many throughout the country could almost take for granted.

We were in his office now. He offered me the chair across from him and sat at his desk. My head was empty of all the things I had known he would say. He had said everything that Ian and I had assumed would be said about his work and the need to have it continue and the pressing needs of our patients.

And then he began saying what I could never have imagined unless I was asked to begin to put words around a miracle and give it present and future meaning. He said he would sponsor me in transplant surgery. He said he would recommend me for training, he would recommend that I be considered for a fellowship to train with the world's leading liver transplant surgeon and his gifted team of surgeons. And when all that was done, he said he would wish that I return and lead this transplant center, the one that he had fathered for so many years.

I must have thanked him because words were exchanged and plans made. But I was too distracted by all who began to enter the room, filling it with their unexpected welcome, desired presence, as far back as the nun who first wrote the first mathematical problem on the blackboard. She was there along with every teacher who wrote in my high school graduation book, and Ms. Diamond, and Daniel and Helen and Louisa May, and Joe, and Dr. Norwood, and my father, mother, and sister. Dr. Brown offered me his hand in farewell, and I took it. I shook his hand, and I embraced all who had come this far with me, and it did not seem any miracle at all that they were there, for it was not a celebration for me but rather for all of them.

CHAPTER 28

Imagine having listened with awe to tales of a magical king-
dom—Camelot, the Land of Oz, Hollywood, take your pick—
and then waking up and finding yourself there, and by
invitation. The city I came to doesn't have the romantic ring
of any of the above, but for everyone who has followed the
history of organ transplantation, it is the place where the miracles are wrought. It was here that the great surgeon who had
performed the first successful liver transplant in 1967 created
the surgical and medical support teams that made his the most
active and successful liver transplant center not only in the
United States but also in the entire world.

I could not be considered a pioneer when I arrived in 1988
to begin my three years of training in the clinical fellowship
that Dr. Brown had recommended me for. The decade of the

eighties had seen the most dramatic increase in transplantation of all kinds—liver, kidney, heart and heart-lung, and even pancreas, the most experimental of all. Because of these great strides, I was in a sense riding the crest. I was going to be able to benefit from the giant steps that the first pioneers had taken, and, most gratifying of all, I was going to work directly with the pioneers themselves. Once again I had the feeling that the covers of the book containing all the wisdom I wanted to acquire had been opened and I was being allowed inside to become a part of what I had read. Often in the past I had used techniques of visualization to project myself into some impending situation and prepare emotionally for its demands. I must confess I had never done that with the situation I was now entering. The notion that I would be present in the same operating room with the legendary figures who had made it all possible was something beyond even my vivid imagination. I wanted to pinch myself to make sure it was really me.

It really was me, and I was really in for it this time. I recalled I felt something like that at every other critical turning point in the past. But nothing in my entire past was in any way like this. Not that I had much time to think about anything as personal as my life and past experience. I was plunged head over heels into the daily round of patient care. I had experience of that before, about thirteen years' worth, as a premed, an undergraduate medical student, and then during general surgery residency. But I had never had to be responsible for so many patients at once, or so many who were so constantly poised on the edge of a potentially life-threatening crisis.

At any period I would be responsible for as many as forty patients, some waiting for a transplant, others recovering after receiving one. It often was impossible to distinguish the degree

of intensive care each group required. Many if not most patients waiting for a transplant were in a desperate state and
often rapidly failing in the days and even hours before a donor
organ became available. They had to be monitored constantly
to prevent or lessen any further deterioration. For days and
even weeks after the operation itself, the patient has to be
guided safely as if through a minefield of potentially disastrous
complications. A mistake or miscalculation about treatment in
the postoperative period is as dangerous as a mishap on the
operating table. There were few moments when my heart was
not likely to contract with anxiety. The intensity of the care
that had to be given made each patient a part of my emotional
life as each patient was in fact a part of daily professional life.
Again I was taken up sharp by something I thought I had already learned and accepted. But I had to learn again the basics:
Transplantation, the branch of surgery that demands the greatest objective technical skills, also exacts the greatest personal
and emotional involvement.

She was always waiting for me in the corridor outside the intensive care unit. I would as usual say something complimen-
tary about what she was wearing. I did not have to pretend.
She always looked fresh and pretty, her clothes were simple
and exactly right for her, her blond hair was parted and held
back on each side with unadorned barrettes. She sometimes
wore a piece of jewelry, a pin or bracelet or charm I hadn't seen
before and wanted to look at closely. There was always a faint
trace of soft cologne when she came close to show me.

We spent a little time talking about these things. She listened to me and watched my reaction so carefully, as anxious
to have my opinion now as when I had first met her weeks ago.
She once said she did not want to come to him looking as
though she were—she hesitated, then said quickly something
like having a problem, getting tired, tired. She was almost

exactly her husband's age, thirty-two, she had told me. The ghastly strain of the last weeks had in some strange way made her seem even younger, like a teen almost, a young girl again. From day to day I had looked for those signs of stress I saw in all the others who waited and suffered. The signs were usually stamped the same no matter how different the face. But her face showed only helplessness, and her candid, clear eyes conveyed only trust, absolute trust in me and everyone else connected with her husband's life-and-death struggle. Every day she came looking so young and fresh and pretty for him, and she smiled a bit shyly when I said how glad he would be to see her. She never said it, but I knew she wanted me to tell her it helped him, made some difference, moved him closer to . . . But by this time I think she did not know what that meant anymore. I think after all these weeks she no longer could tell for certain what she wanted. She wanted him to live, live by some miracle she knew we could make work. She wanted him to live, whatever it would cost, no matter how much time it would take, but only that he live. But as the days mounted into weeks I knew she was fighting herself not to admit the other thought as well. She was terrified to discover she was also thinking of his death.

Two months earlier Vincent had undergone a liver transplant procedure for acute liver failure caused by fulminant hepatitis. Of the three types of hepatitis associated with liver failure, Vincent suffered from the type that had the lowest survival rate after transplantation. But he understood that transplantation was his only real chance of survival, so he and Linda had put all their hopes in it. He had his own small but successful dental practice and was familiar enough with medical terms to be able to understand the details of his own case. He made the inevitable jokes.

"It will be easier than pulling teeth," he told me before the operation. "In fact, when it's over I'll come back and pull some teeth to show you a really complicated procedure."

I thanked him for the offer but declined, even when he added that there would be no charge in my case. In the few days before the operation he remained in high spirits, quizzing me on every occasion for more technical details about the operation and more or less translating these into lay terms for Linda. He would take her hand in his and half raise it in a kind of victory salute, saying things like "If you can't survive a little end-to-end choledochocholedochostomy, you know, duct-to-duct anastomosis, what good are you!"

I'm not sure he always understood what he was talking about, although he was smart enough to ask me about some of the major danger points in the operation and understood why I had put biliary tract reconstruction—the choledocho, etcetera part of it—high on the list. That was how I gave him the medical term he played around with. He did manage to coax a smile out of Linda. And that was probably all he wanted to do. He was trying to convince her that there was no reason to start doubting their good fortune now. He winked across at me, cocky, self-assured, daring anything to shake his belief in himself and his good fortune. He gave you the idea that his being there and our having to save his life was due to some misunderstanding or mistake. Unfortunately, it would take more time to discover the cause of the misunderstanding than to go through the operation that would cancel it out. It all could have been happening to someone else. He wasn't arrogant, he was just self-assured. What was happening to him simply was not in the life he had planned and was making for himself and Linda.

Within a few days after the transplant, he began to reject the liver and developed a fever. We went immediately into action, biopsied the liver and ran all the tests and cultures. The rejection was successfully treated but the infections leaped ahead of us, then were for a time partially contained, giving him and us a brief respite. But they always resurfaced, widening the

breech previously made in his body's defenses, letting the ene-
mies pour in. By the end of the first month we had to open his
abdomen, expose the failing new liver and the bowels, fight
the multiple sources of infection with direct hand-to-hand
combat, his living self the battlefield. The room became his
own operating theater. As we worked over him with warmed
antibiotic solutions, with drains to remove the accumulating
fluids, he sometimes craned his neck to see, looking at himself
in disbelief. What of any of this could he call himself? Why
was this stranger, his body, making such demands on him?

Linda endured the erratic course of small gains and increasing losses, watching him weaken, his spirit growing quieter.
But she came more and more to plead his cause. She began to
ask that he be transplanted again. And when we talked about
the difficulties in the way of that now, she turned all of our reasoning aside as if such medical quibbles were not pertinent, did
not apply to her husband. At first she spoke to me apart. I
thought she feared it would waste his strength if he had to take
up his own cause. Vincent had said nothing about retransplan-
tation since it became apparent that we could not break the infection's hold.

"You think he's going to be one of those liver eaters," she
said to me in a sudden burst of anger one day. I wondered
where she had heard that crude term used to disparage patients
who rejected the first and then sometimes the second transplant. Eating up scarce resources, the cruel words implied. She
didn't wait for me to make amends for the pain they caused.
Her anger faded, and she could only whisper in bewilderment,
"Doesn't anyone think he deserves another chance? This isn't
his fault."

Vincent began to watch us more closely, to ask more questions, almost as if bringing himself up to date on a situation
he had been giving half a mind to. He wanted to know his
chances, how much time, if I had any good estimate. I knew I
had to be honest with him and not evade even the most direct

and painful inquiry. He always thanked me, said he appreciated getting in on the case, getting to know the patient. With something of the old cockiness, he told me it really was about time he got on top of the case, his case. He said it should not have taken him so long to realize he was the person in question. There was no longer any question about it. All of it was really happening to him, in spite of any doubts he might have had about that, and he was in the process of coming to terms with the consequences.

One day he managed to hold my arm as I was trying to take his pulse. I usually had to strain now to hear him, but he said clearly enough, "I need enough time to tell her. Will I have it?"

I knew he meant "How much time will it take her to understand and accept this as I have?"

I said, "Just tell her what you know."

"That there's a patient dying here and it happens to be me and I recognize that now and we'll leave peacefully together?"

"You won't put it that way to her," I said.

"Then I'll just tell her that I finally accepted death as a part of my life. I finally got the whole picture. I was always in the picture, but I didn't want to think about it. Do you think that will be all right?"

It must have told her something like that. Linda was there at the end, and I stayed as well. It was a painful failure after all those weeks of struggle and after all his—no—their and our pain. We held each other and let the others do the final necessary things for him while we cried and consoled each other. She told me what he had been trying to say to her in the last days.

She said it could never take away or lessen the pain she would always feel. It would just help her recognize the place pain and suffering and death, now his death, always has in life. She pulled away and helped me wipe away my tears, and she had her old smile as she said, "He had to say it, you know.

Almost at the end. He had to tell me that the only way he got to join the human race was by dying and leaving it."

It was the kind of remark we both had come to expect from him, and we laughed and clung to one another again. We knew he didn't have to worry. As long as we remembered him, it would be as if he had never left.

I did a lot of traveling during my three years as a fellow, really flying around and getting to know the country—small towns, medium-sized towns, places out in the country where there isn't much of a town to speak of. Not much of it was what you would find on the regular tourist routes. I was never on a tour. I was always on a run to wherever in the country some tragic event had resulted in an organ becoming available for one of the many patients we had on our waiting list. These were often races against time to try to make sure that a life lost would become a life gained.

I made somewhere near four hundred of these trips, flying mostly at night in a variety of aircraft, some of which I considered more airworthy than others but all of which got us safely there and back. The flights often provided a blissful opportunity for snatching some always welcome extra hours of sleep. Not that the accommodations permitted luxurious stretching out on soft cushions. There is a technique to sleeping bolt upright, however, and it can be learned when the alternative is wakefulness.

When the two assistants who would be needed during the organ procurement operation and I arrived, we would be met by the hospital ambulance and taken away quickly. Time was almost never on our side, which was one more reason we had to appreciate the preliminary work done by the hospital's medical staff and by the organ procurement coordinator. Every death is surrounded by legalities and technicalities, and the legalities that must be observed in regard to a brain-dead human being who will become an organ donor are even more complex.

And more demanding than the legalities were the human concerns I could never forget. I always had in my heart the knowledge that our being there at that moment was only because of some tragic event, and that the victim's family and loved ones were still in the first shock of loss. I knew that no matter how much comfort a family could derive from knowing that the dead person would make another's life possible, grief was still the strongest of any emotion and that grief was still fresh. Most of all, I have never lost my wonder at the capacity of the human heart to feel for others in moments of their greatest pain. For a family to interrupt its own grieving to help bring comfort to someone they would most likely never know, never meet, is among the most astounding and reassuring of human actions.

By the time we were ready for our work, such painful tasks had already been completed. The family had been approached, their willingness to donate was confirmed, they were asked specifically about which organs could be procured, they were told about how the donation would be accomplished, they were told how the body would be made ready for burial. They would have to listen as the human being they loved was in this unavoidable way spoken of as so many usable parts, no longer a whole. The wholeness would now be made manifest in their loving generosity. Then we were given the right to proceed; the final moments were turned over to us as a gift for us to pass on.

For many people the whole idea of transplantation, especially of an organ as large and multifunctional as a liver, is still too difficult or upsetting to accept. Surgeons will often point to the statistics to try to give the idea some human dimension. For instance, by the mid-1990s, more than six thousand liver transplantations had been performed in the United States and Europe. Figures don't mean much to many, and even the living thing itself often fails to persuade. That's why I often think of the state police officer who forced us to the side of the road early one morning in some remote rural county. We were in a hospital ambulance rushing to catch the plane back to home base, where the transplant team was waiting for the liver we had just procured.

As senior member of the group, I got out of the ambulance and showed my identification. The trooper's eyes shifted from the ID picture to me and back several times, but I did not offer the usual excuses—a terrible snapshot, no wonder I'm unrecognizable and he is confused, and so on.

I was about to suggest I prove my identity by duplicating my signature for him when he asked, "If you're from there, why are you here? Where's the accident?" I hesitated, and this provoked his curiosity even further. He asked suspiciously, "Why are you headed away from the hospital if there's an accident victim in there?"

I said there had been no accident, but I had to correct this by trying to explain that the liver we were taking to the airport had in fact come from an accident victim. I wasn't surprised that he looked at me with absolute skepticism. All I could manage under that stare was a lame "Yes, we have the liver . . . for transplantation. You've heard of organ transplantation?"

He pointed to the ambulance door. "Open it," he said. It was not a request to be denied. The ambulance driver opened the door. For a moment the officer looked perplexed, as if he had been expecting a body instead of what he saw, a relatively ordinary family picnic-sized ice cooler.

"We have a plane waiting for us at the airport," I began, but he paid no attention. "Open it," he said. I felt a surge of panic. The liver had been cooled during and after removal from the donor by being saturated with a cooling and preserving agent. It had been placed in a sterile plastic bag, which was sealed and placed in two additional bags to provide for maximum safety against contamination. The bags were then placed in the ice cooler and packed with ice. I could not let anything break any of these seals and possibly contaminate the organ. I also could not afford to antagonize the man and run the risk of wasting more time while he decided if he should drag us off to the sheriff's office or wherever they incarcerated criminals.

"It's really only a liver," I said, with more impatience than I had intended, possibly suggesting that his interest was infantile if not morbid.

He just pointed a commanding finger at the ambulance driver, and the man pulled the cooler closer to the opening and carefully held back the cover. He was about to move the ice, but I pushed him aside and got my hands on it before he did. I'm glad it was a liver and not something like a kidney or a portion of a pancreas buried in the ice. Those organs were small and probably would not have shown clearly through plastic and ice water. The liver is the largest organ we have, and this one, at something over three pounds, was unmistakably a liver.

I looked up at him and more or less shrugged. "A liver," I said. He seemed to collapse into confusion as he asked, "But where's . . . where's the body?"

"We don't need a body. We just need the liver. We are going to give this liver to a patient whose own isn't working anymore. Someone else is getting the kidneys."

"But it's not alive."

"Of course it is," I said, not exactly stamping my foot but as if addressing a stubborn child. "It's in preservative solution and packed in ice. It can remain alive and usable for hours." I looked at my watch. "For about the next eight hours. Then it will be useless. That's why we have to hurry now." I pushed the ice back in place and slammed the lid closed, motioning to the driver to pull the cooler back inside the ambulance and get us moving again. The trooper let all this happen without interruption.

He caught up with me as I was climbing back into the ambulance. He began as if still trying to get his thoughts together. "But the body . . . the person's dead."

"Yes," I said. "But in a way not altogether dead. What we have here is living. And we will try to make it go on living for as long as we can." I felt I had to reach him still further. I said, "It happens, believe me. It sounds like a miracle, but it happens."

He hesitated for a second, then seemed to hit on the right words. He motioned to the back of the ambulance and grinned. "I'm sorry I was standing in the way of your miracle. I better get out of your way."

He got into his vehicle and pulled out and ahead and with his sirens going brought us to the airport. We had a few more moments to talk before the plane took off. He gave me his name, and I promised I would send him some things explaining our work. But I told him I thought he had already gotten the essential part of it, he already understood that in spite of death it was possible to save something that would make another life continue.

The daily round of patient care and OR duty filled the days and often the nights month after month. But I was never allowed to forget that I was still a student, still learning. And still held accountable for getting it right. The "it" in the second year of the fellowship referred to the boards, a word that always inspires terror in physicians and surgeons in training. The boards were the examinations of all examinations, the hurdle of all hurdles, the grand finale for which you had been preparing throughout all your medical training. The boards were a daunting prospect. They meant looking forward to hours of written examination and then, a year later, oral examination, with questions being shot at you by examiners you had never seen before, who had never seen you, who were not even from your part of the country. All that guaranteed no prejudice in your favor, no little hints to help you articulate an uncertain answer. You were on your own, and because they had never seen you before and were not likely to do so after, the examiners could be as ruthless as they cared to be. But if you made it, you could put after your title the words that meant you had been accepted by the most demanding of your peers. You were not just a doctor or a surgeon, you were "board-certified." You were finally judged good enough to be stamped with their seal of approval. As a footnote to history, I must add that the year I took the written boards with five others from my alma mater— for the first time in history all six passed.

Preparation for the boards had to be squeezed into the rest of life. As the deadline drew near, I decided to take my coming week of vacation and fly back to D.C. to meet with Dr. Brown. He had agreed to put me through a kind of mock oral examination. Without saying as much, we both assumed that if I could pass that, the real thing held no threat.

The only time he had for me was early Sunday. I went to his house, and we began. I knew I was lost before the hour was up. What seemed like simple questions, more or less theoretical discussion of some aspect of patient care, turned in a labyrinth through which I had to scurry wildly, only to come up to one blank wall after another. Even when I had some grasp of the answer, he found another interpretation of the case that threw my conclusion into doubt. "It's the same patient," he exploded. "Don't you think it is necessary to reconcile possible contradictions before you treat? How are you going to begin treatment if you are not aware of the contradictory signs?"

I had no answer. I hadn't thought of the problem in such terms. I was thinking only of a theoretical answer to a theoretical question. He was talking about a patient in a three-dimensional, real world. I had missed the connection somehow. I had tried to learn too much, think too little.

He slammed shut the textbook he had opened at the beginning of the session but never referred to. "This was supposed to be a dry run, a dress rehearsal. Consider yourself lucky. People are kind at a rehearsal. They want more at a real performance."

He got up, and I knew I was being dismissed.

Ian was doing his best to reassure me, but I think he knew I needed consolation as well. We sat in the cafeteria, oblivious of the students and residents and nurses coming and going. I kept asking the same question:

"Didn't he know he was hurting me? Didn't he care?"

I wound up trying his patience, so he gave me a simple "no."

"No to what?" I asked with anger.

"All right. Maybe yes to one and no to the other."

"He still tries to make me feel I don't belong."

Ian waited a bit and shook his head in a show of disbelief. "He makes you feel you don't belong by trying to make sure you'll be good enough to stay. You don't pass the boards, the hospital doesn't ask you to come back and get on the payroll. Very tricky."

As usual, Ian had pushed me into seeing the irrationality of my emotional response. Then he brought his chair closer to mine. "You know what he was doing."

It was not a question, rather a challenge. But when I did not answer, he continued. "He was letting you taste what failure is like. Make you taste it so that you won't ever think it tastes any less bitter than this. He wants you to know how humiliating defeat can be so that you'll never risk it."

"I know what defeat is like! I went through that," I protested.

He waved this aside. "It's not something you go through and are done with. It's something that's always there, waiting. He wants you to know you always have to be ready for the possibility. And not drop your guard."

And then he leaned closer and almost whispered, "There's something else. You've got to make up for everyone who didn't get the message, or forgot, or got sucked into believing defeat wouldn't be as painful and final as it is. You have to make up for all those who let go and didn't realize they'd never get back. There are all kinds of reasons for the human wreckage that's around us, that people like you and me have to deal with every day. But you can bet not a single one of those poor wrecks ever thought it would be as bad as it turned out."

He got up and then had one final word for me. He said, "Dr. Brown could be called an expert in defeat. He's seen it all. He wants those he loves to protect themselves against it."

I took a few more days and began preparing for the boards as if for the first time. I tried not to answer questions but to see how I would treat a real patient in the theoretical situation I was given to explain. I think I was trying to humanize what had been only abstractions. I prayed, I meditated, I tried to empty myself of every obstacle that anxiety and pride and fear had placed in the way of certitude. I had to open myself to understand what I knew and how I could let that knowledge direct my answers.

I took the oral examination before a panel of men I did not know and who did not know me. By some lucky stroke the first questions were similar to problems I had just been working on. I clung to that coincidence and the confidence it gave me, and I survived the hours of interrogation.

It would take months before the results were sent to me. I had little free time to worry about them because I was back on duty, from 8 A.M. rounds to 8 P.M. wrap-ups. Even though I was well into my third year as a fellow and had attained what was clearly seniority, I was still, and by now perhaps automatically, doing work usually handed over to the lower ranks of interns or residents. I occasionally wondered where the male fellows

‚went when the lines had to be inserted or blood drawn or even some basic patient histories taken. I guessed. They were off in the locker rooms plotting how to take on the stock market or reap another million or so before arthritis cramped their operating style. There was no place for me, literally or figuratively, in such bonding sessions, so I just went along with the nurses, doing nurses' work, all us women closing ranks. Sometimes the nurses forgot or forgave the fact that I was a physician and surgeon and hence could never really be one of them. They were glad to act as if I had earned my place on the team. That was an honor they did not dispense freely or to everyone solely on the possession of a certain title after a name.

The flights continued, taking us back and forth across the country, mostly over black, flat stretches of land, sometimes over cities whose lights held me fascinated as they appeared out of the darkness and then ran swiftly beneath us until it was all night again.

The board examiners notified me that I had successfully completed the requirements that made me now certified. I stuffed the letter into my bag and rushed back to the hospital with little more than a prayer of thanks. I had long since spent enough emotional energy on that episode and had little to give it now. My response was more like I did not fail than I did succeed. In time, of course, the full realization of the milestone I had achieved (or been dragged over) dawned on me and I let my spirit celebrate.

Years before I ever assisted at a liver transplant operation or performed one of my own, I had read about what to expect. The words never left my mind. Not just long and demanding, the task of removing the diseased liver was also one of the most brutal and bloody experiences in a surgeon's life. At any stage disastrous or even lethal hemorrhage was a major threat. As brutal as part of the procedure was, a great portion of it required, by contrast, the most delicate and sophisticated technique. But there was no single best order of steps to follow from one portion of the operation to another. Critical decisions had to be made at the moment, so the surgeon had to be trained to know at an instant's glance which of the many possible steps was the best and safest for the patient. Long, long hours had to be spent on achieving perfect union of every severed vessel until all internal bleeding was arrested. Nothing could be left to anything like a "natural" healing process. Any vein or artery that had been cut had to be made whole again, every source of bleeding had to be secured.

We were at the most complicated sequence of the operation: reconstructing the veins, arteries, and biliary tract, reestablishing the entire system that got the liver to function. Every stitch in every vessel had to be placed exactly, with a precise amount of distance between each suture to guarantee no leakage and no life-threatening rupture, and yet provide union without the kind of tension that would result in a tight-obstructing anastomosis. Bleeding from the reconstructed vessels into the abdomen is one of the most feared complications after transplantation and can threaten the life of the patient even when the liver itself functions perfectly.

I was suctioning away the blood that was obscuring the field for the chief as he and an assistant worked the stitches around the delicate vessels. No sooner had I cleared a minute area than it was filmed over again by blood seeping from the vessels in his hand. I felt the tension increase as his tightly spoken command "Clear it! Suck it out!" grew louder. I started working with two of the tiny suction devices and kept the field clear as he finally tied off the vessel. Then I turned the suctions over to the second assistant and was ready to take the thread as the chief placed the first stitch in the next vessel. The curved needle came through the thin wall of the vein. I caught and pulled the thread, popping it off the head of the needle. My fingers were slippery, and I felt the tension as I forced them to take a firm grip on the edge of the thread so that I could tie it exactly in place. I pulled too tight, and the thread snapped.

In itself the blunder could not compromise the operation's success. But it was a blunder, and it came too soon after my struggling efforts to keep the field free of blood. I didn't get ordered out, although that would have been easier to deal with. I had to stay. I had to continue taking the thread from his hand and tying off. I had to listen as my every move was commented on, made the focus of attention, an occasion for the kind of critique reserved for someone in a beginners' class.

The bitter words did not let up. I thought they were designed to force me into some proof that I could not stand up to them. I thought they were meant to have me break down and pick my weeping self up and rush from the room, a typical hysterical woman. There swept over me that old feeling of being an intruder in a world that barely acknowledged me or any possible contribution I could make. I felt every ancient hurt. And at that moment I made them all die within me. I willed them into silence and then into oblivion. For an imaginary flash of time I pursued them as you would dust under a bed and swept them up and had them in a dustpan and then in the trash.

When I felt my fingers about to tremble out of control, I gathered all the strength I had to cancel out the words, to concentrate everything on the chief's own expert fingers rapidly bringing the fragile vessels together. I silenced everything else about him, forgot all that, forgave and understood all the pressures he bore, not only for the patient but for every one of us there with him. Every one of us was as much in his care as the anesthetized patient before us all, and I had never given him credit for this before he made me feel that he could care enough to let me feel his anger and displeasure.

And then I just seemed to walk into the light. I looked and understood that in all his measured tirade he had never for a second interrupted the exchange between our hands, not for a second did the rhythm of our work skip a beat or falter. The needle entered, the thread was drawn, the knot tied, the vessel secured, and then we moved on, continuing the work but now in silence.

I tried to apologize afterward for my clumsiness, but he brushed this aside. He said everything had gone well, better than expected, given the degree of bleeding, the unanticipated need to reconstruct a new hepatic artery, and other complications. Some patients just bled more profusely than others, and sometimes you can't keep up. Threads snap—and so do tempers. The point is to keep going and not let an occasional slip detour you. You sometimes can see things differently when you're righting yourself after a slip.

I had nothing to offer in return for such generosity. And then I remembered the letter in my bag and knew it was the best gift: Passing the boards meant that the work would go on and I would be among those entrusted with its fulfillment in the future. He threw his arms around me and congratulated me. When I said thank you, he replied, "You're welcome. You are now and always welcome, and we are all honored to welcome you."

CHAPTER 29

I often think back to the state trooper who stopped our ambulance on that lonely country road and looked with such amazement at the liver I had just secured and had so carefully placed in the sterile bags and then into the ice-packed cooler. He saw it all as a miracle on its way to happen. What he didn't realize was how long the miracle had taken to get born and how uncertain it was that it would survive those birth pangs. All this sounds like so much medical history, but for me and surgeons like me, it is history with a most personal meaning. I found that out in the first few weeks of my return.

When liver transplantation was first attempted in the early 1960s, none of the first seven patients survived more than a month. Further efforts to achieve a successful transplantation were suspended here and in Europe, until 1967. In spite of what looked like the eagerly awaited breakthrough, in the next decade anywhere from one half to two thirds of patients died, sometimes on the operating table, often when their bodies rejected the foreign liver. The real success of liver transplantation did not begin until the revolutionary new immunosuppressive agent cyclosporine was introduced in 1978. This drug effectively halted the body's efforts to rid itself of the new liver; it made the incompatible finally compatible. During these years great improvements in surgical techniques also reduced the risks that went with the long and complicated procedure.

By the time my fellowship ended and I returned to my own hospital to continue work as a liver transplant surgeon, I had incontestable figures that proved patients were surviving in numbers that could hardly have been imagined only two decades earlier. Survival, of course, was greatly influenced by the nature and severity of the original liver disease and by the patient's condition when the operation was done (as always, too many patients are not transplanted until they are in extreme danger, at which time they have drastically reduced chances of survival). But when anywhere from almost 70 to nearly 90 percent of patients are alive and healthy a year after transplantation, you know something extraordinary has happened. Transplantation was the only thing standing between each and every one of these patients, regardless of disease, regardless of age, regardless of every claim on life and certain death.

In the long run, you can't put your trust in numbers. I went into my first liver transplantation operation, the first in which I would be chief surgeon, with my mind full of 70 to 90 percent survival and my head turned off to the 30 to 10 percent of patients who did not.

My first patient died on the operating table, suddenly, in spite of what had seemed like proof that she was standing up to the demands of so many hours under anesthesia. I had to fight against the near overwhelming feeling that some of my own hopes and expectations died with her. She was a woman in her mid-fifties and was being slowly, inevitably undermined by primary biliary cirrhosis, not from alcohol abuse but probably as a result of some little-understood destructive inflammation of the vessels supplying the bile ducts. The first signs had crept up on her almost without her being aware of them—fatigue, outbreaks of skin disease, problems with her bowel movements, then jaundice and bone weakness.

She had lived with these problems for some time, then things seemed to go into fast-forward and her liver function tests flashed out an emergency. She was at first afraid of the operation and its risks, but I had convinced her that the disease had one of the highest success rates of any for which transplantation is a cure. I had actively participated in many such procedures before and had the statistical evidence of success.

My patient went into cardiac arrest before the end of the operation and the work of joining all vessels and achieving absolute control of all possible internal bleeding was completed. Nothing we did could bring her back. For days after we studied the case, going back and forth over the cardiac output numbers, the potassium level numbers, the records of her blood pressure, everything that had been closely monitored and recorded at every moment during the operation. She had always seemed to be safely within tolerable levels for everything we tested. At the end we knew what we knew at the beginning. At some point her potassium level began to climb, at some point her heart had been compromised, at some point she had gone into cardiac failure and had died.

If the answer were in any of this, we could not be sure we had found it. But I had to leave it at that because of the demands of other patients on the waiting list for transplantation, patients who had to be prepared for an imminent transplantation, patients who were recovering from one. As usual, each patient as well as each phase of the process required special attention.

Some patients seemed designed to test your strength, dedication to medicine, compassion, forbearance, goodwill, and all the other attributes and virtues assumed to come automatically to those of us in the healing profession. Mr. Huff was over sixty years old, putting him at the very age limit of patients we could consider for a transplant. His age was compounded by his problematic behavior, which also put him at the limit. Far be it from me to judge whether or not he was a good or bad human being; he was just a bad patient. Every doctor has them, but few doctors want to admit to the frustration and anger they cause.

What is a bad patient? For example, all patients are told that certain food must be avoided, overweight patients are told that all foods must be taken in moderation. A bad patient such as Mr. Huff is a patient with poor liver function who not only eats everything on his hospital tray but also goes by stealth to other hospital floors and forages among dinner trays for all the protein intentionally removed from his rations. Is Mr. Huff just hungry, near starvation on the diet prescribed for him? No, Mr. Huff has learned a good deal about transplantation and knows that the sicker he is, the more days in the hospital he has to his credit, the higher up on the list he goes. Being high up on the list means he will have less of a wait for the always scarce organ that will prolong life.

In spite of this behavior, the hospital transplant review committee recommended that Mr. Huff be transplanted. "Before he does himself any more damage" was the unspoken but perhaps universally felt conclusion. He did surprisingly well for a man who had put so much at risk, but some patients will risk everything for another chance. It is important to keep

on believing that everyone should have an equal chance—
difficult at times to do but still important.

Getting away from the hospital for a few days if only to catch
up on daily living, housework, shopping, reading, simple plea-
sures like that, kept you going when the demands of the Mr.
Huffs of the world seemed the only ones with any legitimate
claim on your time. During one such commonplace but to me
blissful interlude I was pushing my shopping cart down a
supermarket aisle, letting myself become hypnotized by the
endless displays. Who invents all this stuff? I was thinking.
And how do you go about inventing food? It all can't just be
natural, out of the earth. Was there this much the last time I
went shopping? When was that?

I had strolled over to the dairy section, relieved to find
things I recognized, like milk in familiar containers. I reached
for a quart and then was caught up short, suddenly recognizing
a gesture that I had probably done so often I never gave it a
thought. I had pushed aside the containers up front and was
checking the ones in the back of the shelf for the "sell before"
date of expiration. As usual, the containers with the sell-by
date closest to the present day were lined up like a solid guard,
protecting the milk with a much longer extension on life.

Given the amount of time I spend away from home, any
milk on my refrigerator shelf needs as much time as possible
between the day I bought it and the day it will be used up. It
was the caution about the sell date that had stayed my hand in
midair. And I thought of blood, units of blood, way up to the
one hundred or so units of blood that were used during the average liver transplantation. I imagined someone in the blood
storage department examining dates and moving units off the
shelf and seeing that they get taken to the OR in preparation
for the surgery. But were the units taken from the front of the
shelf or from the back? All the units were safe and usable, but

the ones closer to expiration were liable to have undergone a slow buildup of potassium. Had that happened? There was no way now of knowing. But a minimal rise in potassium level in itself would not have rendered the blood unusable. But in this case, the potassium, bit by bit, had been transfused into the patient. How much potassium? What effect had it had on her heart? And for such a patient, how much potassium would have placed her at risk of cardiac toxicity and death?

There was no way of finding out now, so the connection was only a supposition, a grim but unproved possibility. But I could never live with even a remote possibility. In the future, every drop of blood that would enter a patient of mine would first be washed free of potassium, right there in the operating room, no matter who had previously attested to its purity.

There were great and unlikely triumphs as well as such defeats. Brandon was a triumph, complete, entire, a vindication of all that had been done before to make transplantation possible. He was young, just a teen, just at the beginning of his manhood, gifted with a sense of the spiritual that few of any age, and fewer of his own generation, possessed. He knew his condition and had kept track of his deterioration—painfully easy to do because of the profuse bloody vomiting that signaled each emergency. The defects in his congenitally underdeveloped biliary tract resulted in liver failure, portal hypertension, and esophageal bleeding. When the portal hypertension reached a peak of congestion within the vessels supplying to his esophagus, his body revolted and he vomited blood until he seemed drained of life.

They were always emergencies I handled because everyone knew he was my patient, for the last three months on the list waiting for the liver that I would transplant. I knew what to expect. His face would be ashen, his body cold and clammy, he would be struggling to remain conscious. Any observer would place him immediately among the desperately, incurably sick, bearing a disease that seemed to have had a longer life than his years suggested.

I would have him in position so that his body would offer the least resistance to the catheter. I would first anesthetize his neck with the lidocaine, gritting my teeth almost in unison with him as the burning liquid penetrated, numbing the flesh but leaving behind a memory so painful it would last throughout the procedure it was meant to ease. Then I would thread the catheter into his jugular vein, hoping that the uncontrollable vomiting would not resume, would give me enough time to begin the flow of blood that would revive him. He would come back slowly, regaining color and complete consciousness. He had come back from the edge once more, and we would be given another respite in which to hope again. He had recorded every one of these days throughout the full three months before he could be transplanted, marking each day that passed on his calender.

When the gift finally came, it seemed almost like something given in trust from brother to brother. The death of the seven-year-old black youngster who made Brandon's life possible was as senseless a tragedy as any I had encountered in all those four hundred or so flights during my years of fellowship training. He must have momentarily forgotten everything he had been taught about crossing a busy street. Why else would he have run heedlessly between moving automobiles? It was, after all, only ice cream that he was rushing away to buy. He suffered massive brain injuries, but the accident left his liver untouched, almost perfectly matched to our needs, black brother to black brother, male to male, race to race.

The operation to save Brandon's life was a success. It would become one of the factors when the statistics on survivals from our transplant unit were compiled. If our work was compared to the results from other transplant centers, it was expected that more than 83 percent of our patients should have survived the most critical three-month postoperative period. In reality, all of our patients survived that period. In comparison with other centers, at least 76 percent of our patients should have survived the first year after transplantation. More than 87 percent of our patients actually survived that first year.

It wasn't that I didn't have any personal life or any world outside the hospital and my patients, it was rather that I forgot about such things from time to time. Surgery was no longer the goal of my life, it had become every meaningful step along the way. Things that were not surgery or were not connected with medicine sometimes took me by surprise and left me wondering where they might fit into life. My life did not appear to have leftover, unoccupied places anymore. I wondered if I had used up all the options, had made all the choices that would be available so that what I had now would be what I would have—this, more of this, and nothing else but this.

I had continued to practice meditation as a means of separating myself, however briefly, from the noise and insatiable demands of the external world. I knew I never dialed out completely; the world was always there, if only a shadow not quite out of sight.

Sometimes rather than trust myself to find my own way to some interior calm, I joined with others, more adept than I, and sought in their company some kind of shared peace and understanding.

The group engaged in no prescribed ritual, held no dogmas, imposed no commandments or codified teachings. That in itself was a welcome contrast with my life, where there was always someone saying, "You have to listen, listen to what has to be taught to you because you cannot know on your own or by yourself. You are not up to that, you have not come along far enough for that. Maybe you never will."

I fell into the habit of going to meetings where others talked about their quest for inner peace and understanding in the most ordinary language. It was as if the quest was the most logical, acceptable thing to be occupying yourself with, and so the language in which it was described had to be the same and offer no blocks to understanding. Then I learned that the reason there wasn't anything like a leader or a set of rules or a prescribed formula was that everyone had something better, something better informed, better aware, better able to communicate if you listened. It took a little listening, but I began to have enough confidence to trust myself to hear myself at last.

I met him there, at one of those gatherings where one came to learn how to recognize what was necessary in life and what was superficial. To begin with, he didn't look as if he had been spending much time meditating. He seemed too packed with energy to stay still that long. I sized him up with what I thought was a cool, critical medical eye. Yes, very healthy, very trim, no chance of any problems related to sedentary living habits, no problems that could be exacerbated by lack of exercise, physical activity. Too bad not many such outdoor types came and engaged in this indoor, insightful soul-questing activity.

I ran through all those things to justify my continuing to stare at him, all the while that recently revived inner voice was shouting in my ear, "This has got to be the most attractive, the most poised, the most vibrant male you will ever find yourself walking calmly toward and introducing yourself to. And if you don't do it, you will have to find yourself another small, caring voice to listen to, if the occasion ever arises again."

I welcomed him to the meeting, and he took my hand and held it without my even feeling the firmness of his grip, and because it did not hurt at all I did not remove my hand as he repeated my name and told me his and went on to say that he was from out of town but he knew the national treasurer of the organization who had invited him to the lodge here.

I had already noticed that we were the youngest couple there but did not see any reason to mention this to him until he pointed it out to me and asked if there was any reason I could suggest for that. "Everyone's out playing basketball," I suggested. Naturally, he said he had done that yesterday and a couple of times a week was enough if you wanted to leave yourself any time for things more important. Did I have another explanation?

I had none and fell silent, and he said altogether simply and believably, "It's so I wouldn't have to deal with any competition."

And when I pretended not to understand, he said, "Things do get arranged, somehow."

They did, but not without some difficulties. I actually forgot the first arrangement because another meeting had to be delayed because of his schedule and mine. He was to come back to town and spend some time. But I had worked late on an emergency call and was still sleeping when he called from the train station.

"Hello," said the bright voice. "It's Michael."

I was still asleep or dreaming. "Michael?"

"Did you forget?" he asked, as if he knew that was a real possibility in the world and he could take that in stride if it were required of him. I tried to apologize, but he brushed this aside and said he would be waiting outside for me so I would not have problems wasting time with parking and such.

As I rushed down the highway, I had a sudden panicky feeling that I had forgotten completely what he looked like and I would never recognize him among the hordes of men sure to be wandering about in front of the station.

Even if there were hordes, which there weren't, I would have recognized him as instantly as we had known one another that first time. We spent the day together. I had not spent a day talking about nonhospital, nonmedical things longer than had been good for me. He said it had been longer than good for me, and I sounded as if I were rediscovering some language I had spoken fluently, naturally, in my youth. I was in danger of losing my native language.

Michael did that. He has told me that I started out inspired to bring healing to all in great need. Then I had made my goal the acquisition of knowledge and had forgotten where I had started from. I had materialized all the spiritual meaning with which I had begun my journey. I would have to learn again why I began.

We have begun on that journey together, as it was arranged we do. Such arrangements among persons are miracles in their own right. Love is the ultimate healer, loving the only lasting comfort in pain. I was given the last great thing to know— loving is the real miracle that one never questions.

ABOUT THE AUTHOR

ROSE-MARIE TOUSSAINT, M.D., earned her B.S. at Loyola University in New Orleans, and her M.D. at Howard University. She did her post-doctoral training in the surgery departments of Howard University, the University of Pittsburgh, and the University of Wisconsin. She is a Diplomate of the American Board of Surgery and a Fellow of the American College of Surgery. She has served as assistant professor of surgery at Howard University College of Medicine and associate director of the Howard University Hospital Transplant Center. She is now in private practice.

ANTHONY E. SANTANIELLO has written and edited publications on nutrition, preventive medicine, the use of computer science in medicine, and general health issues. He has also worked as a producer, researcher, and writer of more than thirty medical films and video programs created for the medical profession.